Redistributing the Poor

Redesigning the Dead

Redistributing the Poor

Jails, Hospitals, and the Crisis of Law and Fiscal Austerity

ARMANDO LARA-MILLÁN

OXFORD
UNIVERSITY PRESS

OXFORD
UNIVERSITY PRESS

Published in the United States of America by Oxford University Press
198 Madison Avenue, New York, NY 10016, United States of America.

Library of Congress Cataloging-in-Publication Data
Names: Lara-Millán, Armando, author.
Title: Redistributing the poor : jails, hospitals, and the crisis of law
and fiscal austerity / Armando Lara-Millán, PhD,
Department of Sociology, UC Berkeley.
Description: New York : Oxford University Press, 2021. |
Includes bibliographical references and index.
Identifiers: LCCN 2020044919 (print) | LCCN 2020044920 (ebook) |
ISBN 9780197507896 (hardback) | 9780197507902 (paperback) | ISBN 9780197507926 (epub)
Subjects: LCSH: Jails—United States—Administration. | Prisoners—United
States—Social conditions. | Public hospitals—United States—Finance. |
Poor—United States—Social conditions—21st century. |
Social control—United States. | Fiscal policy—United States.
Classification: LCC HV9469.L267 2021 (print) | LCC HV9469 (ebook) |
DDC 338.4/3362110973—dc23
LC record available at https://lccn.loc.gov/2020044919
LC ebook record available at https://lccn.loc.gov/2020044920

DOI: 10.1093/oso/9780197507902.001.0001

Hardback printed by Bridgeport National Bindery, Inc., United States of America

Contents

Preface

When I started research for this book in 2009, I came across an article in the *Los Angeles Times* about a yearly mass burial. Every year since 1896, Los Angeles County's government has buried the ashes of around one thousand unclaimed bodies into an unmarked grave in East Los Angeles. In 2009, with the onset of the Great Recession, cities across the nation were seeing increased burials into such "pauper's graves."[1]

Fast-forward nearly a decade later, and I am writing this preface during the 2020 COVID crisis. Local governments in major cities are once again seeing an uptick in the premature death of mostly poor, mostly brown and Black people, necessitating their burial into unmarked graves. New York City has gone from burying 25 to 120 such people per week. It is difficult to know exactly who these people are but—given the contours of American poverty—it is easy to imagine they are the bodies of the under-housed found on park benches, the impoverished elderly living alone, or families unable to afford funeral costs.[2]

I will return to these deaths momentarily, but first a detour into the virus currently raging through America's jails and public hospitals. At the start of the crisis, prison abolitionists and legal advocates were threatening to sue county jails for endangering inmates. Indeed, despite expansive efforts to conduct testing during jail intake, inmates have been falling ill at alarming rates. Less widely acknowledged, though, is that public agencies across the country actually responded to legal pressure by releasing thousands of inmates early, stopped booking many into jail, and moved to issue citations rather than arrest. Such policies have resulted in drastic drops in jail populations; Los Angeles County, for instance, decompressed its jail from 17,000 inmates to 11,000 in just one month.[3]

It will probably become a footnote in history, but early in the crisis, social distancing policies saw many hospitals significantly under capacity and, as a result, hemorrhaging revenue. People were avoiding normal healthcare, and patients are money-makers for hospitals. It was not until late June 2020 that hospitals in major urban areas finally began to hit disastrous capacity limits. In addition to the relaxing of social distancing adherence, officials have quietly noted that prison and jail releases may have contributed to the recent uptick in hospitalizations. Indeed, early research in Chicago showed that jail releases accounted for 55% of the variance in case rates across zip codes. Persons released from incarceration and the people they have come into contact with are filling up the nation's public hospitals.[4]

The standard story we have been given to make sense of this situation is to blame overinvestment in criminal justice and underinvestment in public health. The idea would be that because criminal justice budgets have risen exponentially in the United States, it is no wonder that during a pandemic the sick and poor have ended up behind bars and that our nation's public hospital system would become overwhelmed. Such a theory is rooted in our understanding of the way mass imprisonment has shaped our county's institutions.

In this book we will see how this received wisdom is inadequate for understanding the current moment. While we largely assume that jail officials were pressured into releasing inmates during COVID, the theory offered in this book suggests that officials—for the moment—were likely privately ready and willing to cut costs. We might also assume that public hospitals were decrying the growth in caseloads, but in this book, we will see how these new caseloads are actually a way to earn revenue and renew interest in the funding of public hospitals.[5]

This book argues that we have drastically misunderstood not only this nation's largest jails and public hospitals, but the way that states govern at the turn of the twenty-first century. In short, the idea of "redistributing the poor" draws attention to how state agencies circulate people between different institutional spaces in such a way that generates revenue for some agencies, cuts costs for others, and projects illusions that services have been legally rendered. The concept pushes us away from viewing governance as either a problem of officials being overly concerned with punishing poor people or not concerned enough about extending a helping hand. Instead, public agencies are in the business of redefining problems in whatever way possible with the aim of reconstituting dying public institutions and reproducing the status quo.

By using this new language to describe state activity, we can better understand the premature deaths I encountered at the beginning and end of my research. Redistributing the poor shows how these deaths—what Ruth Gilmore (2007) calls "disposable" Black and brown life—are not simply the result of society's failure to act. Instead, as we shall see, they are the inevitable outcome of the state agencies' *successful* resolution of a particular kind of crisis. When state agencies encounter a crisis generated by a fundamental tension between fiscal austerity and legal demand the social suffering associated with that crisis evolves into some new, legally visible, and more affordable kind of suffering. The fiscal and legal crises generated by COVID are just the latest examples in which the social suffering of huge swaths of people are simply written off on paper.

Armando Lara-Millán, PhD
June 30, 2020
Oakland, CA

Acknowledgments

This book is not perfect. And it is through a lot of love and support that I have come to understand that it is okay for books to not be perfect; that I did the best I could. I had always envisioned writing extensive acknowledgments to thank the people who offered that kind of support and guidance. Some of that made it into the methods appendix, but alas, at the end of this journey, I feel the need to keep things short.

I feel deep in my heart there is no way that I could have researched this project and written this book alongside everything else that occurred in my life without the love of many people surrounding me. First and foremost, to the many who have since passed. You know who you are, but for whatever reason I feel the need to name my grandmother Nellie, who it feels as though if not for the critical thinking skills, intuition, and articulation of all that wisdom, I would not have been able to overcome many obstacles. To the living: there are so many of you that made a difference, both people who are still in my life, who will always be in my life, and those that have since moved on. To my best friend Evan, there is no way that I could have written this book without your confidence in me. To my mother, even though we have had our troubles I love you and thank you for everything you did to help me make this possible. The same goes to sister and brother. I am sorry that this book and everything that occurred alongside it took me away from you at times. I hope that can change. To my step-parents, you have shown me a different way that I can love and while it is difficult to explain, it made finishing this book possible. To John and Cindy, to my many cousins in all of my families, my friends Zack, Daniel, Joe, Manuel, thank you for bearing with me and still being there. To those who have since moved on, you know who you are and your impact on my life, your support and love through it all is still with me. Thank you. To my partner Babi, you have filled me with joy and taught me to kill the self-criticism; to my surprise you made being a happy person possible through the finish line.

There were people, for reasons I do not understand, who were willing to read drafts of these chapters and help me sort through all the mess. To Michael Burawoy, you have taught me what it takes to be good at this job and you challenged me to get this story straight. I am in your debt. To Mary Pattillo, you pushed me to find my voice (and get to the point!). To Lynne Haney, Ann Orloff, Valerie Jenness, Neil Fligstein, Calvin Morrill, Claude Fischer, Josh Pacewicz, Neil Smelser, thank you. Elizabeth Onasch, you were always there to make sure something I had written wasn't crazy. Thank you to my editor James Cook, who believed in my vision from the beginning, as well as the anonymous reviewers for their meticulous feedback.

To the many colleagues and friends that through many presentations, conversations, and feedback, I am also in your debt. Brian Sargent, Robert Vargas, Nicole Gonzalez Van Cleve, John Eason, Amada Armenta, your friendship was just as important as your feedback. Same goes to the members of the Race, Crime, and Democracy Network. I could not have finished without all your support. Thank you to Patrick Lopez-Aguidado, Anjuli Verma, Chris Muller, Issa Kohler-Hausmann, Benjamin Fleury-Steiner, Joshua Page, Reuben Miller, Kimberly Hoang, John Hagan, Ann Swidler, David Harding, Melissa Guzman-Garcia, Phil Goodman, Tony Platt, Jonathan Simon, Julia Adams, Tianna Paschel, Raka Ray, Heather Haveman, Cristina Mora, Monica Prasad, Colin Jerolmack, Christopher Wildeman, Marcus Hunter, Sarah Brayne, Megan Comfort, Stephen Sweet, Margaret Andersen, Elijah Anderson, Karen Barkey, Gary Alan Fine, Victor Rios, Cybelle Fox, Kimberly Morgan, James Mahoney, Forrest Stuart, Corey Fields, Elisabeth Clemens, Annette Lareau, Iddo Tavory, Erin Kerrison, and Anthony Peguero. Finally, thank you to the men and women who opened their places of work to me. It was not easy, but I tried to study your constraints and I hope you will see some of that represented in this work. Forgive me if I have forgotten anyone.

Introduction

On January 10, 1998, the Los Angeles County Sheriff's Department—operator of the largest jail system in North America—moved "all" of the incarcerated persons suffering from mental illness into its newly opened flagship Twin Towers jail. Deputies offered ice cream, cookies, and even cigarettes to entice the "mentally fragile" into leaving their cells and making the trek to the new facility. Throughout the day, 1,500 mentally ill inmates were transferred into the one- and two-man cells of the Twin Towers jail. The moves were accompanied by the doubling of the Department of Mental Health staffing in the jail and the hiring of 100 custody staff to properly monitor sick inmates whenever they left their cells. Concerning the unprecedented jail healthcare expansion, the Sheriff said at the time, "It is an issue that must be resolved. . . . There are no other options, except get it done."[1]

A few months earlier, just down the road, in front of a raucous crowd, another move was being finalized. The Los Angeles County Board of Supervisors—the county's five-member political leadership—voted to rebuild its flagship public hospital with no more than 600 hospital beds. Most concerning for the hundreds of community activists who packed the county's Hall of Administration was that every commissioned study on the issue had shown that a bare minimum of 750 beds were needed to serve the community. An emergency room (ER) physician warned the supervisors about their downsizing plan, "they are going to be dying in the hallways," he said "dying waiting to get into the operating room."[2]

At first glance, these two scenes fit a single idea that comes to mind whenever the topics of urban jails and public hospitals are raised. It is widely believed that because we as a society disinvested in public health, particularly mental health institutions, during the 1960s, the sick and poor are now finding themselves within the purview of criminal justice institutions. Actors on both sides of the political aisle, journalists, and academics generally agree that we have funneled resources into local criminal justice institutions—making it possible for them to take on new duties such as healthcare and other kinds of social services—at the expense of health and welfare institutions.

Redistributing the Poor. Armando Lara-Millán, Oxford University Press (2021). © Armando Lara-Millán.
DOI: 10.1093/oso/9780197507902.003.0001

Making matters worse, places meant to protect the nation's poorest—places like public hospitals, welfare offices, and even public schools—have become more difficult to access. And in some cases, we have even securitized these supposedly helping institutions with police and criminal suspicion to deter people from abusing their goodwill.

While seemingly straightforward, the puzzle of why medicine has expanded in America's largest jails and has been restricted in its largest public hospitals is more complicated. Consider Los Angeles County in the preceding examples. The decision to rebuild the hospital represented a significant investment, using over a billion dollars of public revenue sourced from local, state, and federal funding. Conversely, the expansion of healthcare in the jail took place during significant capacity retrenchment of the jail system—the jail system had been shedding thousands of inmates due to severe fiscal shortfall. Together they seem to contradict the idea that jails are taking on medicine because we have divested in our public health system and overinvested in jails.

It may be surprising to hear that these cases are not anomalous, but actually fit wider national trends in our largest cities. It is a little acknowledged fact that, since the early 1990s, the nation's largest jails have seen declines in capacity, released thousands of inmates, and suffered severe shocks of austerity. It may be equally surprising to know that spending on public healthcare, including the money we have committed to large safety-net hospitals, has grown tremendously during the past 30 years. This holds true even when we control for rising medical prices.

In order to better explain the puzzle of medicine's expansion in large urban jails and its restriction in public hospitals, this book proposes an alternate way of thinking about state action at the turn of the twenty-first century. It is not just "fiscal austerity" that shapes policy, but also the equally constraining force of what we can call "legal demand." In short, contemporary urban governments in the West are in the unique position of having to continuously manage catastrophic budget cuts while also navigating a policy and legal environment that at least ostensibly holds them accountable to the laws of the land, procedural rules, court rulings, watchdog groups, and minimum service requirements. This is the central and least recognized problem of contemporary statecraft wherein officials must routinely solve a mismatch between available public funds and the public's legally recognized right to those resources.

The central argument of this book is that in response to such crisis, state officials *redistribute the poor*. This concept describes how state agencies circulate people between different institutional spaces in such a way that generates revenue for some agencies, cuts costs for others, and projects illusions that services have been legally rendered.

The theory helps us to understand that the move to expand medicine in jails has not occurred simply because jails have more resources and are seeing more mentally ill arrestees, but because reorganizing jails along these lines has allowed public officials to renew dying institutions. Likewise, public hospitals dismantled inpatient capacity not simply because of budget retrenchment, but because doing so allowed local governments to receive huge infusions of revenue from the federal government. New forms of restricting access to hospital services occurred in the wake of these cash infusions. In total, the move to expand medicine in the United States' largest jails and to restrict it in the largest US public hospitals is a part of the same crisis abatement effort.

Theorizing transformations in these institutions as crisis abatement is worth underscoring. Michelle Foucault (1975) and Pierre Bourdieu's (2015) influential work serve as starting points for many accounts of what scholars call "poverty governance institutions," places like jails and public hospitals that spend a bulk of their resources intervening in the daily lives of the poor. In different ways, they argued that what defined such institutions was their effort to acquire more information about the populace and fit people into neatly digestible categories for the purposes of social engineering. The account presented in this book is in fundamental agreement with the idea that state institutions work to socially control, but takes a step away by suggesting that transformations in such institutions are also the result of a series of temporary resolutions to state crisis. Poverty governance institutions may reclassify people, but this is a first and necessary step for redistribution in times of major constraints on the state.

As such, by the end of this book we should begin to think less about the *dismantling* of the state and more about the *disappearing* of crisis. A significant body of scholarship has tried to account for the persistence of social spending despite major political efforts to dismantle the welfare state (Pierson 1994; Thelen and Streeck 2005; Hacker 2004; Morgan and Campbell 2011). By focusing on the redistribution of the poor, we can be attentive to how it is increases in social spending (usually mandated by new laws) that actually shroud structural retrenchment. When welfare states use redistribution to resolve crises a kind of social suffering associated with those crises are disappeared from the public record and transformed into some other, more affordable kind of social need.

It is my hope that by taking the idea of redistributing the poor and the disappearing of crises more seriously we can begin to make sense of other kinds of social problems. For example, in recent years, we have seen mass school closures in places like Philadelphia, where 30 schools were closed in one year, waves of violence in places like Chicago, and unaccompanied minors at the US-Mexico border. Officials usually respond with some kind of service expansion: shifting displaced students around in Philadelphia (Jack and Sludden 2013), funding violence prevention workers or providing community relations training to police officers in Chicago (Vargas 2016; Weichselbaum 2016), and sending hundreds of legal professionals to the border (Hennessy-Fiske et al. 2014). A short while later, these problems become considered publicly resolved in ways that indicate disappearing. After first appearing in 2012 under the Obama administration, the problem of unaccompanied children at the US-Mexico border was partially serviced by losing track of thousands of minors under the Trump administration (Nixon 2018). In Philadelphia, overcrowded classrooms became less of a public concern when many of the transferred children were simply suspended or began engaging in truancy (Steinberg and MacDonald 2019). After a short while, stakeholders stop debating solutions, call off emergency meetings, and produce policy metrics that represent these problems as resolved or at least stabilized; that is, an atmosphere of imminent crisis disappears.

It is the concept of redistributing the poor that can provide us with the language to understand these moments and how, despite the public resolution of crisis, people continue to suffer and underlying economic strife continues.

The Puzzle of Urban Jails and Public Hospitals

What does it mean to say that medicine is expanding in jails, but becoming more restricted in public hospitals? It is important to understand this point in all its nuances, because it is the puzzle we are trying to explain in this book.

Consider the following two scenes, taken from the fieldwork I conducted for a year in two such institutions. On one particularly crowded night in the jail, a sheriff's deputy said something that stuck with me: "Thank god for the nurses." The young deputy I was shadowing made this offhand remark with a chuckle. After what had just occurred, it must have seemed like stating the obvious. The deputy had been called over to attend to an inmate who was huddled in the corner of the "fishbowl," a room surrounded by Plexiglas where a dozen or so inmates await transfer into a bed in the sprawling jail. When the deputy attempted to jostle the inmate lightly on the shoulder, the inmate reacted violently, swinging his arms and screaming, "Just leave me alone!" The deputy immediately pinned him to the ground. Shortly after, a nurse responded to the situation. As I had seen her do before, she quickly administered an antipsychotic sedative. Eventually the inmate calmed down and was carried out of the room. As with hundreds of other inmates on a nightly basis, this inmate would be given a bed in the mental health unit of the jail—highly prized by inmates, extremely expensive from a budgetary standpoint, and very scarce from an organizational standpoint.

On a different night, I observed another provision of healthcare, but this time in the ER of a nearby public hospital. I watched a triage nurse administering another kind of pharmaceutical—opioid pain medication—to a waiting patient who had come to the ER complaining of general abdominal pain. The patient had been waiting for four hours and was among many in the observation room of the triage unit—a room packed with patients who were all qualified to receive a bed but had to wait because of overcrowding. An hour or so later, the patient was called by the nurse to receive a recheck of their vital signs. Indeed, the patient's heart rate had slowed, and she reported feeling a bit better. The nurse looked up at me: "watch, they are going to leave." I was not sure what the nurse meant, so when the patient indeed left another hour later, I asked the nurse how they knew: "a lot of people are in here when they shouldn't be. Just looking to get drugs or whatever. Things are really crowded in here . . . so it's fine."

These were just two of many instances that characterized the fieldwork I conducted for a year in a large urban jail and a large public hospital: in the jail, the ubiquity of medicine as a form of knowledge and technology to understand inmates and run the jail smoothly; in the hospital, the ubiquity of criminal suspicion to understand patients and make the tough choices about who should receive very scarce public hospital beds. In the jail, nurses, doctors, therapists, psychotropic drugs, sedatives, mental health evaluation forms all sprang into action whenever there was a disruption to the normal routine of jailing. When the young deputy told me he was grateful for nurses, it was because he did not have to choose whether or not to use more severe force on this inmate, which put him at legal and employment risk. In the hospital, the triage nurse described the situation as "fine" because, during the year I spent in this public ER, the ubiquity of criminal stigma was all around us. Not only were police, jailers, squad cars, and handcuffs a continuous presence in the ER, so was the suspicion that the patients who overcrowded the ER were not very sick, but instead were out to abuse the hospital as a source of drugs.

We can characterize the role of medicine in the large urban jail in following way: it is the potential of *providing* medicine to inmates that has come to define the way that jailers resolve their key organizational problems. We have to be careful with this characterization, as it is easy to slip into hyperbole. It is distinct from the claim that medicine is nowhere to be found in jails, or that jails do a great job of treating their inmates. Instead of such hyperbole, we can detail how medicine is able to resolve a fundamental tension in jails: the fact that there are too two few specialized beds (both medicalized space and high-security space) for far too many in-need inmates.

We can characterize the situation in the large public hospital with the inverse statement: it is the potential of *restricting* access to medicine that helps to resolve its key organizational problems. Through ethnographic observation we see the ubiquity of criminal suspicion among hospital staff; that patients are not particularly sick, but instead are drug-seeking criminals. This helps them make decisions about who can be delayed access to healthcare resources, which makes it more likely that waiting patients will stop seeking healthcare. Just as in the jail's case, we have to be careful of hyperbole. It is not the case that the ER has become colonized by the criminal justice system, nor is it the case that medical professionals do their work without any contamination from law enforcement or bias against perceived criminals. Instead, we can detail how criminal suspicion helps to resolve the fundamental problem of public ER life: that there are far too many qualified patients in need of hospital beds than there are available beds.

These ethnographic findings make sense given broader trends in the largest urban jails and public hospitals. In 2010, roughly 65% of incarcerated adults in prisons or jails met the medical criteria for an alcohol or drug use disorder, seven times likelier than individuals in the community. One estimate puts the figure at 20% of those in jail who have a serious mental illness (defined as schizophrenia, psychosis, bipolar disease, and serious and persistent depression) compared with only 4% of the general population.[3]

The restriction of medicine in public hospitals also makes sense given their well-known capacity declines. There were 1,691 public hospitals open in 1983, but by 2003 fewer than 60% remained; 19% had closed, while 23% were converted to private or nonprofit organizations. The situation was a bit starker if we highlight urban public hospitals: more than half closed or were converted between 1983 and 2003. Such reductions are significant because urban public hospitals make up a huge share of the healthcare safety net. Private hospitals are often unwilling to pay for undercompensated care and transfer poor patients to public ERs. Moreover, health clinics are unevenly distributed and lack the specialty services offered by a public hospital. Consequently, public hospitals now provide 65% of uncompensated care within the largest metropolitan areas.[4]

The Limitations of Theories of Urban Poverty Governance

The growth of medicine in jails and its restriction in public hospitals is a rare topic in which the explanations we hold about them are widely shared. Consider the similarity between the following two statements. Longtime prison abolitionist Angela Davis—someone dedicated to ending our obsession with locking up poor people and people of color—wrote in 2014:

> The three largest contemporary psychiatric facilities . . . are jails: Cook County Jail in Chicago, L.A. County Jail, and Rikers Island in New York. A direct consequence of the closure of psychiatric institutions called for by progressive deinstitutionalization advocacy.[5]

Compare this to a statement in 2015 by the head of the Cook County Sheriff's Department—someone dedicated to running the notorious Chicago Jails:

> It's a national disgrace how we deal with this . . . this person has a serious mental illness, he's not being treated, his family and him [sic] have been disconnected for years, he obviously doesn't have a job. . . . He will come in contact with law enforcement . . . if they're going to make it so that I am going to be the largest mental health provider, we're going to be the best ones. We're going to treat 'em as a patient while they're here.[6]

Whenever this topic is raised by social scientists, activists, journalists, civil rights lawyers, fiscal conservatives, and even law enforcement administrators, some version of the following idea is repeated: that because we as a society disinvested in public health, particularly mental health institutions during the 1960s, the sick and poor are now finding themselves within the purview of criminal justice institutions.

The idea actually rests on three related, but distinct theories about our largest public institutions: the thesis of "deinstitutionalization," "retrenchment-criminalization," and "mass imprisonment." In what follows, we consider each of these explanations and how they fail to fully account for important empirical trends.

Myth 1: Deinstitutionalization Leads to the Medicalization of Prisons

Scholars have identified the closure of state hospitals in the 1960s as a development that affected many different aspects of US society. Indeed, between 1950 and 2000, the number of people with serious mental illness living in psychiatric institutions dropped from half a million to 50,000. We can call this the "deinstitutionalization" thesis; that because of society's failure to provide adequate traditional healthcare, housing, and social support outside of jail, persons who end up arrested are now sicker than they used to be. The idea is that the mentally ill engage in behaviors that make it likely they spend time in spaces that put them into contact with law enforcement and that new laws criminalize the behaviors that they tend to engage in (disturbing the peace, loitering, drug use, etc.).[7]

A key problem with the deinstitutionalization thesis is that it does not explain administrators' *willingness* to provide healthcare resources in jail. The closure of mental health institutions in the 1960s does not explain why healthcare resources inside of jails in any form (whether they be therapeutic services, healthcare personnel, hospital bills, or psychiatric services) now make up large portions of jail budgets. For instance, D.C.'s jail system spent $33 million on medical services (a quarter of its budget in 2012), Chicago's healthcare department spent $100 million for jail healthcare in 2016, which was in addition to the Department of Corrections's own $327 million budget, and the New York City jail's spending on healthcare per inmate grew by 175% from 2010 to 2020. While representative statistics on jail expenditures on healthcare and mental healthcare are notoriously difficult to acquire, we can indirectly measure such spending through staffing levels. In the only two years that comparable statistics are available in the national jail census, healthcare workers in the largest jail systems grew from 2380 personnel in 1988 to 4214 in 1999.[8]

To think that such resources are related solely to the number of people who suffer mental illness in the jails would be naïve. Why not simply let the mentally ill languish untreated in jails? These numbers relate to the willingness of jail administrators to pay the salaries of medical professionals who work in their jails, to pay for mental health treatment areas that must be accredited, and to invest in continued diagnosis of individuals during their jail stays. For instance, as we shall see in Los Angeles County, we can quite easily trace a move from the denial of a medical problem in the county jails in the 1980s, to the acknowledgement of the problem by 1990, to major action taken on the problem in 1997, to major appeasement of courts on the issue in 2015.

Myth 2: Declining Public Health Expenditure

The deinstitutionalization thesis is usually linked to what we can call the continued "retrenchment-criminalization" of social welfare institutions. Rather than simply emphasize the closure of state hospitals in the 1960s, this thesis would explain the decline of medicine in public hospitals with the attempt of politicians since the 1970s to curb social expenditures. This has meant the retraction of social protections, especially the widespread closure, downsizing, and privatization of public institutions that serve the poor. Scholars point to two developments: the application of market rationality to public institutions and the racialization of public spending. Concerning the former, a major political movement transformed what we think of as good governance, that legitimacy is gained when public authorities make prudent choices that lead to "returns on investment," rather than investment to alleviate human suffering (Schram 2015; Brown 2015). Concerning the latter, the idea is that both national political parties took advantage of popular fears concerning the civil rights movement, urban riots, and social spending during the 1960s that was perceived as favoritism toward the urban poor and people of color. "Irresponsible" spending on welfare was racialized through media images of "welfare queens" and "deadbeat dads" and other images of black and brown persons abusing taxpayer money (Crafton 2014; O'Connor 1998; Block et al.

1987). More or less, both movements are thought to have led to the dismantling of the welfare state.

Scholars have also linked continued retrenchment to the use of crime control techniques or "criminalization" to restrict access to what remains of public institutions. The best-known examples are the use of policing techniques in urban public schools and welfare offices, which have been well documented to use new methods of surveillance, supervision, and deterrence that have led to an increase in the number of expulsions and arrests from both schools and welfare roles. These are instances of what law scholar Jonathan Simon describes as the emergence of crime control as a dominant frame in public policy: in many cases this has meant interpreting the behaviors of the poor as related to criminal activity—especially drug abuse—testing for it, and using it to disqualify them from services.[9]

While it might be tempting to apply the "retrenchment-criminalization" argument to public hospitals, the empirical story of spending on public healthcare is actually quite the opposite. From 1992 to 2008, national and state expenditures on Medicaid nearly tripled, rising from $116 billion to $339 billion, a 90% increase in inflation-adjusted dollars. The growth holds true even if we adjust for increasing healthcare prices (but diminishes to 53%). Spending on healthcare also grew as a proportion of all federal spending from 5% in 1992 to 7% in 2008 and of all state spending from 17% to 22%. Beneficiaries of Medicaid grew from 36 million to 59 million or 66% from 1992 to 2008 (Figure I.1). These increases even square with rising need: Medicaid spending per poor person in 2008 constant dollars nearly doubled, from $4,700 to $8,500.[10]

Astonishingly, exactly during the period of public hospital capacity declines, mechanisms were created to help funnel public money into urban safety-net hospitals. The Omnibus Budget Reconciliation Act of 1981 under Ronald Reagan allowed Medicaid funding to take into account the heavy share that safety-net hospitals took in providing uncompensated care. Through various mechanisms, such as Disproportionate Share Hospital funding and the 1115 waiver programs, states creatively used such programs to funnel dollars to their largest public hospitals, even when those hospitals were not in the most fiscal need. Over time, the 115 hospitals represented by the National Association of Public Hospitals, the nation's largest urban public hospitals, became highly dependent on federal funds to keep their hospitals afloat. This is a story of resilience in public hospital funding in spite of major efforts to dismantle them.[11]

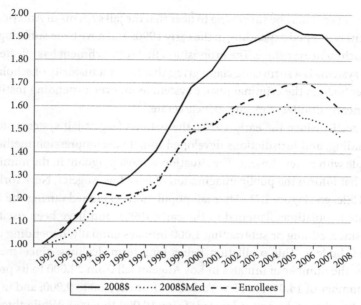

Figure I.1 Trends in Medicaid expenditures and enrollees per poor person, 1992–2008 (no enrollment data).
Source: Thompson (2012).

Myth 3: The Ever-Expanding Penal System

The deinstitutionalization and retrenchment-criminalization theses have been paired with what can be described as the thesis of "mass imprisonment." The idea is that because governments have funneled so much public revenue into criminal justice organizations (e.g., police, criminal courts, jails, and prisons) they are increasingly becoming the site where the urban poor access social services. Megan Comfort calls this "carceralized aid," or social support given to the urban poor on the condition that they enter into contact and surveillance of criminal justice institutions. There is a good reason to believe this as the number of people under correctional supervision grew from 1.8 million in 1980 to 7.1 million in 2005—when combined with those released but still bearing the stigma of felony records the number jumps to approximately 16 million. Many have characterized this growth as "mass imprisonment" insofar as the incarceration rate is now high enough and concentrated enough to affect an entire demographic group: poor men of color from large urban areas.[12]

However, it may be surprising to hear that the jail systems in America's largest cities stopped expanding in the early 1990s and have been suffering from retrenchment ever since. The proposition that retrenchment has affected carceral systems is a surprising claim given that the vast majority of scholarship conceptualizes the criminal justice system as an ever-expanding institution with nearly limitless capacity to incarcerate.[13]

In reality, since the early 1990s, the nation's largest jail systems stopped expanding, and jurisdictions developed inmate decompression methods to grapple with retrenchment. The situation is most poignant in the municipalities that inform the public imagination of jails: Los Angeles, New York City, and Chicago (Figure I.2). After jail populations exploded during the 1980s, inmate populations flattened in the early 1990s, and have been oscillating ever since; adding or subtracting 1,000 inmates annually, depending on the annual budget. This oscillation belies long-term declines: since the early 1990s, the number of inmates in Los Angeles fell from 24,000 to its present-day number of 14,000; in New York City, from 20,000 to 9,000; and in Cook County, where Chicago is located, from 10,000 to 6,000. While this situation is most significant in these three cities, it also characterizes the largest counties in the country's top 50 metropolitan statistical areas (MSAs), which collectively represent 30% of the nation's total jail population.[14]

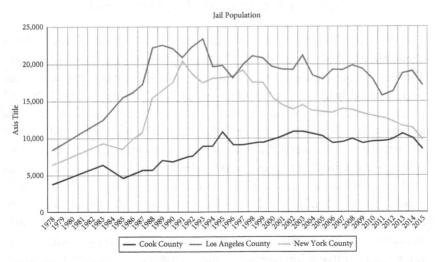

Figure I.2 Jail populations in Cook County, Los Angeles County, and New York County, 1978–2015.

Source: Vera Institute of Justice.

This decline was no mere happenstance. The stagnation represents organizational decision-making amid deep fiscal uncertainty. Large urban jurisdictions innovated with new kinds of early release and "alternative to incarceration" mechanisms, including own recognizance release, home supervision, electronic monitoring, halfway houses, and emergency early release, among many other programs. Scholars of penal state have had difficulty incorporating these developments into their analysis of mass imprisonment.[15]

In total, while these three related, but distinct theses create important backdrops to the expansion of medicine in jails and its restriction in public hospitals, they cannot fully account for important countervailing trends. On the one hand, while jails began spending more money on healthcare, they did so at exactly the time they began suffering from unprecedented—and little acknowledged—retrenchment. This makes it difficult to square the idea that jailers had the wherewithal to take on the new modalities of medicine. On the other hand, in large public hospitals, the provision of medicine is becoming more restricted, but public spending on large urban hospitals has expanded. Thus, we have a much more complicated puzzle, worthy of explanation.

The New Evidence: Historically Embedded Ethnography

As we saw, our three existing theories fail to fully explain the transverse trends of large urban jails and large public hospitals. It is often the case that in place of actual histories of field sites, ethnographers of poverty governance institutions make use of broad theories—theories like deinstitutionalization, welfare retrenchment/criminalization, and mass imprisonment—to explain the origins of what they have found, even if those theories do not fully fit their cases.

The alternative this book proposes is to tie our ethnographic puzzles to archival history. We can call this method of theory building "historically embedded ethnography." While I discuss my methods in greater detail in the Appendix to this book, this is exactly what I did. I spent a year in a jail intake room observing the workers collaborate to process inmates into and out of the jail. I watched from areas closed off from inmates, watching and interacting with clerical staff, medical professionals, deputies, and risk-assessment officers behind Plexiglas as they carted files, conducted interviews, and collaborated to decide where inmates should be housed in the jail. I observed the parallel set of workers in the public hospital. These were the triage staff—the nurses, nurse practitioners, clerical staff, and law enforcement personal—who collaborated to make decisions about who should be given a bed in the ER and who should be made to wait. I did not just ask these workers about what they did on the job, as an interviewer might; I watched them encounter routine problems and come up with a culture that resolved those problems that no single individual could have predicted or might even been aware of. The power of ethnography is to understand the culture of a group—groups that transcend the personalities of any single person.

I embedded what I found in my observations at these two confidential institutions into the archival history of Los Angeles County. This meant scouring thousands of old boxes filled with memos, meeting transcripts, official letters, communiques and emails, official reports, and accounting books—in short, the day-to-day operations of running the largest county in the world.

The history is perfect for us because the Los Angeles County's jails and public hospitals transformed in just the ways we are curious about. Before the crisis, the county's jail system could be characterized as intent on jailing as many people as possible and denying them healthcare resources. During the 1980s, its jail population had exploded from 7,800 inmates to 24,000, and jail officials ignored at least five different health citations. After the crisis, the jail system can be characterized as utterly declining in capacity—relying on the permanent early release of thousands of inmates—and becoming defined by medicine, with entire wings of jails transforming into medicalized space. These two jail trends—capacity declines and expanding access to medicine—came together in the 2015 historic vote to downsize its downtown jail, re-build it as a "correctional healthcare treatment center" fully staffed with medical professionals, and implement an unprecedented diversion program that would send inmates with histories of mental illness or substance abuse into community supervision.

Conversely, despite the immense fiscal pressure, its public hospital system received an infusion of public funds that helped it to stabilize. However, while the new funding helped to build new public hospitals were constructed and kept two from being privatized, all were downsized to dangerous levels in the process. This story of persistence, but restricting access, crystallized in the 2008 opening of a newly rebuilt Los Angeles County + University of Southern California (LAC + USC) Medical Center. The facility costs the county billions of dollars in revenue and was a significant commitment to community health, but had been downsized to only 600 beds—far below the determined community need of 750 beds.

What is key about this case is that it more closely fits the national trends than previously existing theories. While existing theories failed to fully account for the retrenchment of local criminal justice systems and the persistence of large public hospital funding, the history of Los Angeles County captures those countervailing trends perfectly.

The Argument

The Crisis of Fiscal Austerity and Legal Demand

We can use this history to formulate a new theory to explain the puzzle of large urban jails and public hospitals. It is the confluence of "austerity" and "legal demand" that creates the conditions for institutional transformation. As we shall, state officials confronted ever-decreasing resources at the exact same time that new legal rules forced them to expand access, provide more services, and enforce rules that had been neglected.

We have already seen how budget retrenchment affected jail sizes in US cities in the early 1990s, but the problem of "austerity" runs much deeper. No deliberation on urban poverty governance in the United States can move forward without addressing the limits of city resources. In contrast to European nation-states, the drive to gut public budgets in the United States has trickled down to the local municipality. It is towns, medium-sized cities, and major metropolises that have faced the systematic dumping of risks, responsibilities, debts, and deficits. This is what Jamie Peck describes as the "hallmark of austerity urbanism, US style."[16]

Austerity has manifested in different ways. Some cities face extreme fiscal shocks, while others experience slow and less-visible budget pressure. For instance, while only a few cities have actually declared bankruptcy, approximately 300 municipalities nationwide are currently in default on their debt. One study found that for 1,000 local governments between 2001 and 2008, pressures for budget cutbacks and service retrenchment were quite widely distributed. Detroit, the most well-known example, was placed into state receivership, has cut the city's workforce by one-fifth, has designated some neighborhoods for active disinvestment, and is delivering residual services in others on a triage basis.[17]

While many date the rise of austerity conditions in California's public sector to 1978 (the year that a tax revolt in California passed Proposition 13), it was not until 1992 that fiscal crisis severely affected Los Angeles County. In that year, the Republican-led State of California appropriated $1.5 billion from all California counties' property tax revenue. While fiscal crisis periodically re-emerged, it was the crisis between 1992 and 1997 that would forever take expansion off the table for the hospital and jail systems. In its health system, Los Angeles County faced a $500-million-per-year structural deficit. The county's chief administrative officer (CAO) recommended that the county close down its flagship hospital as well as 20 health clinics. The Sheriff's Department would need to absorb a 40% cut, resulting in the closure of eight of nine jails, the release of over 12,000 inmates, and a 62% reduction in patrol services. Edward Edelman, a member of the Los Angeles County Board of Supervisors, described the cuts to a newscaster: "We have to make choices. . . . Hospital, sheriff deputy layoffs, clinic closures. . . . You're talking about cutting services . . . people will have to wait . . . in the long run, jails cells will close, sheriff stations. . . . We are releasing people early. This is sending the wrong message to criminals who are convicted."[18]

Alongside limits on fiscal resources, what is lost in many analyses of poverty governance institutions is what legal historians and political scientists call the "judicialization" of American politics. A large share of policy questions have become judicial questions; answered not through political party representation, grassroots mobilization, or coalition building, but through litigation. Special interest groups often feel that litigation is their only viable option to obtain policy goals, and state officials are at times relieved to have difficult disputes resolved in courts.[19]

The way that legal pressure is manifested in the day-to-day operations of American cities is through the actions of organized, professional agencies populated by legal actors both inside and outside the state. What binds these diverse actors is that they act as watchdog organizations that do not have constitutional access to the jails and hospitals, but rely on ongoing relationships with administrators to maintain their surveillance. Their power is difficult to measure, as sometimes no official legal action ever takes place. Rather, threats of legal action can be communicated informally to political leaders, or county action plans are submitted to these organizations for informal approval, or policy actors formulate plans with knowledge of the interested parties that tend to sue over certain issues.[20]

Key is that while the same austerity crisis would incite the transformation of the Los Angeles County jail and hospital systems, their respective legal pressure took different forms. Concerning the jail, in 1988 a Federal District Court ruled in favor of inmate rights litigants in the *Rutherford v. Block* lawsuit. The ruling was an overall jail population cap—ensuring that every inmate needed a mattress and walls, which prevented inmates from being placed in hallways and on roofs—and provided the Sheriff the ability to release inmates early in order to meet that population cap. This ruling was followed up with smaller lawsuits and legal threats that targeted the issue of medical care in the jails. The Department of Justice (DOJ) and the American Civil Liberties Union (ACLU) threatened to sue, sued, and successfully monitored the jail's provision of health and mental health services in 1997, 2002, 2012, and in 2015. These smaller legal demands concerned how adequate provision of jail healthcare would be defined. In total, legal demand placed limits on overall capacity, orienting the Sheriff's Department to releasing inmates, and later pressure pushed the Sherriff to expand access to medicine in its jails.

Legal force took the inverse direction on the public hospital system. In 2003 a Federal Court specifically ruled that Los Angeles County could not close inpatient capacity if its reasons for doing so were a lack revenue. This means that, in contrast to the ruling that made it possible for the jail to decompress, this ruling barred decompression. Subsequent regulatory pressure came from the Centers for Medicare & Medicaid Services (CMS) and the Joint Commission on Accreditation of Healthcare Organizations (JCAHO) regarding the adequate provision of healthcare during long wait times. In total, legal demand placed limits on the ability of the hospital to cut beds, orienting the Department of Health Services to increasing wait times.

In total, any explanation that attempts to explain the transformation of public institutions must consider how legal advocates make claims on local governments in the midst of immense budgetary cutbacks. Such governments cannot, at least publicly, simply abdicate their responsibility for the poor and those in need of services. This is the central and least recognized problem of contemporary statecraft wherein officials are routinely confronted with legal challenges that force them to expand programs at the exact moment they face insurmountable budget deficits.[21]

Redistributing the Poor

What happens when officials are forced by legal imperatives to expand programs during a budget shortfall? I develop the concept of *redistributing the poor* to illustrate how state agencies resolve such tension. This idea describes how stage agencies circulate people between different institutional spaces in order to raise revenue and project the illusion that services have been rendered in legally adequate ways.

Redistribution unfolds through three processes. First, state agencies work to reclassify the people they are in charge of. This means that public officials will re-articulate the kinds of interventions that their wards are thought to require, for instance, emphasizing the mental health needs of a jail population over their security risks. Second, this reclassification allows the movement of such wards into different institutional spaces or changing the kinds of interventions that spaces provide. By doing so, they can make claims on revenue from other state agencies, both those horizontally located (for instance, such as a mental health department providing services and revenue to a jail) and those vertically located (such as a jail pulling in revenue from a state health tax or renting space to state and federal agencies). Third, it is the continuous movement between old space and repurposed institutional space that projects an illusion that services have been rendered in a legally adequate way. In total, these three processes align officially recognized demand with precious revenue.

The result is not coherent population management, in which the movement of people between state agencies is rationally coordinated for the purposes of punishing, healing, or socially controlling. Instead, the exchange of people is a product of distinct agencies acting alone, often in conflict with other state agencies over which agency will have responsibility for different categories of people and the public revenue attached to them. These are moments of statecraft in which poor people are legally and technically provided with a service, but their needs are also rearticulated into a different kind of need that produces revenue for the state or more conservative budgeting.

This can help us better understand the expansion of medicine in jails and its restriction in public hospitals. Because the legal pressure oriented jails toward decompression, this structured the kinds of redistributions jail officials could pursue. County officials shifted from thinking about their inmate population primarily as violent gang members to thinking about them as mentally ill, substance abusers, and as less criminally threatening homeless persons. Doing so allowed them to funnel in new forms of revenue into their jails from state and federal agencies while also rationalizing the release of thousands of inmates. County officials worked with legal agencies to develop inmate transfer techniques—such as expanded nursing in intake centers, closer observation of transferred inmates, and the use of psychopharmaceuticals that helped alarmed patients temporally feel better during their transfers—which all appear to us as progressive efforts to expand healthcare.

The specific character of legal pressure on the hospital system—oriented toward keeping hospital beds open (as opposed to decompression)—also structured the kinds of redistribution the hospital officials could pursue. County officials shifted from thinking about their patient population as urgently sick inpatients to thinking about them as outpatients, homeless persons, and immigrants who were all less seriously sick. Doing so allowed county officials to obtain revenue from the federal government, while also rationalizing the delay of patients in extremely long wait times. County officials worked with regulatory bodies to develop waiting management techniques to handle subsequent overcrowding—such as police units in intake centers, closer observation of waiting patients, and opioid medication that helped waiting patients temporarily feel better during their long waits—which all appear to us as regressive efforts to restrict access to medicine.

In total, jails have moved to expand medicine not only because they are seeing more mentally ill arrestees, but because reorganizing their jails along these lines has allowed them to tap into new revenue sources and new means of abdicating responsibility for inmates. Likewise, public hospitals moved to restrict access to medicine not simply due to cutbacks and criminalization, but because doing so allowed them to generate revenue from new sources and to rationalize extreme wait times. In all of these developments, the force of law is indistinguishable from the force of austerity; in fact, as we shall see, many of the changes in access to medicine in the jail and the hospital were at the behest of legal efforts to protect the rights of wards.

From Dismantling the State to Disappearing Crisis

The theory of redistributing the poor can help us to understand a wider debate about the resiliency of public institutions. During the past 40 years it has been easy enough for scholars to track major attacks on important social protections. All over the West, governments on both the left and the right have attempted to downsize, marketize, and dismantle the social safety net. The problem with these attacks is that, for scholars of welfare states, it has been much more difficult to find actual retrenchment in public spending. Famously, Paul Pierson (1994, 1998, 2001) showed that many social protections in Western nations have largely been persistent in the face of widespread political attack. In essence, the longer that welfare institutions exist, they accrue important constituencies and self-reinforcing rules that make them ever more difficult to dismantle.[22]

In the wake of this finding, scholars have moved to show that superficial persistence of public spending shrouds deeper, longer-term "structural retrenchment." Sometimes politicians simply take non-actions, and social need eventually outpaces the reach of those institutions (Hacker 2004); other times, old rules get privately put to use toward new ends that curtail services (Thelen 2004); and other times, officials will simply add other, usually private-sector, options in the hopes of making existing social protections less attractive (Morgan and Campbell 2011). By and large, however, we have had difficulty seeing true structural retrenchment because of the low visibility of cutbacks and the overall persistence of public welfare spending.[23]

The transformation of large urban public hospitals and jails in the United States examined in this book are cases of the persistence of public institutions, or what social scientists have called "welfare state resiliency." As health policy scholar Frank Thompson (2012) has shown, the Disproportionate Hospital Funding and 1115 Waiver programs that funneled funds into safety-net hospitals endured through two attempts to convert Medicaid from an entitlement to a block grant. Funding for healthcare in jails has grown exactly during the time that local criminal justice systems faced widespread retrenchment. These are contradictions in spending increases in the midst of widespread retrenchment efforts, fitting the dynamic of welfare state resiliency.

Redistributing the poor focuses our attention not to "blame avoidance" for dismantling efforts, but instead to the circulation of revenue that appears to us as increases in public spending. At times, an agency might suffer from budget shortfall and because of legal requirements will seek to find a way to draw in revenue from other agencies to pay for its services, or will seek ways of sending parts of its caseload to other agencies (which would represent increased spending to that other agency). In essence, because retrenchment is often paired with legal demand, agencies cannot simply dismantle; they change what they do and whom they are responsible for through spending.[24]

While the transformations studied in this book are examples of institution building during crisis, they nonetheless resulted in the shrouding of human suffering. As we shall see, while jails are expanding their provision of medicine, they have to do so in such a way that shrouds the needs of many medically needy persons. While public hospitals are restricting access to inpatient care and creating massive wait lists, they are also persisting, and public spending on them is growing. In essence, because welfare state spending changes the needs of caseloads and rearticulates legal demands to fit those new needs, the social suffering associated with the original crisis becomes administratively disappeared. The people and problems associated with a specific crisis of fiscal austerity and the law are erased from officials' descriptions and are most often turned into some other new kind of problem.

In the United States, this disappearing act is only possible because of racism, but it does not only affect people of color. I mean this in two respects. First, states only have creative possibilities for redistribution because of the existence of racially and gendered thinking about the kinds of needs people under their charge. As we shall see, the revenue-generating and cost-saving possibilities of emphasizing medical need occurred along lines of thought—for instance, that brown women have different needs than black men—that worked differently for raced and gendered groups. Second, redistributions are only possible because the public is willing to tolerate the premature death of black and brown bodies. If we understood these caseloads as primarily made up of white people—or perhaps if we acknowledged the many poor white people that do, in fact, make up these caseloads—the disappearing of suffering would be intolerable, groups would not be reduced to making legal demands in courts, and the crisis would be treated as if it affected all. That is, the crisis would be treated as the real crisis of humanity that it is, not as some particular policy problem. This is how what Ruth Gilmore's (2007) called the "disposability" of impoverished people of color becomes normalized. These are instances when, despite expansions of public spending, the social suffering of huge swaths of people is simply written off on paper as *successful* policy.

Plan of the Book

In Part I of this book we tell our jail story, while Part II tells our hospital story. Both are split into two chapters. Chapter 1 presents ethnographic evidence to understand how medicine relates to the daily problems of filling up a large urban jail. The major problem of jailing is that there are far too many sick incarcerated persons and persons with serious criminal biographies than there are available specialized cells. The chapter shows how in order to resolve these problems, jailers reinterpret inmates' biographies through stigma about the potential abuse of medical services and the widespread use of pharmaceuticals to quell disturbances. It is this work that jailers do—to produce sick inmates—rather than the biographies that inmates bring with them to the jail that ensures the limited space of the jail can always accommodate the demand for space. In total, the expansion of medicine in jails is neither about serving inmates' needs nor about ignoring them, but instead is about using medicalization to resolve the fundamental problems of the overcrowding jail.

Chapter 2 presents the historical transformation of the Los Angeles County jail system in order to explain why medicine has becomes a useful tool for jailers. Jails were successfully pressured into providing expanded healthcare by various legal agencies at the exact same time that they faced unprecedent budget constraint. In response, jails began thinking of their inmates less as violent gang members and more as mentally ill, substance abusers, and less threatening homeless persons. Doing so allowed them to draw in funding from other agencies and release thousands of inmates. In total this resulted in the mere circulation of inmates between general housing and medicalized space as the key solution to the jail's fiscal retrenchment and legal demands.

Chapter 3 presents ethnographic evidence of the restriction of medicine in the large, urban public ER. There are two routine problems facing triage staff: there are always too many urgently sick patients whom staff have no real reason to favor for scarce hospital beds, and far too many less-urgently sick patients who technically should never receive beds. The rational rules of triage do not provide the means to reconcile these two problems and, moreover, mandate that all of these patients be treated. The chapter details how a culture of understanding patients through criminal stigma, the widespread administration of pharmaceutical drugs during the wait, and police presence all work to resolve these two fundamental problems of hospitalization. It is this work that triage staff do—to produce patients that appear less medically needy—that ensures the extreme wait times do not become legally problematic.

In Chapter 4 we present the historical transformation of the Los Angeles County hospital system in order to understand the restriction of medicine in large public hospitals. In contrast to a simple story of underfunding, the chapter details how it was legal demand and austerity that pushed local government to reinvest in public healthcare while simultaneously downsizing inpatient capacity. Officials re-emphasized their patients less as local residents in need of urgent care and more as non-urgent patients, homeless, and immigrants in need of early intervention. Doing so allowed them to draw in funds from the federal government to reconfigure their healthcare systems away from inpatient care. In the process, however, legal and regulatory agencies began threatening public hospitals for dangerous overcrowding. Such pressure led directly to the development of waiting line management techniques—such as policing, closer observation of waiting patients, and opiate medication—that, in practice, worked to restrict care.

The Conclusion pushes us toward a new way of thinking about public institutions and poverty governance at the turn of the twenty-first century. The goal is to provide language for thinking less about how criminal justice institutions are expanding, or public welfare institutions are downsizing or even criminalizing, but instead to think about the disappearing of crisis. This is an important move because unless we can center the reformulation of dying institutions amidst severe crisis, we miss shrouding specific forms of social suffering.

The methodological Appendix presents my vision for "historically embedded ethnography." The findings developed in this book were only possible by linking field work to archival research and theorizing from that link, rather than developing theory from either alone. The chapter spells out how this style of research is distinctive from other ways ethnographers have used history and how it can be used elsewhere.

I want to end this introduction by pointing out the similarity between the concept of "disappearing" and the Latin American word *desaparecidos*. I am indeed taking a que from the sordid word. *Desaparecidos* was a recent linguistic innovation that came out of the Latin American experience of right-wing coups in the post–World War II period. In order to consolidate power, these authoritarian regimes "disappeared" hundreds of thousands of individuals. People would simply vanish, with no record, no trace, or body. The starkest example were so-called death flights in Argentina in which dissidents were taken on airplanes and dropped into the ocean. Families were left in limbo for years, not knowing where their loved ones were and with no perpetrator to officially blame. Thus, the word *desaparecido* came to be invented in Latin American Spanish.

The disappearing of suffering in the case of modern urban governments is in no way akin to the actual murder of citizens in Latin America (though many do experience "premature death" in hospitals and jails that goes unaccounted for). Instead, what I refer to here is the administrative disappearing of a specific kind of person that is tied to a particular context of crisis.

Somehow, despite overwhelming new demands in the midst of budgetary cutbacks, state actors find ways to avoid bankruptcy and keep places like hospitals and jails humming along. Meanwhile, the impoverished people caught up in these dynamics often have a keen sense of their disappearing. That is, no matter how many times policy elites preach reform, and no matter how many times social movement leaders claim that "this time it really matters," the status quo seems to get reproduced and poor people's social suffering gets "disappeared." Ultimately, administrative disappearing pushes us to think about state activity as the continuous resolution of crisis—crisis that moves from one institutional space to the next, while state institutions continue to carry on (when they otherwise might have failed) and the poor continue to suffer.

PART I

THE EXPANSION OF MEDICINE IN LARGE URBAN JAILS

The following two chapters offer an alternative explanation for the expansion of medicine in large urban jails. The "deinstitutionalization" and "mass imprisonment" theses would contend that jails have expanded medicine because the people they jail have gotten sicker and because they have the resources to take on new modalities of social control. As we have seen in the Introduction, both of these theses cannot account for jailers' willingness to fund medical resources in jails (rather than simply allow the sick to languish), nor can it account for the fact that our nation's largest jails have suffered severe shortages of resources.

In Chapter 1, "Summoning the Sick and Violent into Jail," we use ethnographic evidence to understand the routine problems of jailing created by fiscal austerity and legal demand and how jailers go about resolving those problem. In essence, there are far too many sick inmates and far too many persons with serious criminal biographies than there are available specialized cells. The chapter illustrates how it is medicalization—used neither to serve inmates needs nor ignore them—that works to resolve the organizational problems of the overcrowded jail.

In Chapter 2, "The Medicalization of the Los Angeles County Jail System, 1978–2015," we present the history of the Los Angeles County jails in order to find specific explanations for the dynamics uncovered in Chapter 1. In total, the archival record shows that, during each challenge of fiscal austerity and legal demand, a section of the inmate population would have its qualities of medical need and medium risk emphasized in order to generate revenue or diffuse the inmate population.

Thus, it was not simply that more sick inmates began to fill up the jail, as predicted by the deinstitutionalization thesis. Nor was it that the jail simply grew in resources and power to take on the duties of medical provision, as predicted by a thesis of mass imprisonment. Instead, taking on medicine was a form of crisis abatement. The county could—by redistributing the inmate population—use medicine to renew its dying jails, no matter how severe the crisis between fiscal austerity and legal demand became.

1

Summoning the Sick and Violent to Jail

Much has been written about the human suffering that occurs in jails. Year after year, civil rights organizations, prisoner advocacy groups, and the Department of Justice have meticulously documented the extensive patterns of neglect and abuse within detention facilities. The media occasionally presents an exposé of how jails have become the nation's largest mental health providers. These accounts (which appear in public reports, affidavits, lawsuits, and newspapers) always contain descriptions of extreme physical violence against inmates, medieval sanitation issues, undertreatment of severe mental illnesses, and medical injuries that result in lifelong health problems. A simple arrest on a Friday night is not to be taken lightly. Public health scholars know that a stay in jail of any length of time is likely to have a negative impact on a person's mental health. One simply needs to imagine being trapped for 48 hours in a small room with four other grown men and a single toilet—not to mention slow access to medications, constant yelling and screaming, human stink, physical intimidation, and various other forms of humiliation—to understand what a weekend in an American jail might be like. John Irwin in 1985 wrote that the jail is a place "the rabble will continue to suffer our harshest form of imprisonment, the jail—an experience that confirms their status and replenishes their ranks." This is the vision of the jail as a place of social suffering, a place where the state manages the destitute by removing them from the community for short stints, disorienting, degrading, and punishing them, and returning them to the community even less equipped to deal with the instability of impoverished lives.[1]

Conversely, when jail administrators and law enforcement officials think about the jail, they see it differently. For them, it is an administrative problem: making sure that the right inmates are placed in the appropriate type of cell space, such as ensuring supposedly violent inmates are housed only with other violent inmates or that a person at risk of suicide is placed in a single cell and under constant watch by a medical professional. Based on the classification decision-making rubric, an inmate is assigned a level of security risk, placed in housing presumably appropriate to that risk, given special

Redistributing the Poor. Armando Lara-Millán, Oxford University Press (2021). © Armando Lara-Millán.
DOI: 10.1093/oso/9780197507902.003.0002

protection if necessary to avoid being victimized, put on an appropriate schedule for receipt of medication, and tracked for the purposes of court appearances, release date, and medical appointments. If such placements are done correctly, in the administrators' view, there will be, on average, less inmate-on-inmate violence, less need to use physical discipline in the jail, and consequently less social suffering. The administrative problematic is to make sure the jail runs smoothly, not comfortably. In this view, the jail is meant, in part, to punish individuals, most of whom have been convicted of crimes in the past, and to compel some kind of future crime deterrence.

If the journalist works to expose malfeasance and perhaps place jail reform on the public agenda, and the practitioner seeks to amend rules in order to incentivize better decision-making, what is the role of the social scientist? What can an ethnographer who observes a jail for a year tell us, using the tools of sociological theory, that a journalist or practitioner cannot? The journalistic endeavor might expose rule breakers, wrongdoing, and the immense social suffering that occurs in a jail. It might result in a settlement for an aggrieved party, or specific individuals being held accountable. But what of the sociological study of the jail? What can it tell us?

Consider an episode that occurred in the Los Angeles County jail in the fall of 2005. The case received much media attention and was the subject of numerous public hearings. A person was murdered while incarcerated when he cut ahead of other inmates in a food line. The murderer, who had a known history of gang membership, waited until he was alone with the victim in a holding area out of view of the guards.

The episode began with the arrest of the victim—whose name was Cochran—by the Los Angeles County Sheriff's Department. Cochran was arrested as an "escapee" and as a felon in possession of a gun. Because he was an escapee from a correctional facility and was found with a violent weapon, he had the merits for a high-risk classification score that would indicate he was a serious potential threat to jail safety. However, during Cochran's detainment at a local patrol station, the arresting officers noted that he exhibited "aberrant behavior" and should be looked at by mental health professionals upon his arrival at the jail.

When Cochran reached the medical practitioners in the jail intake room, he told them he was bipolar, had been off his medications, and been taking illegal drugs. The officials also noted that Cochran was "somewhat recalcitrant." They classified him at the highest level of risk to jail safety: the designation of "keep away," representing an individual to be kept away from all other inmates. Cochran was placed in the mental health unit of the jail in single-cell housing and was watched closely by mental health staff.

Once in the mental health area of the jail, Cochran refused to talk to the staff and refused any toxicology tests. Staff wanted to conduct tests in order to determine what level of narcotics were in Cochran's system so that they could safely administer bipolar medication. Some time passed, and eventually Cochran calmed down; but because he was bipolar, this was not technically a reason to believe he was no longer suffering from a mental ailment. Individuals with bipolar disorder may seem completely calm at some points. However, because Cochran seemed in control of his faculties, it was difficult for the staff to maintain his status as urgently needy and in need of a scarce mental health bed in the jail. The determination was made that he could be transferred back to intake and reclassified.

When Cochran returned to the intake room, he told the classification officer who interviewed him that he was "not a real escapee" but was just a "walk-away." This distinction is important, because an escapee is someone who has attempted to escape from a secure correctional facility and is therefore in need of close supervision, whereas a "walk-away" is someone who simply leaves or does not report to a non-custodial supervisory program in the community. The intake staff made the effort to verify Cochran's claim. This is also critical, because if such a claim were true, it would likely mean a downgrade from a high-risk classification score of eight to a medium-risk classification score of seven, at which point the inmate could be placed in more widely available and cheaper dormitory-style housing. Thus, there is incentive for classification officers to try to verify such claims. Inmate Cochran was reclassified as a medium-risk inmate and was sent to general population, where he later met his death at the hands of another inmate.

In a meeting about the incident with the Los Angeles County Board of Supervisors, a Sheriff's Department official explained,

> [Cochran] was appropriately classified as a 7, based on his background, based on his arrest, criminal history . . . unfortunately, the amount of personnel and the "real estate," to use a term for amount of space we have in the jail to be able to do that, doesn't always allow us to put just 8s and 9s together. We have 1,400 murderers or attempted murderers in the jail, 630 of them in central jail, so it's very difficult to be able to place them in these single cells and the amount of personnel or manpower needed there to be able to watch them in single cell rather than in a dorm setting is an

enormous cost, and we don't have the ability to have that many deputies or custody assistants there to do that. . . .

We use a very sophisticated system called Northpoint in the classification . . . in terms of putting gang murderers, the more serious murderers, if you can say there's a "non-serious" murderer, but the reality of putting gang murderers separate, the sheriff has directed, if we can do that. Right now, *we don't have the sophistication to determine who's a gang murderer and who's a regular murderer* but we're looking into the ability to do that, to put just gang murderers with gang murderers and keep the other murderers, who I guess are less violent, if you can actually say that, separate from those people. So there's some issues there that we can improve upon in terms of classification areas. (emphasis added)[2]

From the perspective of the journalist or civil rights litigator, the issue is whether the inmate was wrongly categorized as a medium-security risk, whether the jail systematically puts individuals such as Cochran at risk, and whether any illegal wrongdoing against this individual or individuals like him took place. We can also see the practitioner's perspective, that there isn't enough high-security space in the jail to isolate all eights and nines (high-security inmates) from sevens (medium-security inmates) and that better, more precise information is needed about inmates in order to separate them appropriately. Thus, the incident exemplifies both of our current framings of the jail: as a place of social suffering and as a problem of jail administration.

When the Sheriff's Department official mentions the word "real estate," we get our first hint of what social science can offer. That phrase points to the interplay of classification, laws, budget, and space inside the jail. When an inmate is determined to be a "seven"—a medium-security score—he will be imprisoned in dormitory-style housing along with hundreds of other inmates who are watched over by only four or five deputies. Each of those sheriff's deputies has a salary, benefits, overtime, and a retirement plan, all of which translate into a dollar figure that is represented on a budget and paid for with county tax dollars. Such an inmate is thus a cheap inmate who can be placed in more widely available "real estate."

Conversely, if an inmate is given a classification score of eight or nine, which officials consider to be a high-security score, indicative of a significant risk of violence, the inmate will be imprisoned in very restrictive housing. Restrictive housing is characterized as cell occupancy of only one to four inmates, supervised by a much higher ratio of sheriff's deputies. Such housing is made even more expensive by the requirement that when these inmates leave their cells for whatever reason, be it medical care or a court appearance, they must be accompanied by a deputy at all times. The same logic holds true for medical care, but with the addition of medical staff who all have a salary attached to them. Thus, to score an inmate as an eight or nine (violent) or as extremely sick and in need of an inpatient bed is an expensive proposition.

Yet classification decisions technically should have nothing to do with budget considerations. It is supposedly an inmate's history of violence or health symptoms that should determine the classification. Indeed, in my observations of classification and medical intake decisions, discussions of the budget never appear. In the classification interview, inmates are asked about the charges for their arrest, their criminal history, and the kinds of medications they are taking. When intake personnel talk about their jobs, they never invoke the budget, discussing instead issues related to how they figure out whether or not inmates are lying about their history.

Despite the absence of a discussion about budget, a very peculiar phenomenon occurs in jail intake: there is always the right number of high-security inmates for the number of available high-security cells and the right number of sick people who can safely be treated in inpatient beds. This is an astonishing phenomenon. Despite the fact that risk classification and medical evaluations do not consider the budget, and despite the fact that inmates come to the jail with infinitely complex criminal and medical biographies, the numbers and types of inmates produced perfectly match the available jail space. This is what sociologists might call a *looping effect*, when an official categorization changes the way humans behave, and this in turn changes the next iteration of the official categorization. In our case, the budget (how much money has been allocated to certain types of space in the jail) transforms the ways that informational inputs (e.g., criminal history or medical need) are interpreted and, subsequently, such biographies are used to determine budgeting needs. The budget, in part, causes itself, and social science can help us see this effect in the intake room.[3]

For instance, recall the official's explanation about the inmate Cochran. The subtext of the official's comments is that because there are so many murderers in the jail, it makes it difficult to keep an inmate like Cochran in the high-risk category. The official is pointing to how the budget can change the way a jail constructs what it is considered a high-risk inmate; that is, because there is so little space in which to house risky inmates, there is much pressure to downgrade inmates to less risky designations for any reasons that present themselves. We saw this when Cochran indicated that he was not an escapee and was in fact a "walk-away." It is not that the intake staff took him at his word, but rather that they made the extra effort to verify his claim because they knew this was something that would make it easier to house him.

In other words, because the budget limits how many high-security spaces there are in the jail, it raises the bar for the types of information that qualify a classification as risky. The standards change. This was most evident when the Sheriff's Department official commenting on the Cochran incident talked about the need to make a new distinction between more serious "gang murderers" and less-serious "regular murderers."

It is because of this alignment of inmate demand with limited capacity for beds that we need the social scientist. We need to know how, despite all the social suffering, inmate and staff violence, medical uncertainty, and other problematic issues associated with the intake process, a jail can create a budget that always strikes just the right balance between cost and resources. A sociological examination can teach us how available space will always line up with inmate needs.

Who Is a Gang Member, Who Is Sick?

The first step in understanding the daily linking of inmate's biographies with resource constraint is understanding the two routine problems— determining who is violent and who is sick—that emerge during the harrowing process of jail intake. The intake unit is a series of waiting rooms, hallways, and office spaces designed for inmate processing. It is staffed by what we will call the intake workgroup—those individuals who collectively process inmates. The intake workgroup includes sheriff's deputies, classification officers, management, nurses, doctors, psychologists, clerks, record keepers, and even the computer system that tracks inmate information.

In large urban jurisdictions such as Los Angeles County, the intake process can take a full 24 hours from the time an inmate enters the intake room to the time placement is made into a housing location. Although the intake room examined in this chapter is smaller, the Los Angeles County jail processes more than a thousand inmates on days following weekends.

When inmates first arrive at the jail, they are escorted to large rooms where they will await their interview and risk-classification scoring. While the inmates wait, custody staff members use local, state, and federal databases to research their criminal histories. At the location I studied, the waiting rooms had multiple rows of benches where dozens of inmates sat, cuffed at both the hands and feet. Inmates were completely mixed; inmates from different gang affiliations, individuals convicted of murder, and people charged with DUIs (driving under the influence) were sitting side by side. There were very few guards, and often many disturbances. The wait could last for hours. Inmates often fell asleep, got into fights, had traumatic breakdowns, or, as custody staff summarized it, "acted up" or "shut down." Custody staff members only intervened and entered the room when disturbances slowed the ability of classification officers to do their work.

During an intake process, inmates are called one by one to assessment booths, where they are interviewed and assigned risk classification scores. These scores determine the level of housing inmates will be placed into—high, medium, or low security—and contribute to whether inmates qualify for custody alternatives and early release. Conventionally, jail classification assigns a number or risk score to inmates based on their threat to in-jail security. The classification system uses a decision-making tree that weighs key variables such as current offense, relationship to gang activity, institutional behavior, escape history, and criminal history. For example, an inmate with an assaultive felony charge requires a risk score of no lower than seven, which is considered a medium-risk score. If the inmate has a history of behavioral problems while being institutionalized, his security level should rise to eight or nine, which are high-risk scores.

Jail administrators often portray classification as a straightforward, impartial practice. However, as sociologists have proven *ad nauseum* in every other public service setting, frontline processing personnel always have the opportunity for discretion. At several points during their semi-structured interviews with inmates, officers can use discretion to nudge classification to a higher or lower score. First, they can use "overrides" to manually circumvent the decision-making tree. Officers are provided with blank space on the classification sheets in order to explain their justifications for ignoring the rules of the decision-making tree. Second, classification officers have the discretion to identify special classes of inmates (e.g., gang members or the mentally ill) and refer them to more specialized assessment teams (e.g., gang intervention units or mental health providers). Third—and less well-acknowledged—are aspects of the classification tree that require subjective decision-making. For example, when considering a history of assaultive felonies, officers have the discretion to factor in (or not) "elapsed time" since prior convictions. When considering an escape history, beyond noting specific escape attempts from the jail, classification officers have the discretion to include a "walk-away" from non-secure sites (e.g., halfway houses or work release programs) as an escape attempt. Most prominently, when considering institutional behavior problems beyond noting whether an inmate has a specific infraction on file, classification officers have the discretion to determine whether an inmate is cooperating with facility staff, intimidating fellow inmates, or demonstrating positive attitude changes. In practice, officers can, if they wish, emphasize information garnered from semi-formal interviews with inmates to inform such discretionary points.[4]

After their assessment, inmates enter a series of long hallways, where they wait to take a shower, have their clothes removed, and receive inmate clothing. Depending on the level of jail overcrowding, this process can take hours, and inmates often fall asleep on their feet or become very agitated and disgruntled. The problem of inmates acting up or shutting down is often a source of great contention in these hallway spaces; for instance, if inmates fall asleep, they prevent the line from moving forward. Officers patrol the line to ensure that inmates stay awake. There is constant yelling and fighting; it is never silent.

After receiving showers and new clothes, inmates enter into what custody staff members call the "nursing room." This room is staffed with a variety of rotating personnel, including psychologists, nurse practitioners, doctors, and registered nurses. It is a room in which inmates often request or demand medical attention so as to be further processed via what I call the "medical route"—either the medical facilities within the jail or local public hospitals. Medical personnel sit in caged booths where they interview each inmate and make a health assessment. Nurses ask inmates questions about any potential health problems and, if inmate records are available, scan them for known problems. A common problem for custody and medical officials is that many inmates demand intervention from psychologists or claim to be at risk for suicide.

After the nursing room, inmates are sent to wait in what custody staff members call the "fishbowls." These are rooms filled with 10 to 20 inmates who wait to be routed toward either release, placement in different security levels of the jail, or the medical route. A bed coordinator unit (BCU) sits in the middle of these fishbowls. This is the decision-making body that determines the ultimate fate of inmates waiting in the fishbowls. As there is no direct contact between the classification officers in the BCU and the inmates waiting in the fishbowls, the staff of the BCU makes routing decisions based on the information provided by the risk assessments (both medical and custody) and notes provided by nurses and classification officers. Jail spaces or "beds" will become available in certain parts of the jail that are suitable for corresponding classification scores—for instance, the maximum security part of the jail is suitable for inmates with classification scores of 8, 9, and 10—and intake officers will have to find suitable inmates for that part of the jail.

Who Is a Gang Member?

Many people assume that jails imprison only local inmates and arrestees being held for minor crimes; that is, inmates who are not as violent as those being held in state prisons, inmates who have been convicted of misdemeanors as opposed to felonies, and inmates who are being imprisoned for short stints consisting of only few days. With such a vision of the jail, it is tempting to assume that it might be easy to differentiate between a medium-security inmate and a high-security inmate.

Unfortunately, in the modern large urban jail, intake rooms are dealing with a grade of offender far more "serious" than typically thought. First and foremost, jails are filled with inmates who are technically state prisoners or soon-to-be state prisoners, or who would have been state prisoners in some previous incarnation of the law. The reason for this is less complicated than it appears. At a basic level, jails imprison individuals who are awaiting their day in court. This means that individuals who are likely to be sent to state prisons will reside in jails during their attempts to contest their charges. More important, however, is the impact of state prison overcrowding on local jails, where there often is a backlog of inmates who have been convicted and are waiting to be transported to state prison. Further, some overcrowded state prisons contract out to local jails to house their state inmates. Finally, changes to state laws over the years have raised the bar for the types of felonies that can be sent to state prison. A prime example of this is California's 2011 "Realignment" plan in which the state declared that, moving forward, certain grades of offenders would be the responsibility of local jails.[5]

The second factor that creates a more serious grade of offender in county jails is the persistence of county-level early release and custody alternatives. Many local jails are under federal court supervision for excessive overcrowding and have been given the discretion to release inmates as necessary in order to comply with court orders. Thirty-five counties in California have this discretion. In 1988, Los Angeles County was given the authority to release inmates before their sentences were complete. In many of the most severely overcrowded jails, inmates who have been convicted of misdemeanors are almost always immediately released. Even pre-trial individuals arrested for minor crimes are simply cited and released by jail authorities with a promise to appear in court. The types of release and custody alternatives used by counties vary greatly, and include own-recognizance release, home supervision, electronic monitoring, halfway houses, emergency early release, and many other programs. There is also great variation in how these programs are instituted, who is eligible for them, and at what point in the incarceration process they are instituted. Jail administrators might release inmates based on the percentage of time served, the most recent criminal offense, or some kind of risk classification score. Some jurisdictions review files in house, whereas others rely on probation departments to assess inmates. Moreover, release standards can change daily depending on available jail space, fluctuations in arrests, and inmate behavior. In order to diffuse overcrowding amid budget constraints, many jurisdictions are moving toward the greater use of assessment tools (instruments that score social, familial, and mental health status alongside criminal risk) to evaluate need as well as risk in determining who is best fit for release.[6]

Practically, the problem of higher grades of offenders in local jails presents itself in the question of how an inmate relates to gang activity. Although readers unfamiliar with the jail population may find it ridiculous to think that gang members cannot be identified based simply on appearance or a note on their criminal record, there is an incredible amount of uncertainty related to this question. The problem is twofold. First, many inmates at the jail have the types of markers that classification officers use to identify gang members. For example, many inmates have tattoos on their neck and face, have shaved heads, fit racial stereotypes of gang members, and have some specific mention noted in their criminal records of gang involvement over the course of their lifetime. However, even the presence of all of these indicators is not enough to prompt a classification officer to call in the gang assessment team. There are simply far too many inmates with such indicators than there are available high-security spaces in the jail.

Second, inmates have incentive to cast behavior in a light that either minimizes or exaggerates indications of gang involvement. Classification officers are very cognizant of the fact that self-reporting by inmates can work in either direction. Why would inmates desire to exaggerate their gang involvement? Some inmates might want to be located in a specific unit or part of the jail in order to be near friends or individuals they know. Some inmates might also want to be placed in the more restrictive single-occupancy cells and thus would exaggerate the extent to which they are targets of gangs. Former gang members, gang dropouts, or gang members testifying against other gang members may claim to be the targets of gang retaliation. They could also be exaggerating their involvement in order to receive extra protection from jail staff. Some individuals in charge of gangs might want to hide that fact in order to facilitate ongoing gang operations. It might be important for staff to remove and isolate such a person because violence is about to occur. But staff do not always have enough space or resources to isolate all shot-callers; moreover, even if they did, some new shot-caller would simply emerge. Thus, it is important for the jail intake staff to be as up to date as possible on ongoing gang politics, rumors, and machinations.

When a classification officer believes an inmate is hiding or exaggerating his gang involvement, the work of a special gang assessment team becomes critical. This team is made up of deputies who are tasked with identifying gang members among the jail population, developing intelligence about ongoing gang politics, and making recommendations about where those inmates should be placed in the jail. The gang assessment team is responsible for interviewing inmates sent to them by classification officers, regularly communicating with state prison officials about statewide gang developments that may be impacting the jail population, taking photographs of inmates while they shower in order to spot gang tattoos or "uniforms," and observing how inmates interact in the intake waiting room areas in order to identify gang members.

Actionable information related to gang placements is incredibly fluid, and the flow of information between the assessment team and the classification officers is not without error. Sometimes gangs devolve into all-out war and the job becomes easier. However, sometimes gangs can simply have some "beef" or are involved in a minor skirmish between specific members of a gang. In such instances it is not always clear that a certain gang is a high priority. In the Los Angeles County jail there are hundreds of gangs with constantly evolving relationships to one another, and this changing context informs what constitutes actionable information for classification officers.

Suffice it to say that the gang assessment team has significant time constraints and cannot reasonably respond to every request made by the intake staff. Classification officers know that they must have a solid hunch before calling the team to take a second look at someone.

The final source of uncertainty related to gang involvement is that it is actually unclear whether such involvement should warrant extra attention, security, and a higher classification. At times, intake staff see an individual's history of violence as more relevant to their risk classification than their mere connection to a gang. For instance, should an inmate with known gang membership who does not have any recent violence-related charges be considered a more serious risk to jail safety than an individual with no gang involvement but a recent violence-related charge? To make matters more complicated, what if the former individual claims to have left the gang life? This can actually work in the reverse as well: staff know that even a person who has left the gang life and has not had any recent episodes of violence might, once placed in the high-pressure jail system, be called upon by current gang members to participate in violent attacks, might be the target of gang violence by rival gangs, or otherwise may be more at risk of being pressured into violence. Thus, gang membership could be construed as an indicator denoting extreme risk to jail safety, or could be simply a factor to be weighed against the context of the individual and current intelligence on gang politics. In sum, inmate relationship to gang activity is a complex and highly uncertain proposition.

Who Is Sick?

For the intake workgroup, the other major source of uncertainty stems from the legal mandate that all inmates must be provided with adequate medical care. Because the jail population, for the most part, has cycled in and out of the criminal justice system, that population has a lifelong experience of relatively low access to healthcare, is extremely poor, and is therefore sick, both with chronic long-term ailments such as high blood pressure or hypertension and with complicated specialty care needs. Indeed, because of their relative poverty and low access to healthcare outside of correctional institutions, inmate populations have significant health needs.[7]

Jail staff view the inmate population in three ways: as inmates who clearly need to be placed into a general or specialty inpatient medical bed; as inmates who clearly do not need such placement; and as inmates whose diagnosis is unclear and who can wait for "sick call" and be treated through outpatient jail health services or pharmaceuticals. It is this third group that presents medical staff with a large share of its problems.

"Sick call" is a service mandated by law whereby an inmate housed in general population at any correctional institution can create a medical complaint that medical staff must respond to. At overcrowded jails such as the one I observed, staff know that if an inmate with a medical issue is sent straight into general housing, that medical issue will probably not be addressed for weeks. After evaluation by a nurse, such an inmate would be sent to the outpatient jail medical clinic, seen by a doctor, treated as necessary, prescribed medications, and sent back into general housing. There is no system of triage for sick call lists; it is often up to the sheriff's deputy in charge of specific cell blocks to collect inmate medical complaints and send a list of those to nurses. The intake staff are generally aware that individuals can fall through the cracks once they move into the sick-call pipeline because their complaints are often treated frivolously by deputies, who can decide if someone is "crying wolf" or should be punished in the context of security issues.

The alternative is to mark individuals as medically in need as they pass through the intake room and place them in inpatient beds. In jails there are different types of medical inpatient bed housing that all have different levels and types of care. For instance, in the Los Angeles County jail there are five types of mental health housing. There are 46 very limited mental health beds that are a part of the larger 200-bed licensed correctional treatment center. These beds are reserved for inmates who need acute care because they are either an immediate danger to themselves or others, or have a serious disability that prevents them from functioning at a basic level. Inmates will receive extensive psychological intervention by trained staff in this level of housing. The next level of medical housing are single- and double-cell observational mental health units. Here, inmates are observed by custody staff or medical personnel in order to keep them from hurting themselves or others, but they do not receive serious medical interventions. Next are large dormitory-style housing reserved only for mental health patients who can be cared in a less intensive way by a smaller number of professionals. Such spaces in the Los Angeles County jails are serviced by social workers, psychiatrists, psychologists, and private-sector treatment providers who attempt to treat substance abuse and mental health needs and plan for an inmate's release and subsequent needs. Inmates suffering from mental illness who continue their medication are placed into general housing.

Another key medicalized space is that of specialty care offered in nearby public hospitals. For example, if an inmate needs to see an orthopedic surgeon or a specialist for a neurology exam, intake staff must determine prioritization for such placements. If inmates are sent out to nearby hospitals for care, they will be transferred there and their space in the jail will be taken by another inmate. Such transfers are quite literally extensions of jail space.

Although the jail I studied did not have as many differentiations of medicalized space as the Los Angeles County jail, it did have a ladder system of different acuity levels that inmates are sent to and cycled through; that is, inmates are upgraded or downgraded among these levels as their condition changes. A key fact about these spaces is that they are very limited and there are many more inmates who could qualify for services than there are spaces. Recall how inmate Cochran moved from medical space to general population. How very sick individuals move from intense medical supervision to general population give us an indication of how this pressure works to redefine medical eligibility criteria.

Another source of uncertainty in medical decision-making is the relative lack of medical information about inmates. Medical intake staff have limited access to diagnostic procedures and equipment and limited time in which to gather the full range of an inmate's medical information. Because much of an inmate's medical history could be missing, medical staff must rely on self-reports. In addition, there is the belief among the medical staff that many of the inmates probably have something that could be—or needs to be—treated. The uncertainty this creates for the workgroup is twofold: it is both a medical uncertainty and a legal uncertainty. Medically, professionals must make daily assertions about which patients can or should receive the limited number of medical beds. Legally, this conundrum is of grave concern because the jail is, by law, mandated to provide healthcare to all who are deemed to require it. Lawsuits from inmates are a constant concern for medical staff.

The Jail Intake Conundrum

Is an inmate who is clenching his fists and in an aggressive posture when he approaches the classification booth someone who should be referred to medical professionals for evaluation and possible placement in medicalized space? Or is he someone deserving of placement in a maximum-security cell? If such an inmate is positively determined to be needy from either a medical or security perspective, he will need to be placed in some of the most scarce bed space in the jail and be attended to by a greater ratio of expensive deputies, nurses, and doctors—all of whom have salaries. As we saw, the task of the intake workgroup is not easy.

At their core these problems are symptoms of the trends we are examining in this book: the expansion of the duty to provide medicine, and the great decline of capacity. The scarcity of high-security and medical space represents the budget constraints, and the complexity of health and criminal biographies of inmates represents the nearly limitless demand to provide services to inmates. Inmates classified with risk scores of seven (medium threat) and those who are sick but can await services are the hinge upon which jail "real estate" hangs. Such classification decisions are significant to jails because the seven category makes up the majority of inmates, and many inmates can oscillate at their boundaries with more expensive space.

Given the immense complexity related to determinations of gang activity and sickness, how is it possible that the intake room always produces the exactly right number of inmates for the available "real estate" in the jail? To solve the mystery, we must turn to the intake workgroup and its solutions to these routine problems.

Reimagining the Jail as a Welfare Institution

The starting point for understanding the alignment of demand with constrained space rests in a cultural innovation among the workgroup. Intake staff members view a portion of the jail population as purposely committing crimes in order to receive "jail benefits"—what staff members construe as shelter and safety from the streets, food, showers, protective housing, and medical services. As intake staff have come to understand it, their role, in addition to the more traditional jail concerns (e.g., appropriately assigning risk scores, maintaining security, and meting out punishment), is in part to keep people whom they primarily understand to be the undeserving poor from entering the jail and accessing these resources. This stereotype centers on the belief that poor people abuse public resources because such people are morally deficient; that is, there is an expectation that poor people—especially poor people of color—tend to be lazy, lead mismanaged lives, and hail from dysfunctional households. This stance requires decision-makers to reimagine many individuals in their caseloads as mainly welfare abusers rather than as true criminal threats. It is common among the intake unit to refer to inmates as "regular customers" and to be on the lookout for inmates who try to "game the system." Officers also refer to the cells or units of space within the jail as "beds," which emphasizes a characterization of the jail as housing. The following quote from an intake officer illustrates the numerous components of this orientation:

> Look, sometimes they will just come out and tell you [that] they robbed or did something to get thrown in here. A lot of the fire department guys, the paramedics, they know that they get called in and a guy has drugs on him just so he can end up here. . . . It's such a waste. We are overbooked with murderers, gangsters . . . who do this for a living, who don't care about hurting people [pause] and we have to deal with these people who can't control themselves, can't take care of themselves.
>
> I've seen some guys here for years. You're telling me you can't get your act together in 15 years? We have programs to help them out . . . they get sentenced to these programs and just drop out. They'd rather be in here 'cause they don't have to do anything. [They] just want us to take care of them.
>
> You see it in the way they complain in here. It's this whole entitlement thing. They are always, like, yelling at us: "Take care of me! Take care of me!" to make sure they are safe. And the moment something happens that's out of our control, it's like "Oh, I'm gonna sue you, I'm gonna do this and that." One guy told me he gets arrested to come in here just so he can get a settlement and make some money. That's the attitude . . . we have to pick out the real criminals, the people who are out to actively plan and hurt people.[8]

This elucidates how custody officials conceptualize their jail as a welfare institution of sorts. Note the use of the phrase "entitlement." This parallels the prevailing political rhetoric about welfare institutions and the people who cheat and abuse public aid. Additionally, the officer describes the characteristics of lazy criminals: a desire to be incarcerated (going so far as to fake crimes), infantile nature, and ability to manipulate the jail and legal system as a resource.[9]

This reimagination of the jail is constantly maintained by the sharing of enduring stories of specific inmates well known to the staff. These stories mostly involve specific homeless individuals who frequent the jail and gang members who supposedly seek jail time in order to communicate with their gang brethren. Custody staff members share these stories in the break rooms, hallways, and during key moments of decision-making. While stories of "jail abuse" may be true for some of the individuals described in them, what is more sociologically interesting is that the recasting of jail time as entitlement is used to understand an entire inmate population.

Stories of inmates commonly unfold in two ways. The first storytelling device involves gang members who actively work to make their charges seem more serious. According to the stories exchanged between jail staff members, these inmates are attempting to communicate with gang members already in the jail. Such inmates know where specific classification levels will place them in the jail, and they attempt to "game the system." Additionally, according to the stories, gang members will claim they are ex-gang members in order to be given special handling status and be placed in protective custody. Custody staff members believe protective custody to be a jail benefit. Further, these stories include moralizations about inmates who do not mind receiving higher classifications—and even go so far as to admit to inciting violence inside the jails—because they are "career hardcore gang members" who are committed to a life of crime and have abandoned any future of earning a legitimate living.

The second common storytelling device among the workgroup involves homeless people. Officers continually share stories of specific homeless individuals who frequent the jail and purposely abuse its resources. Rather than viewing the arrest of a homeless person for minor offenses as caused by over-policing or other criminological explanations, jailers blame crime on poor moral character, such as an unwillingness to overcome addiction or mental illness. The following exchange illustrates the role of storytelling. In this instance, an officer gave an inmate with a felony-level drug charge a lower classification. As the officer explained,

'There's no way that I give this guy a bump on this ranking . . . he won't get a bed on my watch. No way. I've seen that guy in here, in and out of here, for the past month. He's no kingpin . . . he's just looking for a shower and meal. Too lazy to go wait in line at the shelter, [he would] rather just get dropped off here.'
'So the felony drug charge? That's not serious?' I asked.
'For him? No way. Look. . . . There is a guy in here. . . . He comes in here every week ranting and screaming that he is playing tricks on us . . . that he

plants drugs on himself so he can get a free ride in here. No lie, he admits this. He just sits right over there . . . and mocks us.'

In this excerpt, despite the fact that the cases are unrelated, the story about another inmate is used to justify a low classification for an inmate charged with a felony-level crime. The classification officer believed that this inmate was seeking a shower and was too lazy to stand in line at a shelter. The story about some other individual is used as rationale for making sense of the inmate's lazy moral character and low classification score. The workgroup continuously shares humorous stories that reinforce a belief in "jail benefits" that must be protected from poor people. The key here is that the individuals featured in these stories serve to stereotype the inmate population as a whole.

The New Category of "Non-Gang-Related"

The effect of this cultural innovation is best understood by detailing its deployment in the otherwise rigid inmate classification system. Because classification officers know that their scores have a direct and indirect effect on the jail's ability to meet its population cap, they informally work to prevent inmates from being "nudged" from a medium ranking of seven to a high ranking of eight. The workgroup deploys its belief in "jail benefits" by using the more practical informal label of "non-gang members." This is not an official category on the decision-making tree. Although there are other examples of how officers put welfare stigma to use in classification, this label is particularly important because it is malleable, fitting many types of criminal backgrounds. To be sure, as we detailed in our discussion of the classification system and its opportunities for discretion, officers do not have free reign to alter scores—they must follow the strict rules of the decision-making tree; but when discretion allows for the subjective interpretation of an inmate's criminal history, officers will make use of their informal understanding of inmates as "non-gang members."

When officers understand inmates' felony-level charges as emanating from a culture of poverty—especially from what they perceive to be dysfunctional family culture—such crimes are susceptible to being labeled as "non-gang-related." A broad range of case circumstances pushes officers to designate some serious crimes as "non-gang-related," but the following are the most prevalent: domestic arguments resolved by police, inmates with cases pending in the child welfare system (e.g., paternity, child support, and children in the care of the state), homelessness, and most importantly, drug addiction. For instance, if officers learn that inmates have cases pertaining to child support, they associate their current charges with dysfunctional family culture. If an inmate blames a domestic partner for causing an altercation related to his criminal charge, officers can find ways to nudge the scores downward or prevent scores from being nudged upward. The following excerpt from a classification interview illustrates these points:

'. . . You have a court date in family court?' asked the classification officer of the inmate.

'Yeah, I'm having paternity issues . . .' replied the inmate. 'You know how these ladies are, man? I'm not trying to be a dad right now. That's not my responsibility. I didn't ask for that.'

'Why don't you just pay the payments, get it over with?' replied the officer. The inmate did not respond.

'. . . You pled no contest to a year in here, three years' probation . . . let's see . . . what did you do? They put possession for sale . . . hmmm.'

The officer stopped reading from the database and suddenly asked the inmate, 'How come you stopped going to the drug program?. . . What happened?'

'No, no, I was trying to do it, but my brother died so I couldn't make one of the sessions,' replied the inmate.

'Uh-huh. Is that when you got that girl pregnant?. . . I see what this is. What a waste, man. You are just messing around.'

After giving the man a classification of six (a medium-risk score), the officer clarified his reasoning to me: 'He's not really a danger to anyone. I mean, yeah, it says possession for sale, so I guess he COULD be a serious gang guy, if that's what you're asking me, but I don't think he is . . . 'cause you saw all the custody issues with the girl and some kid. He's just a deadbeat dad. He's out there doing coke or whatever and he knows to stay away from that girl. I mean, he wants to stay away from her. . . just the cockroaches fighting over crumbs. That's it. He's no big deal.'

This excerpt illustrates a downgrade that results from an officer's use of welfare stigma; that is, from his belief that an offense was related to dysfunctional family culture. The inmate's supposed familial dysfunction supersedes his robust criminal history. As the officer said, this history could have been used to indicate a more serious classification score. Instead, the officer mobilized welfare stigma, characterizing the inmate as drug addicted and a "deadbeat dad" who was unwilling to rehabilitate.

The following excerpt is taken from a classification interview in which an inmate had many indicators that classification officers use to identify gang involvement: violent charges on his criminal record, a specific mention of gang involvement, a "cholo" aesthetic, a shaved head, and prominent tattoos:

'Look, man, yeah, I was involved with a crew back in the day. I won't lie, but look, that's not what this is about. . . ." said the inmate, as he leaned in close. "I was out there with my lady and the guys got into some stuff; I had to say something . . . and I ended up here.'

The officer responded, 'But why did you have the gun on you? That's a deadly weapon. . . .'

'I'm not the only one in here with charge, man. That's status quo; that's just living, man; you know that.'

After the classification officer moved the inmate along, I asked him, 'Not that serious?'

'Yeah, I mean, he's obviously been mixed up in gangs in the past and the case involves a deadly weapon, but look, on some level he's right; lots of guys are like that,' said the officer.

In this example, the framing of the arrest as related to the inmate's girlfriend (e.g., dysfunctional family culture) is, at first, insufficient to downgrade the inmate. The officer notices the various markers that indicate gang affiliation and pushes the inmate to account for the firearm. The officer nudges the inmate's classification downward only after he concedes that this type of case is "nothing special." That is, among the overabundance of similarly situated inmates, he believes the case is unremarkable. I pushed the officer to elaborate on the exchange:

'What about the incident . . . what if that's gang-related?'

The officer said, 'You can just tell . . . like that incident, he's there with a girl. . . . These jokers are just out there; [they] can't control themselves, and they get into it and now we have to deal with them. Pretty much all filled up with these lazies in here . . . he's not special.'

At this juncture, the officer mobilizes welfare stigma to justify the downgrade post hoc. The violent assault is framed as a fight over a female partner, as a squabble with other "lazy" criminals, and as occurring in a world where all poor people carry firearms as a part of their normal, mismanaged lives. The officer views the incarcerated person as part of a category of "lazies" that he must dutifully manage and deal with as part of his job. Welfare rationale works to label this incarcerated person as a "non-gang member."

In the following excerpt, I provide an example of an incoming inmate who was moved into high-security housing. Although this inmate was in a position similar to the inmates discussed in the previous examples—who were cast as non-gang members—he was upgraded into the high-risk category.

The inmate approached the classification desk with shoulders held high. I noticed his aggressive tone when he arrived at the booth: 'What do you want from me?' The intake officer moved forward in his chair. 'Says here you had another assault? And there was possession for sale in the car you guys were in?'

'What do you want me to say?' said the inmate, raising his left eyebrow. 'Cooperate,' said the officer. 'You been through here before. What was the altercation about?' The inmate responded, 'We got caught into a disagreement with some others . . . we were using, just hanging out and they came hard at us. I dunno what you want me to say. You gotta do what you gotta do,' said the inmate in a frank tone.

'Alright then, here you go,' said the officer.

'What was that about?' I asked the officer. 'He, like, barely said anything.'

'Yeah I know, that guy knows the routine, look at his rap sheet here,' said the classification officer as he scrolled through the arrest history. 'Drugs, drugs, selling, assault, robbery . . . ha, he's been in the system for years, look at this guy. This guy is a hardcore dealer, he's not going anywhere, this, this is the type that I been telling you about, it's the type that we gotta keep off the street for as long as possible.'

'A lot of these guys have long records like that, though,' I countered.

'Well, see, he's not, like, begging to get out of here. Did you notice that? He knows what's in store for him. He's just gonna serve his time and get right back on the street and go back to his little game. All he knows is punishment. There's nothing left for a guy like that. And that story, what did he say? He got into a dispute? What do you think that was? They weren't users, that is a dispute over money or territory or whatever.'

In this excerpt, we see a moment of discretion that results in the casting of an inmate as a real criminal. It is instances such as these that push the classification officers to call upon the aid of the gang assessment team. The charge, a felony-level assault, presumably could have been associated with drug addiction when the inmate indicated he and his friends were "using." Instead, the charge was framed as the most recent in a long career of narcotics distribution. The inmate's seeming unwillingness to defend himself against such an interpretation and the indication of a "disagreement" that could easily be framed as a drug deal gone wrong were all used to upgrade the inmate's charge. He moved from being a drug-addicted individual who happened to get into a violent assault to being a gang member who perpetrates violent acts whenever he can.

As we see with these two examples, officers produce downward nudges in classification scores based on their understanding of whether they perceive an inmate to be a "non-gang member." The uncertainty involved in interpreting an inmate's gang membership and violent biography is regulated by this cultural innovation. Key is that the "non-gang member" category is an informal cultural innovation whose features constitute extralegal inputs related to welfare abuse; that is, stigma about social service provision changes the way practitioners view criminal history. In the end, officers' deployment of this informal category improves the chances that inmates will be assigned to the more widely available medium-security score of seven—thus providing the jail with a systematic way of funneling more inmates toward more widely available and cheaper space.

Turning the Violent into the Sick

We have now learned how the vision of the jail as a social service provider aligns criminal biographies with high security space. We now turn to the specific problem of limited medicalized space—but doing so does not mean we should forget how the problem of gang membership is solved. In fact, as we will learn shortly, security issues are intimately connected to who is likely to be considered medically needy. That is, from a sociological perspective, information related to security threats works to resolve medical uncertainty related to inmate health needs.

For jail staff, the biggest obstacle to the smooth functioning of the intake process is, in the colloquialism of the staff, the frequent "acting up" or "shutting down" behavior of numerous inmates. "Acting up" refers to yelling, cursing, screaming, fighting, getting out of line, disobeying staff direction, refusing to cooperate, and otherwise causing a commotion during the process of intake. Inmates who engage in "shutting down" behavior may enter into depressive-like states or appear to become lifeless, and, as a result, do not move forward in line or follow commands. In short, inmates with these behaviors slow down the machine-like flow of intake.

These types of disruptions represent two kinds of uncertainty for intake staff: scarcity and legal uncertainty. On the one hand, there are not enough jail staff, isolation rooms, and equipment to simultaneously neutralize all of the inmate activity that disrupts intake. That is, the deputies and teams who patrol the intake hallways and are responsible for security in each of the holding rooms cannot possibly hope to respond to or neutralize disruptive behavior or spend the appropriate amount of time it takes to force intransigent inmates to comply with the intake process. Moreover, there are only so many isolation rooms, spit guards, restraint chairs, and other devices designed to punish and immobilize disruptors. Sheriff's deputies cannot possibly hope to respond to all disruptions and must be able to quickly move on to address other disturbances. This represents a deep source of organizational uncertainty for deputies, who must determine which disturbances truly deserve their time and how much time they can spend on a disturbance without jeopardizing a response to some other more serious disturbance.

On the other hand, disruptions also represent deep legal uncertainty. "Use of force" is a legal category referring to instances when deputies physically act upon an inmate in order to force behavioral compliance. In many jurisdictions, staff must report and explain any use-of-force instances, and jail administration keeps regular statistics on such instances. These are legal problems because watchdog organizations and civil rights groups keep track of such statistics and periodically use them in lawsuits. Individual reports of such instances are reviewed whenever there is a complaint of deputy wrongdoing or an actual lawsuit about deputy maltreatment of inmates. This situation represents a deep source of legal uncertainty for deputies, who must determine if use of force is allowable under jail guidelines or could potentially be illegal and cost them their jobs.

In short, the widespread administration of psychotropic drugs, pain medication, and mixes of sedatives serves to ameliorate situations in which inmates act up or shut down and to ensure the machine-like flow of the intake process. First, the sedation or elevation of disruptive inmates solves organizational uncertainty in that it allows custody officers to quickly move on to the next disruption. Second, it decreases the amount of time custody officers are faced with in their legal conundrum of whether to use force or not. Custody officers know that without the widespread administration of medication they would be unable to control many interruptions in the intake process. The following example illustrates this link.

The classification officer was calling an inmate up to the booth. None of the inmates got up. We both looked out into the room where dozens of inmates were sitting, as no one was moving to get up. After a few more tries, the classification officer eventually notified his watch commander that the inmate he was calling to be interviewed for classification was not responding but should be in this room. The watch commander moved to request that deputies go into the classification room and locate the inmate.

After entering the room, one of the deputies immediately shouted in a deep, authoritative tone, 'Everyone be quiet!' With the exception of a few murmurs, the room fell silent. The same deputy called for the unresponsive inmate to 'show himself.' After a brief silence and no activity from the sitting inmates, the other deputy jarringly shouted, 'Alright, everyone against the wall.' Everyone got up and followed the command except for one inmate.

This lone inmate was curled up so that his head was between his hands and knees. One of the deputies walked over to him and pushed down on his shoulder a few times in order to jar him awake. The deputy then tried to verbally coax the inmate into responding. I could see the inmate briefly look up from the ground, but not high enough to look at the deputy, before looking back down. The deputy made eye contact with the other deputy, who then exited the room.

I asked the classification officer standing next to me what was going on. He replied, 'He's going to get a nurse.' After some time passed, with one of the deputies remaining in the room, a nurse entered the room. The nurse approached the inmate, got down on one knee so that she was eye level with the inmate, and began talking to him. The inmate was not responding at first, but after a few minutes, he nodded. The nurse helped him stand and, along with the deputy, led him out of the room.

'What happened?' I asked the classification officer. He said, 'He's most likely in a depressive state, and I'm sure they will take care of that so he can be processed.'

Here we see an example of custody staff relying on medical professionals to deal with a disruptive inmate. In this case, the disruptive inmate was despondent rather than aggressive, and the situation allowed for a more orderly removal of the inmate by nursing staff. Later on in the day, I followed up with that nurse, asking her, "What was all that about in the classification room, why did you have to take him away?" The nurse replied, "He's probably clinically depressed, well, we determined that once we got him over here [the nursing station] . . . we gave him some meds to get him through the process. At some point, once he is placed, we will follow up on him and make sure he gets appropriately treated." "He went back into line?" I asked. "Yeah," she said.

On one occasion, as an inmate was pinned down by several officers and a nurse administered a sedative, a supervising officer said to me,

'In a way, if you think about it, we really wouldn't be able to get all this done without that. . . .'

'What do you mean?' I replied.

'Think about it, I only have so many guys on this staff right now, guys that are specifically ready to deal with someone acting up and not following directions. We can only respond to so many incidents at the same time. We can only do it for so long, too. If we are in a room in here with 50 guys and we have to subdue someone. . . . There are 50 guys in this room alone. If we cannot put this guy down immediately, then it will be trouble. We couldn't respond to other situations. Sometimes our guys are all over the jail from one situation to the next.'

'Thank god for the nurses, right?' I blurted out.

'Yeah,' said the officer.

We can see how the medical staff are useful for deputies. The administration of pain medication, psychotropic drugs, and sedatives has the effect of ensuring that intake can continue despite numerous and frequent disruptions. Such administration of medication is by no means unethical or "bad" medicine. It is easy to see how this routine, in situations where inmates act up, is a good use of medical services in place of deputy tactics that can range from full physical restraint in chairs to physical violence or isolation until the inmate becomes cooperative. The goal here is not to evaluate good or bad medicine, as a whistleblower might, but instead to discover the key sociological fact that security requirements and lack of organizational resources determine the provision of medical resources. That is, the flow of information that leads to the provision of medical care originates from the organizational and legal uncertainty faced by custody deputies and their goal of ensuring the machine-like flow of intake.

The Medicalization of Jail Inmates

We now know how medicine helps to solve security problems for sheriff's deputies. But are there downstream consequences to doing so? Does the initial medicalization shape the provision of medical services later in the intake process? In short, it is those inmates who are medicated for security concerns who are likely to be transferred into medicalized spaces. What is critical is that this securitization of medicine helps to solve the problem of knowing who is a sick inmate. The following excerpt describes an instance in which a nurse was asked to intervene and deal with an inmate who was "acting up."

I was shadowing a nurse named Michelle when she was called over by an officer to 'go check up on a guy bugging out in a bin.' She dropped what she was doing and reached for some latex gloves. I asked her, 'What's this about?'

She replied, 'Sometimes they just need us there as a witness, to make sure everything is ok health-wise when they are coming down hard on a guy. But other times they need us to figure out if a guy is suicidal and needs to be dealt with.'

'Oh, yeah?' I said.

'Yeah. Lots of these guys are in here claiming they are suicidal, trying to make it into better conditions inside the jail, but we are here to kind of look for real signs,' she replied.

When we got to the fishbowl, one of the inmates was quiet and solemn in the corner. Apparently he had been 'flipping out, screaming, and running around the bin' before the nurse was called over. After the nurse interviewed him, which I was unable to listen to because I was not allowed to enter the fishbowl, I asked 'What do you think was up with that guy?'

She replied, 'He's just having a hard time being in here. He's young . . . hasn't been through here too much. He did say to another inmate [that he] apparently wanted to get out, even if it meant hurting himself to do it . . . so we are going to give him some medication to kind of calm him down, *before* he becomes a problem.'

'Is that a useful thing to be able to do?' I asked.

'It helps him and us . . . he wants to calm down, you know? Some of these guys, though, are looking for a fix so we have to watch out for that. This kid is young, he clearly doesn't want to be in here. So he doesn't really know the routine. I think he just needs to calm down before he actually does want [to] hurt himself. He just said that he *might* hurt himself if he can't calm down. Not that he was *going* to hurt himself. So if I can calm him down, that is the medical intervention.'

At first, the excerpt demonstrates the difficulty faced by medical professionals in diagnosing mental health problems among inmates during the intake processes. The young man suggested he was considering suicide, but within the context of limited time, space, and resources, the nurse was not able to provide a full diagnosis or the needed mental health treatment. Moreover, such a complaint is not atypical and does not warrant immediate special treatment. Nurses are aware that many inmates use formal language about suicidal ideations, and that some are faking in order to receive favorable placement in health wards. Pain medication or sedatives become a useful tool with which the nurse can simulate medical certainty, because the drug momentarily delays ailments that might otherwise necessitate sending the inmate toward the medical route. The nurse suggested this when she stated that the medication is necessary 'before [the inmate] becomes a problem.' Therefore, sedatives and pain medication or psychotropic drugs are stand-ins for what otherwise might be more extensive health treatment in the fast-paced world of jail intake.

There is another avenue with which inmates can make it into medicalized space: at any point, inmates can tell deputies about their medical complaints either informally or through "sick call." These requests are directed toward deputies who do hourly checks of holding rooms, fishbowls, and other spaces. This creates uncertainty for medical staff because deputies start from the baseline assumption that inmates requesting healthcare are simply lying and trying to manipulate their way into the more comfortable medical spaces of the jail. While the most severe cases normally find their way into medical space, it is the borderline cases or inmates with a great deal of missing medical information who often go a long time before gaining the attention of security staff. This includes suffering through days of pain, making repeated requests, and employing other tactics to get the serious attention of security staff.

The key finding is that if security staff are able to note that an inmate has received medication earlier in the stay—including medication administered to quell disturbances in the intake process—the security staff have some organizational rationale for taking an inmate's complaint seriously. Essentially, deputies can say to themselves that they have at least some reason to take an inmate's medical request seriously if there is some previous or initial "medical mark" (as I call it) on the inmate's record. These medical marks are ascertained by deputies in nebulous ways; often, deputies will note visually that an inmate is receiving daily treatments or will make inquiries through word of mouth with other deputies or nursing staff as to whether an inmate was the subject of some previous medical intervention. A big source of organizational uncertainty for deputies is the fear that they will be blamed for wasting the scarce time and resources of the health evaluation teams or even, more seriously, wasting a scarce medical bed. An initial medical mark is an intervention at the point of intake that may have been made for non-medical reasons (i.e., disruptions to the intake process) but that later helps an inmate accrue additional health information and interventions.

For inmates, the consequence is clear: many who are sick but who missed the initial mark at the point of intake will be less likely to receive future treatments. For the organization of the jail, the consequence is also clear: Medical marks help to solve the uncertainty around providing healthcare and scarce medical beds to many borderline patients with limited health information. Administering medication during the intake process provides a solution to security threats and also works to help restore medical certainty in the selection of some inmates for care over others.

The downstream effect of these medical marks is something we can gauge. A critical organizational task is accomplished when an inmate is actually transferred into a medical space or bed. By examining the decision-making that takes place when an inmate is moved to medical beds in the jail or into specialty care in outside medical institutions, we can understand the process as an expansion of incarceration space in the jail. There are two key components of this decision-making.

First, when notified of a medical bed becoming available, medical professionals will begin to re-examine the list of inmates, including those inmates who had previously been marked for care, and then attempt to identify those inmates who would be justified in receiving a medical bed. Beyond obvious cases where medical need is indicated, this process requires professionals to re-examine or revisit the medical records or bodies of the inmates. Professionals will recheck records or previous diagnoses, engage in discussion about potential candidates with nurses who made daily rounds, and look at various sources of evidence in order to identify a qualified inmate. This re-examination may seem like an obvious process, but to the ethnographic gaze it brings to light an important fact: that the availability of a medical bed causes the medical professional to look at the medical record and the inmate's body or mind in a new way, one that alters the diagnosis to fit the qualifications for a bed opening. Take the following example:

> Two nurses were discussing a patient. Pointing at the computer screen, one nurse said, 'What about him?' The other nurse paused, scrolled through the record, and said, "His treatment has been pretty regular.' 'We should have a look at him,' replied the first nurse.
>
> Interrupting, I asked, 'What's so special about him?" One of the nurses responded, "Don't worry, we are just looking at him because we have an opening. . . . He's not in any danger. . . . He's sick, is what we are saying, but it's not gotten worse. It's not a special case, if that is what you're asking."
>
> I didn't understand what she meant, and I sort of nodded my head in confusion. The nurse touched my shoulder to reassure me. 'No, no, you are misinterpreting us, it's not that his condition has changed. . . . It's that we have a bed, and he's qualified. . . . It's available, and we think he could benefit from it.'

This instance shows how an inmate's condition is not the sole determination of his routing toward a medical bed. Instead, it is the opening of a medical bed that causes the medical professional to reconsider an inmate's medical history—his "medical marks"—and then reinterpret them and determine that he is now qualified for a bed. Key is that this patient's medical experience is unchanged; it was obtained in a non-medical space (the intake room) and is based on the same symptoms and diagnosis. If the nurses are correct, and according to medical standards this inmate could always have qualified for a bed, but he is only now getting one because a bed has opened up, then the causality for transfer is clear: the organizational capacity for medical beds determines the transfer of a borderline inmate.

The finding here is that when inmates, at early stages in the intake process, are administered some form of medication, they begin to obtain a medical record that provides legitimacy to any of their future medical complaints. From the perspective of the ethnographer, there is a direct causal line from inmates who cause disruptions during the intake process to acquisition of medication, to deputies taking inmates' future desires for medical interventions more seriously, thereby allowing inmates to benefit from continued treatment and improved health.

Summoning the Sick in Jail

Sociologist Iddo Tavory, in his recent study of Orthodox Jewish life in contemporary Los Angeles, developed a concept about identity that he called "summoning." The idea is that the Jewish men in his study (and, in Tavory's view, all people) have an identity not because of some decision they made, but because of whom they interact with on a daily basis. That is, they do not carry something Jewish around with them at all times and invoke it when they encounter just anyone; rather, they come to develop what it means to be Jewish in a certain situation through interactions with other people. By extension, this means that being an Orthodox Jew—or being Black, White, gay, or an inmate—is not enough to tell us how to behave, for example, in a Jewish student group on a university campus, as a member of a Black church, or as an inmate in a jail. Elements of these contexts would alter how such individuals behave. "Summoning" means that individuals are called into being by other individuals, consent to this calling, and develop an identity that neither party could have predicted beforehand.[10]

What does this have to do with interaction in a jail intake room? One of the main criticisms of Tavory's concept is that he studied a group of individuals with not much inequality between them. Given that he specifically studied only the male relationships in the Orthodox Jewish community, it is easy to see how he came to view culture as a mutually agreed-upon summoning. Can we think about summoning between parties such as inmates and intake staff, which are characterized by huge power differentials?

It is easy to think that the inmates who come into the jail are already predefined; that is, how the intake officers think about them is already set. Yes, it is true that the inmates are mostly Black, brown, and extremely poor, with long criminal records, and many have tattoos that are identified with gangs. Yes, it is true that staff, before interacting with inmates, make assumptions about them that are drawn from larger cultural frameworks (Van Cleve and Mayes 2015). Staff may have racist opinions or classist ones; they have training about what backgrounds should be placed into high security or medium security;

and medical staff know what kinds of ailments need immediate attention and which ones can wait.

But then why is there an interview at all? Because those predetermined characteristics do not provide enough information for staff to make the evaluations necessary to decide if someone is a high-security inmate or if someone is medically needy. For instance, as we saw, information about inmates' potential abuse of medical resources help staff nudge inmates toward lower classification scores, and inmates who disrupt the waiting line help staff understand which inmates need medical attention. Predetermined precepts might inform the interactions, but quite literally each classification is an instance of summoning between an inmate and a classification officer.

Understanding that classifications are instances of summoning between inmates and staff across huge power differentials allows us to see how it is medicine that resolves the fundamental problem of jail "real estate." As we learned, the problem was twofold: there are too many persons with criminal biographies that necessitate their placement in high-security cells, and there are too many sick incarcerated persons that need to be placed in spaces of the jail devoted to healthcare.

Both of these problems get resolved through the summoning of medical knowledge about inmates. First, concerning potentially violent inmates, during interviews used to determine their security risk, jailers work to cast inmates less as serious criminals, but rather as people who purposively commit crimes in order to gain access to the jail's many social provisions, such as shelter, food, and, especially, healthcare. We learned how staff culture redefined the jail as a welfare institution, using the novel category of "non-gang member" to nudge the security level of inmates from eight to seven. This medicalized stigma reinterprets criminal biographies in a manner that pushes inmates into more available general population housing.

Second, it is security events—disruptions to the normal routine of jailing like fights, slow-downs, or other forms "acting out"—that draw the attention of medical authorities; nurses and jailers work to medicate inmates who act out, and it is those inmates whose medical conditions are taken seriously while jailed. We learned how security disruptions result in heavy medicalization of inmates, which in turn provides initial "medical marks" that help inmates accrue new health information that can make their placement into medical housing more likely. This resolves the issue of deciding who to place into limited medicalized space. Others are left to their own devices in the general population and are rationally disqualified from scarce medical space.

  Thus, the expanded availability of healthcare, provision of pharmaceuticals, and medicalized reinterpretation of inmate's biographies help to resolve key problems of the jail. This gives us the answer to our question about a looping effect that opened this chapter. It has less to do with the rules about what counts as a true medical ailment or true security threat than with how these formulations are accomplished through "summoning." The informational inputs taken from inmate biographies, the current circumstances of the jail (how many beds are available in particular units, what the current gang situation is like, etc.), and the highly contingent interactions between inmates and classification officers all work to create these demarcations. This is the "summoning" of the sick and violent into the jail.

2

The Medicalization of the Los Angeles County Jail System, 1978–2015

In the previous chapter we saw that the expansion of medicine in jails has a particular function. It is not that medicine has expanded to the point that it serves all of the inmates' health needs; in fact, we saw that many purposively go untreated and are left to suffer. Nor is it the case that medicine is absent in the jail. Many persons receive medications and are admitted to medicalized space. What we found instead was that the continuous medicalization of security events resolves fundamental problems of overcrowding. That is, medicine is a useful tool, allowing the jail to resolve its problems of too little space and too much demand.

How could this be? One criticism of ethnography is that it offers only a snapshot of the social processes we are interested in. We can detail quite well the routine problems confronting the actors in our field sites and the patterned ways they go about solving those problems. But what ethnography is less successful at is explaining why the people in our field sites have the options available to them that they do. These are what we might call "lines of action," or opportunities inherited from the past that make it difficult for the workgroup to choose alternatives or, even further, to even perceive alternatives.

In this chapter, we need to explain three specific things from our jail ethnography. First, why was the production of medium-risk scores for inmates an important feature of the jail intake process? Second, how did the production of medium-risk scores become associated with a medicalized understanding of inmates' criminal biographies? Finally, why did security events become a key input to how inmates become medicalized? In total, we want to know how the opportunities we saw in the previous chapter become so integral to the jail.

For answers, we can turn to archival history; in particular, the administrative history of the Los Angeles County jail system at the turn of the twenty-first century. It is a perfect history for our purposes: the jail system moved

Redistributing the Poor. Armando Lara-Millán, Oxford University Press (2021). © Armando Lara-Millán.
DOI: 10.1093/oso/9780197507902.003.0003

from a place almost entirely devoid of medicine and intent on locking up as many people as possible to a place defined by medicine and reliant on the permanent early release of thousands of "medium-risk" inmates.

This transformation was remarkable. Consider a 1983 letter that the then-sheriff Sherman Block wrote to the *Los Angeles Times*. The newspaper had just published a negative article about the jail's health services, and the sheriff was incredulous. He wrote: "It is true that no form of psychotherapy other than medication is provided inmates in the observation modules, but it must be remembered that we operate a jail not a mental hospital, and our primary concern is the safe confinement of persons in our custody." This statement underlies the perspective of the Los Angeles County Sheriff's Department on the issue throughout the 1980s: a rejection of the very idea that a jail should be responsible for health treatment.[1]

More than 30 years later, on September 1, 2015, the Los Angeles County Board of Supervisors—the political leadership of a county that controls a budget larger than that of 37 states—voted to downsize the largest jail in North America, to rebuild it as a "correctional healthcare treatment center," and to implement an unprecedented diversion program that would send inmates with histories of mental illness or substance abuse into community supervision. The historic vote was meant to transform the jail from a dungeon-like facility built in the 1960s and under federal investigation for inhumane conditions into a licensed medical facility with complete step-down medical and mental health treatment areas, downsize it from 4,885 to 3,885 inmates, and create 1,000 community treatment beds for mental health and substance abuse diversion. As one board supervisor said about the landmark vote, "There has been a movement for such a long time to try to convince people who have authority and power, jail isn't the answer, it's part of the problem, it exacerbates the problem . . . we are making such a beginning today. . . . That will all be for services related to diversion, not only medical and mental health and substance abuse but in some cases housing, other kinds of training, things that really help people stay out of jail. It's historic."[2]

How did this transformation happen? The argument presented in this chapter is that Los Angeles County officials shifted from thinking about their inmate population primarily as violent gang members to thinking about them as mentally ill, substance abusers, and less criminally threatening homeless persons, because to do so became organizationally expedient in the face of constant tension between fiscal austerity and legal demand. By studying actual policy implementation as it unfolds, we can see how health-care was an adaptive organizational solution for a correctional system under crisis and helped to keep a sinking jail system afloat.

In calling this shift expedient, I reference three specific phenomena vis-ible in the archive: (1) The pushing of inmates into medium security allowed the county to generate revenue from other government agencies when it otherwise lacked it. This explains the nudging toward medium-security designations in our jail ethnography. (2) The quality of "medium security" became associated with medicalized rationale as it allowed officials to con-tinuously release inmates early en masse in a way that was politically palat-able and could obtain funds for incarceration alternative programs. (3) The pharmaceuticalization of security events became the key signal used to re-solve legal demands around inmate healthcare with limited available funds. In total, the archival record shows that, during each challenge of urban aus-terity and progressive law, a section of the inmate population would have its qualities of medical need and medium risk emphasized in order to generate revenue or diffuse the inmate population. By doing this—by emphasizing the health of its inmate population—the county could make claims on state mental health funds inside its jails and justify the release of thousands of inmates.

This chapter begins with a brief primer on the long-term crisis of austerity and legal demand facing the Los Angeles County jail system. The chapter is then divided into three sections that trace the three aspects of this trans-formation: a reliance on medium-security inmates to generate space and revenue; the association of medium security with a medical rationale in the development of what I call a "permanent medicalized early release system"; and the medicalization of the Twin Towers Correctional Facility and the pharmaceuticalization of use-of-force incidents. By viewing these three seemingly disparate developments in their proper historical context, we can see them as part of a broader shift that ultimately resulted in the 2015 vote for a downsized hospital-jail. Over the course of three decades and through successive bouts of progressive law and austerity, Los Angeles County officials moved from identifying county inmates primarily by the attributes of maximum-security violent gang membership to identifying them as mentally and physically ill, as substance abusers, and as less risky homeless persons.

The Long-Term Crisis of Austerity and Law

It is a little-recognized fact that the inmate population in Los Angeles County has not exceeded the level it reached in the late 1980s. After exploding in size from 7,500 inmates in 1978 to nearly 24,000 inmates in 1988, the total inmate population has since oscillated between 14,000 and 22,000 inmates, depending on the year's budget.[3]

This decline is the result of an ongoing crisis between fiscal austerity and legal demand. On the one hand, as noted in the Introduction, these bouts with austerity have come from property tax shifts from the State of California, the inability to raise taxes, and periodic global financial crisis. On the other hand, progressive legal advocates have continuously forced the Sheriff's Department to spend revenue in new ways. First, in 1988, a federal court ruled in favor of inmate advocates and issued an all-encompassing jail population cap. Second, the Department of Justice, the American Civil Liberties Union (ACLU), and State of California health inspectors successfully threatened, sued, and monitored the jail's provision of health and mental health services in 1990, 1997, 2002, 2012, and in 2015. In 1988, the then-sheriff summarized the confluence of pressures his department would face in perpetuity: "By law we must comply with federal court mandates and state minimum jail standards. We must release sentenced prisoners out of necessity. The dilemma is this: If we could house all of the sentences and pre-adjudicated prisoners society demands, the Los Angeles County jail population would approach (and might soon exceed) 39,000. We have staffing and resources for approximately 20,000."[4]

The county has been stuck in this long-running legal and resource quagmire, in which it has been responsible for the health and safety of 40,000 inmates, with only enough budget and space for 14,000 to 22,000 inmates. Occasionally, the tension of this long-term problem boils over into crisis situations. Three have been instrumental: 1994–1997, 2004–2007, and 2009–2015. In the run-up to each of these periods, the Sheriff's Department was forced to close thousands of jail beds, which included closure of entire jails, release of inmates, and searches for new ways to manage the jail population.

The most important of these periods, and the one that would set precedents for how the county managed the tension between law and austerity, was the crisis of 1994–1997. This crisis centered on the struggle to open the county's state-of-the-art flagship jail, the Twin Towers Correctional Facility, in downtown Los Angeles, which was the last of the jails the county had planned and

built during the 1980s jail boom. When the facility's construction was completed in 1994, it remained empty for three years due to a lack of operational
funding. The next crisis (2004–2007) saw closures of three jails, riots, and
murders of mentally ill inmates, and would see the expansion of the logics
created in the initial crisis. Finally, the crisis created by the Great Recession
in 2009 was rendered inert by formalizing these long-running administrative
adaptations.[5]

In each of these crisis periods, county officials responded with new
adaptations to accommodate the fundamental tension between austerity and
progressive law. As we shall see, the ingeniousness of the county's successive
adaptations was that, in the long run, capacity expansion was never required.
Instead, officials learned to manipulate the security risk rankings and medical need of inmates in such a way that jail bed space and revenue could always be generated.

Generate Revenue from "Medium-Security" Inmates

In our jail ethnography we saw the importance of "nudging" inmates from
high-risk scores of eight into medium-risk scores of seven. In the intake
workgroup culture, this was accomplished by interpreting criminal biographies as less criminal and less risky and more in need of the jails' social
resources, especially that of medicine. In this section, we learn how this development was born out of an administrative solution to this legal and fiscal
crisis of the mid-1990s.

In 1997, county officials produced a convoluted plan to open the Twin
Towers Correctional Facility, which sat empty for three years due to budget
shortfall, and it was the tenets of this plan that helped the county realize it
could manipulate the distinction between medium- and high-security
rankings. The jail was designed as a state-of-the-art jail for 3,992 maximum-
security inmates. Its specific purpose was to house thousands of serious, violent offenders (including those awaiting trial and those sentenced to the
county jail). The facility was named Twin Towers because of its two side-by-
side towers, one eight stories high and the other seven stories high. A third
tower consisted of a four-story, 200-bed medical facility. The jail also included an inmate reception center, similar to that in our jail ethnography,
that would continuously process 800 additional inmates around the clock for
the entire Los Angeles County jail system.

The effort to open the jail started with the convening of a "Custody Study Group" in the fall of 1996. This group comprised a staff member from each the five Board of Supervisors' offices, representatives from the Chief Administrative Office, Auditor-Controller, County Counsel, District Attorney's Office, Presiding Judges' Association, Municipal Court Judges' Association, Los Angeles Superior Court, Probation Department, Public Defender's Office, Alternate Public Defender's Office, and Sheriff's Department. In short, this group represented the collective knowledge of the entire law enforcement community in the county, political leaders, and top bureaucrats.[6]

What came out of this group was a convoluted plan that would set the county on the dynamics we are interested in. The county's own rather useless visual representation of the plan—known as "Option 6"—is reproduced in Figure 2.1. At its core, the plan involved a series of inmate transfers among three jails, grouped by security risk, that would free up space that could then

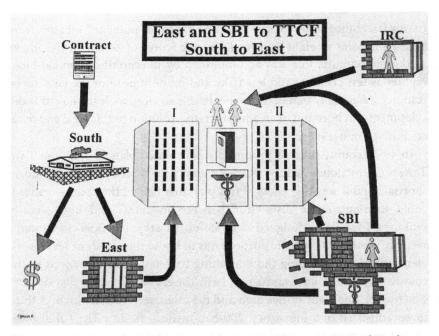

Figure 2.1 "Option 6" visualization of the Twin Towers Correctional Facility opening plan, "Twin Tower/Custody Study Group Recommendations."
Source: Burke Papers: 436/15.

be contracted out to state and federal authorities for revenue. The revenue can be noted in the bottom left of the figure.[7]

First, the plan moved 1,650 "high-security" inmates from an outlying county jail (called Pitchess Detention Center [PDC]-North) into 1,972 beds of one of the towers of the empty Twin Towers jail. The emptied space at PDC-North was filled with an equivalent transfer of what the county called "medium-security inmates" from an outlying third county jail (called PDC-South). The plan justified this move by explaining, "Housing medium-security inmates, rather than the previous high-security inmates, will increase the number of available beds by 196. Because of the dormitory-style housing, these beds were previously vacant for security reasons. . . . This program would allow the use of currently unused common area space to provide 300 additional jail beds for medium-security County prisoners." The move turned on the specific logic that so-called medium-security inmates required less supervision and could be guarded in larger bunk rooms (including common areas).

But what kind of inmates replaced those medium-security inmates from the outlying third jail (PDC-South)? The entire purpose of these transfers was to sign a contract with the State of California's prison system—at a profit of $37 million annually—to imprison state inmates in county jails. An additional, smaller contract was signed with the US Immigration and Nationalization Service to house immigrant detainees, also at a profit. These two revenue-generating contracts, in particular the plan with the state, were not an unintended consequence of the jail reorganization, but rather an explicit linchpin in the plan to open Twin Towers. The state contract became a sinkhole that the county could count on for more funding to fill budget gaps in this plan.[8]

Comparing this 1997 maneuver to the following crisis in 2004–2007 is instructive. In the crisis of 2004–2007, officials had learned that the 1997 shift of medium-security inmates for state inmates was primarily an administrative manipulation. That is, Sheriff's Department officials revealed to county political leaders that, astonishingly, jail inmates had never actually been housed according to their security classification, as was purportedly the case at the end of 1997. Over the course of a year, each of the supervisors took time in open meetings to question Sheriff's Department officials about this fact. Consider the following quote from a high-level Sheriff's Department official about why inmates had not previously been housed according to risk:

Chief Klugman: . . . when the inmates go to the different housing locations in the different facilities throughout the county, that they are housed differently, depending on the kind of facility they're in and the needs of that facility. And that's something that we haven't been able to get away from. For example, in the north facilities where we have dormitory settings, we have to—we have to balance the population in the dorms racially. Otherwise, if they're imbalanced, it becomes very dangerous. So we have to—and that requires us sometimes to mix classifications that north point has given us. For example, we might have highs and lows in the same dorm setting, but it's safer to do that than to unbalance the environment by keeping all the highs together and the lows together but having a bad racial mix where one is dominant and the others are not. So we have to—we have to make some very common sense, frankly, decisions as to how to house, depending on the style and the type of facility we're using, which sometimes negates some of the ability to do what north point would seem to require . . .[9]

To be clear, what this means is that in 1997, jail officials had been classifying inmates according to risk at the point of intake—and doing so allowed them to resolve that crisis—but were not actually using those classifications to assign inmates to specific housing locations in the jail system. Many high-security inmates were being held in low- and medium-security spaces. In other words, officials' claim in 1997 that they were moving medium-security inmates into PDC-North in order to generate revenue from state inmates was an administrative maneuver that existed only on paper.[10]

This underscores how the distinction between medium and high risk is less related to the actual circumstances and qualities of inmates. That is, the existence of a certain number of medium-security inmates or high-security inmates is predicated more on the needs of the budgeted available bed space and less on how many actual inmates fit into those categories.[11]

We can connect this finding to our jail ethnography: the "summoning" of medium security inmates in the process of intake. As we saw, the criminal biographies that inmates bring to the jail are too serious for the limited available high-security bed space and they must be nudged toward medium risk. This finds itself in organizational adaptations to crisis: In the 1992–1997 crisis period, the Sheriff's Department was able to resolve the conflict by emphasizing the medium-risk classification of its inmates in order to generate space and sell that space to other government agencies. In the next crisis of 2004–2007, they resolved the crisis by revealing they had never actually housed persons according to risk and could then suggest a different solution to resolve the crisis (the funding of a new computerized classification system to be able to actually house people according to their risk). Thus, the ability to manipulate high- and medium-risk scores is something that originates out of the political process, the production of a sound jail budget, and resolutions to policy crises.

The Rise of a Permanent Medicalized Early Release

While we have seen why the medium-risk category became an administrative priority, we have yet to see how that category became "medicalized." We do so in this section. The move to emphasize the qualities of medium security as medical need among inmates coalesced in the Los Angeles County jail system in what is best described as a permanent medicalized early release system. Austerity and legal demand would push the county to develop procedures to empty jail beds by releasing inmates early, placing them on expanded probation caseloads, and utilizing medical rationale to do it. Practitioners may not see a link in the programs I discuss here—the Sheriff's early release program, the Probation Department's Community-Based Alternatives to Custody (CBAC), and the Department of Mental Health's various diversion programs—but by viewing these policies in their proper historical context, we can elucidate a link.

In 1988 a federal judge, William P. Gray, ruled in the *Rutherford v. Block* case in favor of inmate rights' litigants. The order issued an all-encompassing jail population cap and gave the Sheriff unilateral authority to release sentenced county inmates early in order to comply with that population cap. The sheriff could no longer pack inmates into hallways, roofs, and communal spaces, needing to ensure that every inmate had a mattress.[12]

Since the order, county inmates have served, depending on a year's budget cuts, between 10% and 80% of their sentences. As one presiding judge wrote in a letter to a county supervisor in 1994:

There are courts in the land which have jurisdiction over custody and probation. Los Angeles County is not in that category. Once our courts sentence a defendant to jail. The person becomes a guest of the sheriff who, as you know, is over the jails. . . . We cannot even control the length of stay of a defendant in the county jails. We sentence them, and the sheriff decides how much, if any, time they will serve. We set bail, and the sheriff decides who will be held and who will be released without posting the amount of bail set by the courts. We are not being critical of the sheriff in this regard. He is under federal court orders regarding the size of the inmate population in the jails.[13]

Contemporary observers assume that this early release policy affects only a small portion of the inmate population. Although the "Gray order" technically permitted only the release of sentenced county inmates (who make up less than 10% of the current inmate population), the archival record shows that the order was inextricably linked to the sheriff's periodic denial of entrance into the jail to pre-trial inmates. Over the course of the next two decades, when the jails became too overcrowded, Sheriff's Department officials either simply refused to book certain classes of arrestees—namely, misdemeanor arrestees—or they moved the minimum bail threshold and then released arrestees on their "own recognizance" (OR). Consider the document represented in Figure 2.2, which shows OR cite-out policies explained alongside the early release policies – even added them together. In county documents, this expanded administrative latitude—which was above and beyond the power granted by the federal court order—was justified on the logic that these pre-trial inmates were low risk and not a threat to the community. This ability to designate a certain class of inmates as less risky was critical to the endeavor. As a 1993 Sheriff's Department memo stated, "Each day, all inmates will be updated, sorted, and filtered to categorize the inmate population into groups deemed of least danger to the community to target for release."[14]

In addition to the release of county-sentenced inmates and pre-trial inmates, during crisis periods officials have periodically released, en masse, thousands of other inmates onto expanded probation caseloads (through CBAC programs). Such releases occurred during each of our three major crisis periods—1994–1997, 2004–2007, and in 2009. In each period, the Sheriff's Department released approximately 2,000–4,000 inmates using early release, decreasing the time served by inmates from highs of 60%–90% to lows of 10%–35% of sentences, and sending many inmates to expanded probation caseloads.

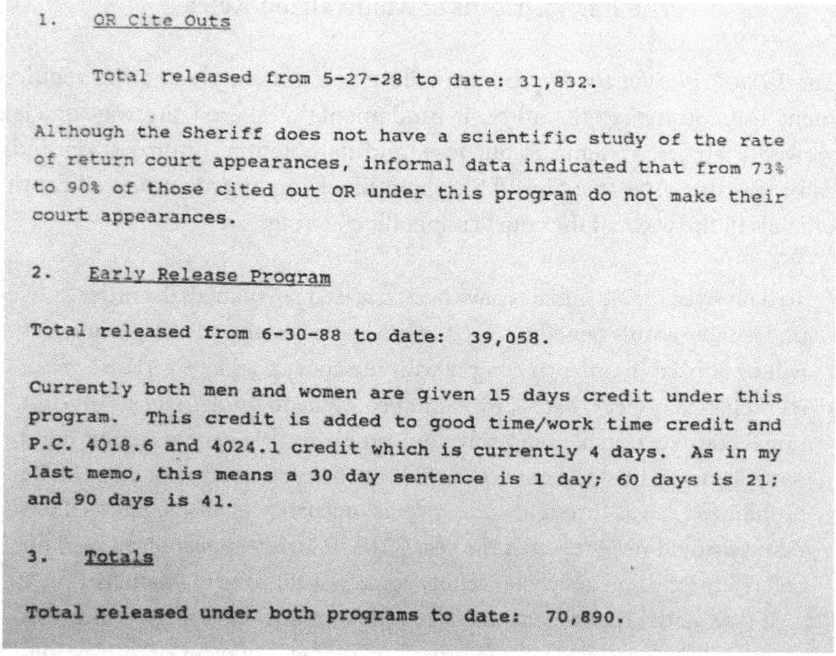

1.   OR Cite Outs

    Total released from 5-27-28 to date: 31,832.

Although the Sheriff does not have a scientific study of the rate
of return court appearances, informal data indicated that from 73%
to 90% of those cited out OR under this program do not make their
court appearances.

2.   Early Release Program

Total released from 6-30-88 to date: 39,058.

Currently both men and women are given 15 days credit under this
program. This credit is added to good time/work time credit and
P.C. 4018.6 and 4024.1 credit which is currently 4 days. As in my
last memo, this means a 30 day sentence is 1 day; 60 days is 21;
and 90 days is 41.

3.   Totals

Total released under both programs to date: 70,890.

Figure 2.2 "Own recognizance" cite-out and early release program policies and released inmate totals.
Source: Edelman Papers: 534/17.

In this section, we will examine how the ability to release inmates early under these programs was justified by medical knowledge and the push to categorize inmates as less seriously risky to the community. To underscore how crucial this early release authority was to how the county managed its jails that, consider what one supervisor said in 2013:

On the issue of Rutherford . . . and I am being told . . . there is an interest by our lawyers and the sheriff for it not to go away. . . . Without it, I am told . . . that otherwise everyone would have to serve their full term, their full sentencing. And if they did that, we would need 30,000 beds on average, 25 to 30,000 under the report that was here. So right now, we do it and we have Rutherford, which is a pain in the behind already, but now we want to keep it because it's our safety valve. That way, the sheriff has the determination to let out people early.[15]

The Early Origins of Medicalized Release

The 1988 *Rutherford v. Block* court ruling was not simply another requirement the county faced; rather, it fundamentally altered the way officials
viewed their jail system, its purpose, and its potential future. A key indicator was the letter that Sheriff Sherman Block circulated among all county
officials in the wake of the court ruling. Block wrote:

> To date, over 11,500 inmates have been released pursuant to the order . . . as
> undesirable as this remedy is. . . . It is inevitable that the releasing standards
> will be revised in order to comply with the court mandate. I **MUST** make
> it emphatically clear that . . . we cannot continue to think in terms of addi-
> tional construction alone to solve our problems. We simply cannot build
> our way out of this dilemma. The cost of construction and housing will be
> prohibitive. . . . If through some magical occurrence, all the jail facilities
> that we would need through the year 2010 suddenly appeared, all paid for
> and ready for occupancy, the County could not afford to maintain them.
>
> It is essential that we examine the type of crimes that lead to incarcer-
> ation and then actively pursue programs that will prevent or at least sig-
> nificantly reduce these violations of the law. It is apparent that substance
> abuse is the leading cause of jail overcrowding . . . 44% of inmates in the
> County have as their primary charge some form of substance abuse. As
> much as 30% more are in custody for crimes directly related to substance
> abuse. This includes such crimes as burglary, robbery etc. . . . which are
> committed to support drug habits. When the abuse problem goes away, so
> will jail overcrowding.[16]

Noteworthy are the sheriff's statements about the impossibility of building
jail capacity to meet projected needs and the desire to medicalize the inmate population. The sheriff's letter marked the beginning of a slow process
that would come to normalize penal downsizing and medical alternatives to
jailing that would become so important in the present period.

The sheriff's letter was not simple rhetoric; it was taken very seriously
by county officials. Committees were convened to study it, internal memos
debated it, and, in short, its underlying logic of medicalization began to per-
meate county officials' understanding of their jail problem. Directly after the
letter was circulated, the Los Angeles County Board of Supervisors revived
a committee on jail overcrowding (the "CRASH" committee) that was made

up of representatives from all law enforcement agencies in the region. This was no perfunctory report; "an attempt was made to include all relevant comments and recommendations even where there was not unanimous consensus."[17]

Consider how the report and the sheriff's letter were discussed in one Board of Supervisors internal memorandum (see Figure 2.3). The inmate population is framed as connected to substance abuse, which is discussed as the leading cause of jail overcrowding. The following excerpt is taken from another county meeting in the wake of the Board's order (the excerpt is from shorthand notes written by a supervisor's aide who attended the meeting):

Need to get message out to be "tough on crime," not the wrong message, such as not serving time. Support "percentage release" program started by Block (i.e., all inmates serve some percent of sentence). Need to reduce availability of drugs and to produce more drug treatment resources for abusers and addicts with a view to reducing drug-related crime (currently, 80% of jail population has substance-abuse-related crime).[18]

Prevention/reduction of crimes leading to incarceration by pursuing programs to provide reductions.

- Example, substance abuse connected crimes (now, 44% of inmates in custody have substance abuse as their primary charge) are the leading cause of jail overcrowding. (Prevention should take the form of apprehension, prevention and education). Our international borders must be the first line of defense.

) Alternative sentencing proposals need to be developed and encouraged.

  - more feasibility study of electronic home confinement must be conducted.

  - accelerated sentencing of defendants procedure such as Probation 14-day court report turn around project, should be explored for greater use in courts.

  - alternative to custody sentences, such as expanded work release program efforts (stay home, but be required to work off sentences in public works jobs and supervised by D.P.O.'s).

Figure 2.3 "Agenda Item No. S-1 for Tuesday June 6th, 1989, Consideration of Sheriff Block's Letter."
Source: Edelman Papers: 534/7.

The memo coincided with the late 1980's development of the first medicalized early release program in the county. The Probation Department, asked by the CRASH committee to develop programs that would address jail overcrowding, created a program to save 1,025 beds, based largely on placing less serious offenders in home detention, but it included a small "Medically Restricted Prisoners" program. As described, "This program is designed to reduce the jail population by 125 inmates by placing paroled and medically restricted inmates on home detention. Since released prisoners will utilize their own doctors, there will be significant medical savings."[19]

This early program of 125 people would be expanded during the action plan of 1994–1997. As a part of that plan, the county created an entirely new system of programs that provided alternatives to jailing—the six CBAC programs—and released 1,324 inmates to expanded probation caseloads. The six CBAC programs—Early Disposition, Own Recognizance Release, Bail Deviation, Supervised Release, Electronic Monitoring, and Drug Court— were explicitly linked to the county's 1997 jail overcrowding plan. In order to put the release of these 1,324 inmates into perspective, that number of inmates was approximately the same as the number of new state inmates on the revenue-generating contract. A memo from an early planning meeting underscored how important the expanded probation programs were: "it was in agreement by all that the mere opening of Twin Towers would not have any impact on overcrowding issue unless some or all of the Probation programs are put into place."[20]

Officials learned that they could always cheaply expand and justify releases through the use of supposedly fail-safe risk-assessment tools and by designating inmates as medically needy. In order to illustrate this point, I highlight two of the six programs: the Electronic Monitoring Program (EMP) and the Supervised Release Program (SRP). Although the EMP was responsible for only 79 additional inmates released, it is critical to study because it established the use of a risk-assessment instrument that program staff would use to determine which inmates would be considered "low-risk [and] non-violent" and because it linked the Probation Department to the jail in this endeavor. The program was described as follows:

EMP provides an alternative sentencing/probation violation sanction, in-lieu of or in conjunction with, county jail time. It is designed for the low-risk, non-violent defendant who must have a residence and a telephone to be eligible. . . . The defendants are referred to the EMP by either the Court, or Sheriff's Department. Defendants are interviewed, their complete criminal history is accessed, and a risk assessment scale is administered to determine suitability for program participation. If found suitable and approved by either the Court or Sheriff's Department, the defendant is ordered to report to an approved electronic monitoring vendor.[21]

Here we can point to two aspects of release logic that would come to play a larger role in the following years. First is the equating of the low-risk/non-violent offender category with fitness for release. The new risk-assessment scale was sophisticated, measuring 20 different risk levels grouped into low, medium, high, and "high +" risk categories. Approximately 50% of inmates were placed in the medium-risk category. This was the first entrenchment of "non-serious" or "medium risk" as a broad and amorphous category in order to expand "releasability" beyond what was traditionally permitted. Second, the expanded program created a new administrative procedure whereby Sheriff's Department officials could refer inmates to the Probation Department using a risk-assessment tool administered directly in the jail intake room. Traditionally, pre-trial inmates would be referred to the EMP program through the courts. The expanded program provided administrative capacity at a county policy level for the sheriff to release sentenced individuals into some form of community supervision.

The second program we examine is the SRP. This program was an extension of the massive Own Recognizance (OR) program, with one major difference: it was intended for pre-trial inmates who had been denied OR by the courts but who had substance abuse issues. The program description is as follows:

> SRP provides Court with an alternative option to incarceration, pending trial, for defendants identified as those who may benefit from an intensified plan of supervision and treatment. . . . These conditions may include . . . 1) urge testing for drugs or alcohol; 2) intensive supervision by SR staff; 3) referrals for substance abuse counseling/treatment; 4) job referrals; 5) electronic monitoring.[22]

Thus, the main difference between OR and SRP was not additional risk-level criteria or higher criteria of criminal status, but rather an unspecified and highly fungible determination of the need for substance abuse "treatment."

This program was stated as saving an additional 199 jail beds for the sheriff in addition to the 695 saved by the regular OR program.

It is important to understand that these increases in probation caseloads included no new probation officers to supervise released inmates in the community; instead, they simply made existing caseloads much larger. We have two pieces of evidence to suggest that newly released inmates did not receive much, if any, probation supervision. First, consider that in fiscal year 1980–1981, the Probation Department had 242 deputies to service a caseload of 40,000 offenders—slightly more than 165 offenders per deputy. After the expanded probation caseload was created in 1997, Los Angeles County maintained approximately 250 probation deputies (depending on the year) for approximately 77,000 adult probationers. Second, after the 1988 *Rutherford v. Block* federal court order, the Probation Department created two types of adult supervision caseloads: "High-Risk Offender" caseloads and "Automated Minimum Services," or what was referred to by officials as "bank" caseloads. The "bank" caseloads made up 86% of the entire adult supervision caseload and included 2,000 probationers per officer. In 1991, 65,000 of those on "bank" caseloads were required only to mail the Probation Department a postcard once a month telling officials where they were physically located. "Bank" probationers not required to mail in cards saw probation officers for 15 minutes each month. The department was well aware of the lack of supervision on "automated" caseloads and, at least internally, acknowledged that these probationers were not simple, low-level offenders: "The potential risk to victims in the community would escalate, as Automated Minimum Service Caseloads size do not permit the needed amount of personal contact with felony offenders." The report added that 20% of the minimum service caseloads—9,000 offenders— "never report for probation orientation in the first place."[23]

Releasing Thousands of Inmates into Community Treatment

In addition to these Probation and Sheriff's Department programs, an entire ecology of Department of Mental Health and Public Health Services programs were created to alleviate jail overcrowding. The medicalization that occurred inside the Twin Towers jail was a critical part of these new programs. This is a somewhat controversial claim, because these programs were publicly advertised as affecting the jail population only indirectly through treatment to already released individuals so that those individuals would not reoffend. However, by examining the archival record closely, we can see how this medical infrastructure allowed the release of thousands of inmates annually.

In essence, county officials became attuned to pushing the state legislature to support funding dollars for community treatment programs and infrastructure that would make it possible to diffuse the jail population. Among a plethora of smaller grants are two sets that are most instructive: the demonstration grants that invented this diversion infrastructure on a smaller scale (AB 34/AB 2034 and Mentally Ill Offender Crime Reduction [MIOCR] grants, phases I and II, respectively), and two major propositions that scaled them up (Propositions 36 and 63). The demonstration projects created the county's first real experiment with directly linking the mentally ill jail population to extensive community-based mental health treatment and developed its innovated "do whatever it takes" treatment model that, in the words of the county application, included "substance abuse services, housing or residential assistance, vocational rehabilitation, benefits assistance, money management assistance, access to healthcare, and other non-medical programs necessary to stabilize homeless severely ill persons who may either go untreated or come into contact with the criminal justice system."[24] Proposition 36, in effect between 2000 and 2011, gave the county $30 million annually and mandated that individuals who were convicted for possession of controlled substances and crimes committed under the influence receive treatment as a condition of probation instead of incarceration. Through Proposition 63, in effect from 2006 until the present, the county received $90 million per year (29% of the state total) to create 68 community-based mental health programs whose aim was to provide temporary, supportive, and permanent housing, counseling, assessment, and other services to mentally ill individuals.[25]

Propositions 36 and 63 latched onto the infrastructure created by these two demonstration programs and scaled them up to a level that significantly impacted the jail population. Proposition 36 produced 2,000 case dismissals per year and Proposition 63 diverted nearly 4,000 inmates from jail per year. These are not trivial numbers, as they were roughly the equivalent of the population of the Twin Towers jail.[26]

To prove that these programs, beyond their recidivism effects, actually decreased the jail population and mobilized the medicalization occurring in the Twin Towers jail, we must look at the two types of infrastructure they created: the "Jail Linkage Team" and the building up of community treatment and medicalized supervision methods. The Jail Linkage Team consisted of personnel whose job it was specifically to "identify and link" mentally ill inmates in Twin Towers to community-based treatment and/ or supportive housing services. The motivating logic of this team was that by contacting individuals before release, assessing their needs, creating placements for them, and physically transporting them to supportive services, an inmate's willingness to engage in treatment post-release would increase.[27]

When we look at the detailed job descriptions of this team, we can see how the team's activities actually work to alter the level of inmate sentencing. Specifically, these staff members were in court advocating for leniency and reduced sentencing for the inmates they had worked to medicalize. As noted in one report, "AB 2034 team members enter the jail and initiate an engagement process with the referred client that includes . . . attending court hearings to advocate for them and to work with the Sheriff's Department to coordinate an effective release/discharge plan from [Twin Towers Correctional Facility]." Thus, through engagement with individuals who had been through the medicalization process in the Twin Towers, jails created information and biographies that pushed court actors to reduce sentences.[28]

Once inmates were approved for diversion, they were ordered to reported to newly created Community Assessment Services Centers (CASCs); the county developed 11 such centers. At these centers, for the first time, probation officers and treatment providers would jointly assess offenders. Probation staff used a three-level risk assessment that combined a criminal and addiction inputs to assign the required duration and intensity of treatment and supervision. The county ultimately contracted with 100 certified and licensed treatment agencies that provided services across 194 sites throughout the county. While each agency had a different treatment modality, all were places where released inmates could report and receive some kind of intervention, and where a staff member of that agency would statistically indicate that the individual had been provided services and was made accountable to the county's supervision.[29]

These programs exemplify the utility of framing inmates with medical attributes in order to avoid the need to use precious jail space. Their expressed logic was to preserve jail space for violent offenders and to release less serious substance abusers and mentally ill inmates. This is the linking of medium security to medically releasable: an outright redefinition of a population in order to justify its removal from the incarcerated population (and use community health funding to do so). If we view probation release in its proper historical context, we see that this medicalization was a space-saving and revenue-generating measure and not a feat of increased correctional control.

The Medicalization of Twin Towers

In our jail ethnography we uncovered the processing of security threats into healthcare events—what we called "medical marks"—that resolved key problems of scarce specialized jail space. Here we detail the origins of the pharmaceuticalization of inmates who "act up" in its ability to project limited healthcare into legally satisfactory levels. As we shall see, officials can meet legal requirements to provide inmates with massive amounts of health services, despite having very little money to do so.

In the spring of 1997, at the exact time when officials were implementing the plan to open the Twin Towers jail, county officials were stunned to learn their jail healthcare system was the subject of a new Department of Justice (DOJ) inquiry. The Civil Rights Division of the DOJ had retained a panel of medical experts to tour the jail facilities, interview inmates and medical personnel, and write a report about the jail's delivery of healthcare. At the time, the report was not made available to the public because the DOJ was only threatening to file a lawsuit, and the report was only meant to be a starting point for a dialogue. However, in the spring of 1997, the *Los Angeles Times* obtained a copy of the report and escalated the situation to a crisis level. The Times reported:

> the panel has assailed the Sheriff's Department and county mental health officials for housing scores of mentally ill inmates in cramped, dingy cells where they receive little treatment. . . . What's more, the panel wrote, some prisoners languish for days and even weeks without the medication they desperately need to keep their illnesses under control, while other mentally ill prisoners are given drugs—such as lithium and Depakote—to treat conditions from which they might not suffer. . . . Mental health personnel admitted to investigators that little or no effort is made to treat the mentally ill inmates who are not "high impact" or actively suicidal.

The administrative procedures created in the wake of this 1997 DOJ inquiry represented its first significant action on the issue of jail mental healthcare. In the archival record, we can quite easily trace a move from the denial of a medical problem in the county jails in the 1980s, to the acknowledgment of the problem by 1990, to action taken on the problem in 1997. In this section we examine the administrative responses to every progressive legal challenge on jail healthcare from the 1980s to 2015. It is only in reviewing these responses sequentially that we can see medicine as an organizational solution and asset.

The Expansion of a Limited Jail Medical System

The initial period was marked by outright denial on the part of Sheriff's Department authorities that anything was wrong with medical care in jails and the presumption that little could be done. In 1980, as part of the *Rutherford v. Block* case, the ACLU complained that the Los Angeles County Sheriff was not pursuing Correctional Treatment Center (CTC) licensure in good faith. Throughout the 1980s, the sheriff ignored the order by maintaining that the standards for licensure were more appropriate for community hospitals, such as the requirement to provide windows in each cell. Sheriff Sherman Block wrote to the *Los Angeles Times* in 1983, the first time that state health officials toured the jails:

> The areas of the jail referred to by [the *Times*] are no "ding tanks"; they are called behavior observation modules because . . . not infrequently inmates entering the jail system display behavior patterns that indicate to both officers and medical staff that they require a period of closer observation before being integrated into the general prisoner population . . . their actions can be monitored and they can be interviewed by mental health professionals, including a psychiatrist. "Most" of the inmates in the modules are not "heavily drugged," as was indicated in the article, and those who do receive drugs have them prescribed by a physician and administered by qualified medical personnel. . . . Inmates deemed in need of psychotherapeutic treatment are transferred to either state mental hospital or the forensic in-patient unit . . . this unit is fully staffed, 72-hour designated mental health treatment facility.

Here we see the level of certainty in medical provision that defined the 1980s. In it are public claims about the ability of frontline personal to always be able to detect the difference between those inmates in medical need and those not in need. Overall, there is a denial of interest in an organizational mission of healthcare within jails throughout the 1980s.[30]

By 1990, the refusal of Los Angeles County Sheriff's Department to pursue licensure pushed the State Department of Health Services to develop specific jail standards on licensure. The State Department of Health Services toured the jail's facilities and in 1990 issued a critical report on the jail's medical provision. The report found that the jail infirmary failed to meet minimum hospital standards in 11 areas of patient care, such as "taking precautions to prevent the spread of infection; disposing of dressings, syringes, and other medical waste properly; keeping thorough medical records, and providing ways for patients in distress to summon medical help." In contrast to the sheriff's letter to the *Los Angeles Times* in 1983, in the 1990 *Times* write-up of the story, county officials are quoted as "acknowledging . . . some legitimate problems with the jail's health care services." However, department officials deflected the allegations: "he and Dr. Clark defended the quality of medical care provided for inmates at the hospital, saying it was equal to or better than the care in many county hospitals." The Board of Supervisors convened a jail taskforce, but its report was filed and ignored. Thus, in 1990—before the onset of austerity in the Sheriff's Department—we see acknowledgment of possible issues with medical provision in the jails, but an unwillingness to act upon it.[31]

In 1997, just after the county opened the Twin Towers jail, everything changed. Internal county discussion of the DOJ report on the jails and the *Times* article covering the leak of the report was significant. The Sheriff's Department officials quietly wanted to hold a private meeting with the Board to discuss the *Times* report before going to the public. After that meeting, the Board quickly moved to reconvene the taskforce that had been ignored in 1990. This time, the taskforce came up with a staffing plan and budget, and the entire issue was made actionable. The sheriff was quoted in the *Times* as saying, "It is an issue that must be resolved. . . . There are no other options, except get it done. We are going to do all we can to expedite a resolution to this problem."[32] This was a far cry from the sheriff's position in 1983.

The administrative response to the DOJ plan was threefold.[33] First was the movement of "all" mentally ill inmates into Tower One and opening of the

200-bed third medical tower (which had been left closed in the original Twin Towers plan). The idea was that inmates could be better served by health professionals in the updated jail. This was a major redistribution of the inmate population. Recall that a linchpin of the county's 1997 crisis abatement plan was to house "high security" inmates into the empty Twin Towers jail. No county documents at that time described any medicalized knowledge about this high-security population being moved into Tower One. At the time of the original plan, these high-security transfers were defined solely by the security threat they posed to deputies. Consider the following description in the original Twin Towers plan:

> [Twin Towers] will provide a much higher level of officer safety. Officer safety has become a critical issue during the past 15 months with a large increase in the number of violent prisoners caused by the passes of the Three Strikes Law . . . our need for maximum security beds has increased substantially. With its large number of single cells, [Twin Towers] fulfills this need much better than Men's Central Jail.[34]

In this original description of the planned opening of Twin Towers, the single-cell space of Tower One is considered safer because it will better protect the guards from violent inmates. With this shift—replacing high-security inmates with inmates primarily defined by their mental illness—the single-cell spaces of Tower One are re-envisioned as the perfect spaces to keep mentally ill inmates safe from others or themselves. As diagnosed by one supervisor, "My understanding, the last I heard a report on this, was that part of Twin Towers was housing those people who also had additional issues in terms of mental disabilities or drug problems, that part of Twin Towers, and those people are—tend to be some of your maximum-security people."[35]

The second component of this plan was the expansion of staffing to serve the redistributed mentally ill inmates. The Sheriff's Department hired 142 new positions at a cost of $13.2 million in the first year. This was followed by similar expansions in 2001 and a substantial, four-year expansion plan for 2004–2007. The original plan included 44 Sheriff deputies, 51 custody assistants, and 30 individuals to implement a new medical information system, and an additional 17 medical staff. A major component of this original plan was the introduction of mobile "teams." These teams were to roam the jails in search of inmates who had slipped through the cracks and transport them safely into medicalized space. As reported in the *Times*,

"Two mental health evaluation teams have been formed. One will work at the Men's Central Jail, and the other will work at the Peter J. Pitchess complex in Castaic to try to identify mentally ill inmates who are not getting proper care."[36]

Third, the DMH staff was doubled in Tower One of the new jail from 100 to 200 workers at a cost of $8 million in the first year. This expansion created a true mental health facility, complete with full-service "step-down" facilities. Each level of the tower was meant for a different level of mental health acuity. The highest level was a 46-bed facility that provided care for individuals who presented an immediate danger to themselves or others or were so disabled that their ability to function was compromised. Other floors were dedicated to single and double cells of "high-observation housing" for individuals who did not need inpatient care but "required an intensive level of observation by custody to maintain their safety and security." Finally, the tower included dormitory mental health housing for inmates whose "mental health needs can be cared for in a less intensive and more open setting than the high-observation areas." These dorm settings were indeed different from general population areas because they were fully staffed with "social workers, psychiatrists, psychologists, nurses, and group treatment providers including specialists in co-occurring mental health and substance abuse disorders [and] release planning."[37]

Given that the county was in fiscal shortfall, how were these three maneuvers paid for? In short, by medicalizing the inmate population, county officials were able to draw upon medical funding that otherwise would not have been available. The $8 million for Department of Mental Health staff was taken directly from a 1991 State Mental Health tax source—it was revenue intended to be used in the Department of Mental Health's budget for community healthcare. The county received numerous inquiries from community stakeholders about the funds and the impact on community healthcare. The transfer would set a long precedent in the county for using state funds to pay for jail mental health services: by 2014, this amount had reached approximately $40 million in various state mental health funds. This amount accounted for the entirety of the Department of Mental Health's jail expenditures.[38]

The $13 million in spending by the Sheriff's Department for medical services was funded by a new revenue that would not have been available had the county not used the funds for healthcare. Officials discovered in 1997 that telephone profits in the jail had been previously tied to the Inmate Welfare

Fund (IWF), which could only be used for costs that benefited the education and welfare of inmates. Such funds were specifically barred from being used for required conditions of confinement, including, critically, medical expenses. As a result, the fund had significant unused revenue attached to it.

Faced with the pressures of the moment, county officials pushed to exploit legal ambiguity in the law so that IWF funds could be used for medical needs. In order to provide itself with a plausible rationale for using the funds, the Sheriff's Department changed the contextual meaning of "required expenses of confinement." Documents illustrate that officials reasoned that they had always fulfilled "required" medical care; that is, that they were always providing what was required by the State of California, and the DOJ response plan in 1997 was actually a voluntary addition to healthcare. This was an administrative innovation, because the meaning of "required services" appears as malleable in our analysis: the new medical plan was in response to a regulator that was threatening to sue the Sherriff's Department for not providing required healthcare; later calling those expenditures "voluntary" therefore constitutes an administrative maneuver. As a grand jury report stated some years later, "IWF has grown from a special fund with limited revenues and application into one with significant revenues and considerable latitude."[39]

How a Limited Medical System Satisfies Legal Requirements

It is important to understand that although these moves were substantial increases in the medical capacity of the jails, they were inadequate to fully meet the needs of the jail population. We can see from the archival record that top county officials knew very well that there was not enough capacity to serve everyone in the jail who was medically needy. The following exchange between the Director of Mental Health (DMH) and a member of the Board of Supervisors illustrates this point:

SUP. ANTONOVICH: Let me ask Dr. Southard. The Vanir report indicates that there's going to be a 40 to 50 percent increase in the need for jail mental health care over the next 5 years. That's being projected by your department and staff . . .

MARVIN SOUTHARD: Supervisor, it's been our experience so far *that the pressures in the jail mental health program, both on the high end and the lower end, needs are greater even though the population has remained essentially about the same...*

SUP. ANTONOVICH: If you had a correctional treatment facility, what type of staffing would you require?

MARVIN SOUTHARD: ... well, the percentage here, if you look at it, Supervisor, it's about 15 percent of the population. If there are 20,000, we're looking at about 3,000. And the bulk of those would not be the intensive needs services, the inpatient type services, or the high observation. The bulk of those would probably be individuals with a relatively minor mental health problem that is complicated by a substance abuse problem. I think that's the typical inmate that we see in our jails, is somebody that has a mental health problem, but it wouldn't be really a big mental health problem but for their addiction issues that complicate it.[40]

This was the fundamental tension of jail health and mental healthcare: there existed a population of inmates that could be deemed eligible for health services if those services existed. As the director of the Department of Mental Health stated, these individuals were in the general population and their needs exceeded the amount of medical resources and space provided by Tower One and the 200-bed medical facility. This was the same tension we saw in our ethnography; that is, in addition to those inmates who clearly need care immediately, a substantial portion of the general inmate population could use the care if it was available. It is the limited space that creates this tension, which in turn must be solved on a daily basis. As another official stated, "You wouldn't have to be a clinician to see that there are people that are currently housed at a lower level of care than they should be housed at . . . in your jails, because you do not have the high-acuity beds in the jails, people that are in the high-observation housing and the moderate-observation housing that clearly meet the critical needs for that higher-acuity inpatient beds."[41]

If progressive law caused the sheriff to expand medical services in the jails, but austerity limited that expansion. We must ask: how is it that austerity limited medical resources were able to the satisfy the requirements of progressive law? By answering this question, we will see why medical provision took the form it did in our ethnography.

A majority of the newly hired personal for medical and mental healthcare were almost entirely made up of security and processing personnel, *not* therapeutic personnel. The new funding provided the sheriff with 44 new deputies, 51 custody assistants, and 30 individuals to implement a new computer inmate information system so that the 200-bed medical tower could finally be opened. Thus, if we view this expansion in its proper context, it allowed the jail system to expand capacity through a move of security personnel into a part of the jail that had yet to be opened.[42]

The new medical staff and mental health officials mainly constituted processing personnel in the intake rooms or mobile "teams." These types of positions were tasked with continuously upgrading and downgrading inmates between the limited medical spaces and general population spaces of the jail. These staff were experts specifically trained to work with a large mass of inmates whose medical attributes they could emphasize or de-emphasize in order to produce some selection of inmates lucky enough to receive limited healthcare. That such staff were grouped in "teams" was especially important. These teams were mobile squads of specially trained deputies and mental health staff who would respond to "crisis situations," "communicate with a mentally ill inmate in an effort to defuse a situation," transport declassed inmates out of Tower One into general population, and conduct sweeps of general population housing areas to look for inmates who might need mental healthcare and transport into Tower One.[43]

In 2013, of the 284 mental health staff in the jails, 136 were in the form of these mobile teams and another 32 were intake room staff, compared to just 54 therapeutic staff and 19 administrators. The teams consumed half of the mental health jail budget. Time and time again, in response to litigation after the 1997 period of administrative activity, we see medical response take the form of these types of processing personnel.[44]

In order to prove how the sheer processing power—visible in our jail ethnography—became the key means to resolve legal demand, I reproduce one extended, annotated exchange between the Board of Supervisors, the Sheriff's Department, and Department of Mental Health officials. The discussion underlies how these logics addressed the tension between limited medical services and legal demand. First, the general problem of limited mental health services emerges:

SUP. MOLINA: What is the determination that is made as to when one exits that [mental health] tower ... and it's based on what?

SHERIFF LEE BACA: Their psychiatric and their psychological evaluation interviews and discussions and the things that they do in their medical profession.

SUP. MOLINA: Well, like what? I just want to know how you stop being mentally ill . . .

KATHLEEN DALY (DMH): They have an evaluation by a mental health clinician to determine if the acuity of their symptoms is mild enough . . . when people come in, they are often psychotic. They need to be on medication. Once they stabilize on medication, they'll need to stay on medication but don't require the ongoing treatment that they get in mental health housing . . .

SUP. MOLINA: You release them into the general population? Is there knowledge amongst the people who are maintaining custody of these individuals that they have mental health issues? Do they know because of their medication?

KATHLEEN DALY: They know. And we also do the mental health units that provide services on the general population side, as well. And they do follow-up with them, as well. So they're seen by a psychiatrist if they're on medication.

The supervisor rightly questions how any inmate deemed mentally ill could suddenly no longer be in need of services and be eligible for transfer into general population. In response, the high-level department officials rely on the logic of processing: that their frontline personnel can assuredly tell the difference between those who need medical care and those who do not. As we see, the Department of Mental Health officials consider the placement of sick inmates into general population non-problematic because the deputies who watch over them know such individuals are receiving ongoing medication—what I have called the "medical mark" of medication. The mark becomes an easy way to keep tabs on these individuals and take their medical complaints more seriously. Next, we see the organizational logic that resolves the legal problem of mentally ill patients in general population:

SUP. MOLINA: You say you need more money to get more [teams].

SHERIFF LEE BACA: Because they don't want to go back and they resist going back to the general central jail housing area. What I've done, in order to avoid that issue, as well, is to have them report to the inmate reception center and send them to another facility that doesn't alarm them to the degree that the old central jail has alarmed them. . . . And deputies are telling me that they often have to use force that they don't want to use because someone is dragging their feet and reluctantly becoming resistive to going to the housing . . . they still require a professional to deal with them because they act rather erratically and they act violently . . .

SUP. MOLINA: . . . You return people into the regular population. But they're still acting out. Isn't that a kind of a problem? I mean, because a custody official is going to use force if he's in the regular population. *If he's acting out because of mental health issues, maybe he shouldn't be in the general population?*

KATHLEEN DALY: *I would agree with you.*

What emerges in this exchange is that transferring sick inmates into general population produces a secondary legal problem: inmates often "act up" and resist being downgraded out of medicalized space and deputies must use force against them. The acting up is itself a symptom of the limited medical space; that is, this is the behavior of individuals who have only been downgraded because there is a scarcity of medical space. It is the "teams" and the medication they provide that allow the jail to consider such a problem resolved. So long as these inmates are stabilized with medication during their transfers, the transfers themselves become non-problematic.

In the archival record, we can see that this specific problem—"use of force" incidents (the use of violence to discipline non-compliant inmates) against mentally ill inmates—became a focal point for the Sheriff's Department, ACLU, DOJ, and other progressive legal monitors. If mentally ill inmates acted up and force was applied to stop them from doing so, it became a sign of poor healthcare. These incidents became the primary indicator determining that mentally ill inmates were not receiving enough care. The creation of the mobile staffing "teams" and their expansion throughout the following decade were designed to mitigate that problem.

As we saw in our jail ethnography, such mitigation meant taking any security issue (whether it was medical in origin or not) and diffusing it with medical knowledge or medication. The teams become the key legal way of both safely handling any violent situation and projecting limited medical resources out of medical spaces and into general population. The supervisor, not to be outsmarted, follows up on the admission by the DMH official:

SUP. MOLINA: I know you would agree with me, but that doesn't resolve this issue. . . . Because what has happened, and some of the issues, particularly in some of the ACLU cases, there were mentally ill people, including one that was killed, in the general population. And so I'm trying

to understand as to why we're releasing them into the general population and yet we have constant problems. And one of the solutions that the
sheriff is presenting is that we give you half a million dollars to hire more
social workers that are going to help escort these people . . .

MARVIN SOUTHARD: . . . I think the idea of the [teams] . . . that the sheriff is
talking about has a function that is more than merely escorting for the
transportation. It's also to augment the ability to provide mental health
services for the individuals as they are a part of the general population. . . .

KATHLEEN DALY: . . . My understanding is that the [teams] would actually be
used in the other direction, as well. So when someone who's in general
population, who may or may not have been identified as a mental health
client, is acting out, that sometimes it's difficult to remove that person
from their cell, to move them to mental health housing. And that that's
when the support of mental health personnel and specially trained deputies would be called upon . . .

SHERIFF LEE BACA: . . . That's when the individual has to be removed. Not
in all occasions but on enough occasions to bring it to my attention by
deputies. That's where inmates start to act up and get resistive and then
violent.[45]

As this exchange concludes, we see a resolution emerge that addresses the
supervisor's concern about the threat of ACLU lawsuits. The two Department
of Mental Health officials rely on the fact that the "teams" extend the power
of medicine out of medicalized space and into general population areas because those teams also work to transfer inmates in the other direction; that
is, from general population into medicalized space. *It is the continuous circulation of inmates into and out of medicalized spaces—the mere act of processing inmates—that becomes the policy solution to the legal problem.* That is,
the lack of medicalized space is resolved by relying on the logic that "teams"
can squelch disturbances as inmates are transferred between the space, even
though, by the admission of county officials, they probably are still medically
needy.[46]

This provides us with an explanation for what we saw in our field site: The
medicalization of inmates who act up is actually an administrative solution
developed as a resolution to legal demand and austerity. Limited medical
space in the jail is projected out into non-medical spaces when inmates are
downgraded and sent into general population with "medical marks"; this, in
turn, creates security threats in the general population that are then resolved

through the processing power of teams—what we saw in our ethnography as the pharmaceuticalization of security events. The actual therapeutic effect of teams is limited as they are charged with escorting inmates into and out of limited medical space.

Conclusion

This chapter started with the 2015 vote to replace and downsize the 5,000-bed Men's Central Jail in downtown Los Angeles with a 4,000-bed correctional treatment facility and the diversion of 1,000 spaces into community treatment housing. This downsized jail, known as the Consolidated Correctional Treatment Facility (CCTF), was virtually a "hospital-jail" and is described over and over in county documents as "a treatment facility for inmates instead of a jail providing healthcare." The primary way this new jail was defined by medicine was in the design of its housing units, which placed treatment staff in each of 100 bed pods. By placing mental health, substance abuse, and other programing staff in each pod, it was thought that tradition-ally lengthy "sick call" waits would be eliminated and connections between staff and inmates could be facilitated.[47]

The county was able to move forward with its 1,000-bed smaller jail—amid long-standing jail overcrowding problems—because it simultaneously funded 1,000 community diversion beds that were rationalized through medical knowledge. To be clear: this was not a side diversion program or an addendum; the creation of these treatment beds was the main way that officials, responding to two and half decades of jail overcrowding problems, justified building a jail that was too small.[48]

All of the strands traced in this chapter—the reliance on medium-security inmates to generate revenue, the medicalization of medium-risk categories through an early release system, and the medicalization of jail space—coalesced into the vote for the new, downsized hospital-jail. As we saw, over three decades and successive bouts with progressive law and aus-terity, Los Angeles County officials moved from identifying its inmates pri-marily by the attributes of maximum-security violent gang membership to attributes of mental and physical illness, substance abuse, and less risky homelessness. In short, county officials created a permanent medicalized early release system because it became a utility to keep a sinking jail system afloat.

It was not that simply that more sick inmates began to fill up the jail, as predicted by the deinstitutionalization thesis. Nor was it that the jail simply grew in resources and power to take on the duties of medical provision, as predicted by a thesis of mass imprisonment. Instead, taking on medicine was a form of crisis abatement. Essentially, the county had a large number of inmates who could be endowed with the qualities that made them less seriously risky and more medically needy whenever it was fiscally and legally prudent to do so.

By viewing these three strands in concert with our ethnography, we see how the redistribution of the poor explains the expansion of medicine in jails. First, our archival history shows that emphasizing medium-security needs of inmates was necessary to sell emptied space to outside agencies. This explains why our intake room revolved around the need to nudge inmates toward a less serious ranking of eight to seven. With space at a premium, ranking inmates as less serious at the frontline level became a utility that helped the jail maintain legal requirements with limited funds at the administrative level.

Second, this push to nudge the inmate population toward lower security risk occurred alongside the medicalization of release. By examining the archival record, we saw how a system of diversion mobilized the intake-processing staff inside the jail to identify inmates in need and get them out of the jail and into community treatment spaces. The need to create space in the face of fiscal austerity interacted with legal demands to provide care, and this pushed the jails to make use of diversion.

Finally, the medicalization of space inside the jail explains why, in our ethnography security, events were pharmaceuticalized, endowing inmates who "acted up" with medical marks. In the archival record, we saw that as long as the county could fund enough "processers"—frontline workers, especially mobile "teams" whose job it was to transport inmates safely into and out of medicalized space—the county could project fiscally limited services into legally viable budgets.

All of these practices produced funds from other agencies where the jails otherwise lacked them. Nudges toward medium risk were intentionally undertaken in order to sell freed-up space to other state agencies for profits that allowed jail space to be opened. Diversion programs also were made possible by newly available state mental health and substance abuse funds, which only further created space inside the jails. Finally, the state funds for mental healthcare–funded services were brought into jails, helping to open previously unavailable space and to appease legal regulators—even when it siphoned funds from community healthcare.

The implication of this is dire. The transformation has created a situation in which an entire jail system has fulfilled its substantial legal requirements to provide healthcare while many inmates go untreated or underserved. We see many inmates with medical need slip through the cracks because they miss obtaining an initial medical mark at intake processing. It was the extent of the resources at hand that created the demand; in other words, inmates' biological need and security risk were manipulated to fit the budget. No matter how overcrowded the jail was, no matter how far the budget was stretched by progressive legal advocates, redistribution allowed Los Angeles County to always claim it was safely housing inmates and providing them with adequate care.

PART II

THE RESTRICTION OF MEDICINE IN LARGE PUBLIC HOSPITALS

The following two chapters offer an alternative explanation for the restriction of medicine in large urban public hospitals. The "retrenchment-criminalization" thesis would contend that public hospitals have restricted medicine because they are subject to the same neoliberal political forces downsizing other public institutions and the same racist ideology motivating crime-control techniques in institutions that serve the poor. While such an explanation no doubt preconditions the changes we are seeing in public hospitals, they fail to explain the persistence of funding in our public health system. As we saw, spending on healthcare, especially mechanisms that funneled federal money to urban healthcare safety nets, grew exactly during the time we would expect retrenchment.

In Chapter 3, "Opioids, Observation, and Restricting Access in the Public Emergency Room," we enter the daily life of the modern public emergency room (ER) where new legal rules mandate that all patients receive care and patient safety is monitored carefully, and yet fiscal austerity has limited bed space to critical levels. We use ethnographic evidence to understand two routine problems that emerge from this tension: there are always too many urgent patients than available bed space and far too many less-urgently sick patients who technically should never receive beds. We see how it is, counterintuitively, the provision of costly services during the wait—opioid administration to manage vital signs, increased triage staff observation, and police presence in the ER—that provides the hospital with the ability to resolve these problems. In essence, each of these developments has the effect of providing technical reasons to delay qualified patients, which makes it more likely that patients will simply stop seeking care.

It is the origins of these dynamics—which all represent additions of healthcare spending—that we work to uncover in Chapter 4. In "Building a Hospital That Everyone Knows Is Too Small," we return to the history of Los Angeles County. The chapter first details how redistributing the patient population as less urgently sick (primarily made up of immigrants and homeless persons who inappropriately use the ER) enabled the county to obtain billions of dollars in new revenue from the federal government. The chapter then details how this new revenue came the requirement to downsize inpatient capacity, so much so that it drew the ire of federal courts concerned about the county's ability to meet its legal requirements. In the end, we see how it was only by making use of other federal regulators' concerns about patient safety—innovating with the kinds of waiting line management techniques of the kind seen in our ethnography—that the County was able to achieve downsizing and placate courts in its attempts to close inpatient capacity.

Thus, it was not simply that the public disinvested from public hospitals that led to downsizing, or that racist politicking led to criminalization, as would be predicted by the retrenchment-criminalization thesis. Such factors surely enabled what was happening, but the restrictive dynamics of the modern public ER are born out of an iterative dynamic between the need to acquire new fiscal resources and the need to send legal signals that appeased healthcare regulators. The County could—by redistributing its patient population—use the provision of medicine during the wait to both restrict expensive medicine and to renew its dying hospitals.

3

Opioids, Observation, and Restricting Access in the Public Emergency Room

One evening in the front-room entrance to the public ER, a woman limped through the security gate. She was being propped up at the shoulder by a man. He wore a dirty trench coat, and as I looked at them more closely, I took note of their ragged hair and weathered faces. They stopped for a moment and scanned the room around them before noticing the black arrows painted on the floor. The arrows pointed them toward the entry nursing station—the station where I and the nurse I was shadowing stood behind a desk. The entry nursing station was a small, rectangular room of about six desks with computers. The primary job of nurses in this room was to create files for incoming patients that would then follow those patients during the rest of their stay.

Open 24 hours a day, 7 days a week, and unable to refuse care, public hospitals and their ERs are where we would expect healthcare to be widely available. It is in the large public ER where the urban poor—like the two I would observe on this night—begin to accrue medical lives. In the best-case scenario, they see doctors, are referred to clinics, and are signed up for different forms of public insurance. If patients leave the ER before seeing a physician, their ailments can get worse, more expensive, and deleterious to their lives. The stakes are high.

The couple approached our desk. The women mumbled a string of indecipherable sentences. She seemed to have a speech impediment, I thought to myself. The nurse looked up at the man and he said matter-of-factly, "She cut her hands on nails."

Upon hearing this, the nurse looked up at me with a smirk. While maintaining eye contact with just me, she addressed the man. "Ooook, why would she do that?" The question had been delivered with subtext. I knew from experience that cutting one's hands on nails was something an emergency room (ER) nurse would, on first inspection, deem to be an

Redistributing the Poor. Armando Lara-Millán, Oxford University Press (2021). © Armando Lara-Millán.
DOI: 10.1093/oso/9780197507902.003.0004

inappropriate use of the ER. It did not seem to be a life-threatening ailment and was probably something a potential patient might make up to get into the ER. The man made no gesture and there was an awkward silence. The nurse obtained the woman's name and some other identifying information and began to create her file.

The two walked away as the nurse clicked on the computer entry box titled "Stated Reason for Visit" and typed "cut herself with nails to get into hospital." Looking up at me, the nurse said, "Just the typical con-artists." I laughed in response. The nurse looked at me. "Did I ever tell you about the diabetic guy? He drinks a Coke can right before he goes into triage!" "No, tell me!" I said. She recited a story about another patient who knowingly spikes his blood sugar just before being triaged so that he can be immediately admitted to the ER. This would, apparently, make his vital signs go haywire. She began to click on the computer and showed me the file of the man in her story. It appeared he had been to the ER 10 times that very month. "That's how you learn to see through these guys," she said.

I was interested in what would happen to the man and the woman, so I left the nurse to try to track them down. I moved into the general waiting lobby and looked around. This was a crowded room with dozens of people standing, leaning against the walls, and milling about. There was a crying baby and a line several people deep at the restrooms. There were also two police officers standing in the corner.

For the next hour, I positioned myself in the waiting room so that I would not miss the couple being called for an assessment. Finally, a different nurse walked into the waiting lobby and called out a woman's name three times. I knew that after about three times the nurse would give up and would return with a different name—skipping whomever she had previously been calling. I felt bad and suspected it was the name of the woman I was trying to see. After some consternation, I moved to the nurse and told her that I thought it might be a couple that was in the overflow room.

I did this not only because I felt bad for the patient, but also because I knew that it might give me a chance to build some equity with this nurse and get the chance to follow the patient's care.

I walked with the nurse to the overflow room. It turned out that, indeed, this was the same person the nurse had been calling. Lucky me. I knew the nurse would have a problem with the man coming along, but after a brief exchange, the nurse said it was okay for him to come along because she could not understand the woman.

We walked slowly into the assessment room—the room where patients are first evaluated and given triage scores. The room had about eight interview booths, separated by semi-private partitions. Each booth had a desk, a computer, and vital signs equipment. There was a row of waiting patients along all four walls of the room.

After another 20 minutes, the woman was called to an assessment booth. Yet another nurse said hello to the couple and began to scan the woman's medical file on his computer. At first, the nurse did not ask them any questions, but started taking the woman's vitals, attaching heart rate and blood pressure monitors. He took her temperature as well. This was key, because it turned out that the woman had a dangerously high fever. "What happened? She has a fever," said the nurse. The man responded, "We collect cans, it's not her fault, she got stuck by nails that were in the can . . . look at her hands." The nurse looked at the hands, which were extremely swollen. "Those could be infected . . . ?" The man nodded yes. "Okay, we were are going to have to get her back right away, that infection could be anything."

I was asked to escort the couple to a third waiting area called "observation." This room was a waiting area beyond security checkpoints (it felt inside the ER but somewhat closer to admissions) and was the location for individuals who had been given a "B" triage score. Had patient received a "C" ranking, she would have been asked to wait in the main crowded waiting lobby with the police and the crying babies. Here, in observation, she would be watched over by the head triage staff and continuously checked by nurses. I knew this meant that her condition was considered more urgent by the person who triaged her and that she was "on deck" for a bed in the ER (if one became available).

For a couple of hours, I continued to meander between observation and the assessment booth, periodically checking on the couple so that I could continue following them. Eventually, the couple was no longer in observation and I was told that she had been placed in a bed. This meant that she had been admitted and was going to be treated by a doctor.

I moved to the room where she had been placed. I stood near the entrance as there was no medical professional attending to her just yet. I noticed that the man was now gone. A different nurse, a receiving nurse in charge of getting patients ready to see the doctor, came up to the door, took the chart off the wall, and flipped through it.

He began shaking his head vigorously. "You have got to be kidding me." He quickly looked at me and then moved into the patient's room and yelled at her, "Have you been shooting?" "No!" she mumbled defensively. "Can you help me . . . my hands . . ." The patient turned her palms up to show how swollen her hands were. "I was digging through the trash and hit nails!" she tried to repeat. He ignored her comment and repeated his original question. "Why are you REALLY here . . . have you been using drugs?" "No, no!" said the patient, now shedding tears.

The receiving nurse walked out of the room and approached the attending physician and a group of nurses. Shaking his head, he said, "I can't believe this . . . we cleared this room . . . finally cleared it out just to get this . . . I don't know who is running things up there [referring to triage]." The physician responded, "I know. And they did the whole MSE up there [medical screening exam by a nurse practitioner in triage] . . ." Another nurse who was in earshot joined in, "I mean, I can just tell by looking at her . . ." "I know," said the doctor, chuckling, "what a waste of a bed . . ."

"Where do you live?" asked the receiving nurse, as he came back in. He looked at me each time he asked these questions—not making eye contact with the patient. "I live at the shelter," responded the patient. "Ooooh, you live at the shelter . . . how long have you been homeless for?" he asked, continuing to look at me. "Two weeks," she mumbled back. The nurse shot a look of exasperation in my direction and said to her, "Why are you homeless? You can't work? You have no job?" The patient tried to explain her speech impediment as a reason for her lack of a job, but the nurse shook his head in disbelief.

After about 20 minutes, the nurse returned to take the patient's temperature. "Wow," he immediately said, upon reading the result. "You have a fever? Ma'am, you can't be wearing all those clothes, that's not going to keep you here by wearing all those clothes like that." After a few minutes, I played naïve and asked the nurse why the sweaters were important. He said, "I mean, she can manipulate these vital signs, they need to be more discriminating up front, in my opinion."

After finishing up his initial check-up, the nurse asked her how her hand had gotten so swollen (this time looking directly at her). She replied, struggling to be clear, "I was digging through the trash and got hit by nails . . ." "So you weren't doing coke?" said the nurse. "No! No! No shooting!" she said. "I can't believe this, man," said the nurse, looking in my direction and shaking his head once more. "Why did you do this to yourself, you need to be more careful, you can't be doing that to yourself. Then you get in here and you clog us all up." "Nails! Nails! Nails!" the woman cried out in desperation.

I left the area, and after a couple of hours had passed I paid the room another visit. When I returned, the woman was gone and the room empty. I walked up to the nurse who had berated her with questions.

'So what is going to end up happening to her,' I asked.

'Oh ya, it's really bad. . . . She is going to have to have surgery. . . it's really bad, she could lose her hands,' said the nurse.

In the end, the patient ultimately received the care she needed. I present this extended excerpt from my field notes because it exemplifies the tensions of life in the contemporary public ER. On the one hand, we saw how, at several steps along the way, staff assumed that the patient was an illicit drug user, probably attempting to get pain medication from the ER, and interpreted the cuts on her hands as resulting from shooting up illicit narcotics.

On the other hand, we also saw the very real medical uncertainty that staff have about patients. Limited tests and time make missing medical information—the true biological nature of the patient's ailment—uncertain. Moreover, staff need to know what is in the patient's system—including drugs that may interact with treatments—so that they can properly care for the patient. As we saw in the excerpt, as more tests were conducted, the patient's infection and life-threatening fever were revealed to the ER staff.

This tension is what we must grapple with in this chapter. How can we characterize the public ER as a place that attempts to restrict medicine, when its entire makeup is built for identifying sick patients and providing them with healthcare? As we shall see, the modern public ER, in contrast to its older incarnations, has a great deal of rational rules set up to protect patients from bias and to make sure that they do not needlessly suffer during their long waits. In fact, the modern public has more expensive services available to waiting patients than at any other time in its history. The healthcare providers reading this chapter may ask themselves how such bias is even possible given all the safeguards, training, and surveillance on staff that exist in the modern ER.

In this chapter we are going to see how it is the very *provision* of costly medicine and medical services that result in the restriction of access to the ER. This is a counterintuitive process in which healthcare is provided during the wait—in ways that protect patient's rights—but that ultimately work to deter patients from accessing more expensive hospital services. By the end of the chapter, we shall see—just as in jail intake—the qualities that make one eligible for an institutional bed are, in part, constructed in the process of being qualified for that bed. That is, patients' ailments are reinterpreted by the budgetary limits of the hospital in a reciprocal process that leads many patients into leaving the ER early. This is the modern-day restriction of care in the very place we should expect it to be widely available: the extremely expensive, highly regulated, but downsized public ER.

The Rational System of Triage

When sociologists and anthropologists studied ERs in the 1970s, what they found was a very informal place. It was non-medical clerks who were in charge of admissions decisions, free to favor some patients over others. The rules for vetting incoming patients were unspecific, learned on the job, and applied inconsistently.

This all changed with the passage of the 1986 federal Emergency Medical Treatment and Active Labor Act (EMTALA). At a time of widespread public health retrenchment, this law actually mandated that indigent patients could not be refused care when they are in an unstable medical condition. Moreover, in 2001, the Joint Commission on Accreditation of Healthcare Organizations (JCAHO) revised their standards of care to include pain assessment and management. The new standards required pain management at every stage of the patient visit. What modern-day patients will find now when they enter public ERs is a triage process that is heavily rationalized: it is registered nurses and nurse practitioners who now conduct triage, must make pain management decisions, and conduct initial testing that was previously unavailable during triage. ERs are periodically visited by state health agencies with the power to cite the ER and disaccredit the hospital if they disobey the mandates of the law.[1]

Thus, any discretion that we uncover must account for the modern-day heavily rationalized process of triage. Simply put, staff cannot do whatever they want. While triage processes are not standardized among hospitals, there are basic processes of evaluating that all ERs must fulfill.

When patients first entered the ER I studied, they pass through a security checkpoint (with X-ray machines and metal detectors) and are directed to an initial screening room. This screening room contains 3 to 10 interview booths (depending on staffing). Patients typically wait an hour to be called to a booth. The room is tense, as patients are told very little about the admissions process; every few minutes, security guards wrangle with weary patients who demand to be informed of their fate.

Eventually, nurses call each patient to a booth, conduct oral interviews, and administer vital signs checks. In these interviews, nurses push for specific symptoms and the reasons patients chose to seek care on that particular day. Patients, however, often annoy nurses with the wider social circumstances of their pain (e.g., lack of housing, unemployment, and stress) and more general health problems. Finally, vital signs checks (blood pressure, heart rate, and temperature measures) are given to patients. The vital signs tests are a key source of triage's purported objectivity:

> 'It's how we know whether or not a patient is faking, if they are really in pain,' said one hospital administrator. 'It also allows us to differentiate between patients with the same presenting medical issues. If one has a heart rate over 200 and another one with 195, we can make a distinction. The machine does not lie.'

These oral interviews and vital signs checks constitute the rational rules that guide nurses in assigning urgency rankings.

Assigning patients urgency rankings (A, B, C, or D) is the critical goal of these interviews. Patients are admitted in order of their rankings; the sickest patients should always receive beds first. Most patients are given a ranking of B (urgent) or C (non-urgent) and sent to two different waiting rooms. The C-list patients, who constitute the vast majority, are sent to the front-room lobby, where they are placed on the "general wait list." These patients are admitted based on their order of arrival.

The front-room waiting lobby—where people on the C-list wait—is an unpredictable setting. At times, people sleep and patiently await their admission. At other times, it is a chaotic space, with police officers threatening the removal of patients and confrontations between frustrated patients and nurses. The bathroom always has a long line. Children are a constant source of noise. For most patients, the 8- to 18-hour wait in the ER I studied was harrowing.

Critical to the fate of C-list patients is the process of "reassessment." Reassessment refers to re-checks of patients' vital signs during their wait. The goal is to monitor changing conditions and upgrade or downgrade patients' rankings accordingly. Reassessment is particularly important because nurses have the discretion to expunge patients from the waitlist if they do not respond when called for reassessment.

Alternatively, patients given B rankings are considered "urgent" and are sent to a separate waiting room called the "observation waiting room." To gain access to this room, patients pass through a separate security checkpoint. In the observation waiting room, head nurses deliberate over patients who are near the point of admission. This separate waiting room allows nurses to maintain continual observation of B-list patients. Because these patients are considered more urgent than their C-list counterparts, they are, technically, always admitted before C-list patients— regardless of arrival time.

It is in this observation room that the head nurse makes final admissions decisions. When beds become available, the nurse receives a phone call from a bed coordinator with information about how many beds are free. During such moments, many head nurses claim to remember all patients and the seriousness of their conditions. This information is built up from their review of patient records, their own observations, and conversations with other staff. Once a decision is made, patients are called and, if they have not left in the interim, are led to a bed.

There is also a "back room" entrance to the ER. This entrance is available for patients brought by ambulance, fire departments, police departments, and sheriffs from local jails. This entrance has a separate nurse whose primary responsibility is to negotiate access to beds for these public safety arrivals. The back-room entrance has a small waiting lobby where there is almost always a congregation of public safety officers. Nurses befriend these officers after repeated interactions, and it is a collegial setting. It is also a gauntlet of sorts for incoming arrestees and inmates, who are often taunted and questioned about criminal activity.

Two Conundrums of Overcrowding

Triage staff must find solutions to two organizational conundrums created by extreme overcrowding. The first is the rule that B-list patients (those with more urgent medical conditions) should always receive beds before C-list patients. A problem emerges in that the B-list is never empty; there are always urgent patients in the ER I studied who populate the B-list. As a result, technically, no one on the less concerning C-list should ever receive a bed. If staff do not find informal means of thinning the C-list, the general lobby patient population would swell even further and the hospital would risk losing accreditation.

The second conundrum is that there are more B-list patients whom triage guidelines categorize as urgent and in need of a bed than there are available beds. That is, nurses must choose between patients who, according to medical criteria, qualify equally for beds. This constitutes insufficient specificity in the conferral of "urgent" rankings.[2] For example, a head nurse is told that two beds are now open, but the nurse previously determined that three patients were all equally in need of beds. Over the course of their approximately eight-hour wait, all three patients had at least one concerning electrocardiogram, or EKG (a diagnostic test that measures the electrical rhythms of the heart), some shortness of breath, intermittent chest tightness, and high pulse rates. A head nurse said in such a situation,

'These patients . . . are most likely not going to have a heart attack during their time at this hospital. But, you never know, and it only takes one patient to die here in the waiting room to spark a lawsuit. From my perspective, with the information I have on them and what they have provided me with, they all have an equal chance, albeit a small chance, of that happening.'

The nurse is faced with a conundrum: Which two patients get a bed, and which patient will continue to wait?

What is at stake when a bed is given to one patient over another? Those who are made to wait are more likely to leave the ER before being seen by a physician. Although available data show no medical differences between those who leave and those who continue to wait, patients who leave are far more likely to develop serious medical problems in the short term. While the medical community is at a loss to explain why some patients "choose" to leave the ER, in what follows, I show that patients often leave because of dynamics related to crime control and criminal justice.[3]

Restricting Access in the Public ER

Because these two conundrums of overcrowding must be resolved, the triage department must come to restrict admission to the emergency department. But this restriction cannot occur overtly and must fulfill the legal obligations to provide anyone with who seeks out care. Disobeying the law (EMTALA) would risk the hospital's accreditation. As we shall see, restriction manifests through the *provision* of expensive medicine, medical supervision, and safety requirements during the long wait.

This counterintuitive claim—that restriction occurs via the provision of resources during the wait—unfolds through four processes. First, general patients are delayed through the widespread administration of pain medication. This has two effects: pain medication temporarily alters patients' vital signs and provides staff with valid medical reasons for delaying patients and subsequently confers criminal stigma upon waiting patients. Second, additional staff observation of waiting patients—staffing meant to protect patients during long waits—results in the deployment of this criminal stigma in ways that reinterpret similarly situated medical biographies. We can see how criminal stigma is refracted along race and gender lines to compensate for ubiquitous "missing medical information" about incoming patients. Third, hospital-based police aid in keeping waiting rooms orderly, even helping to identify patients who are next in line, but this has the inadvertent effect of pressuring patients to stop seeking care. Fourth, at the back-room entrance to the ER, police and jailers bring in a significant number of arrestees, inmates, and witnesses who are rushed to hospital beds ahead of general patients— even when they are less medically qualified for those beds. As a result, front-room patients lose beds to the endless supply of drug arrests and inmates being given medical resources at the back-room entrance. I will expand on all four processes in turn and illustrate them with common examples taken during the course of fieldwork.

Pain Medication and the Expansion of Criminal Stigma

When it comes to prescription opioids in the United States, we generally acknowledge two facts. First, it is well known that the United States is experiencing a major opioid epidemic, with a 200% increase in opioid-related overdose deaths from 2000 to 2014. Even though ER physicians provide only 4.7% of the total number of opioid prescriptions in the nation, it is well known that long-term opioid use often begins with the treatment of acute pain from clinical settings like the ER.[4]

Second, it is also the case that we know that patients from low social-status groups are less likely to be prescribed pain medication at the point of hospital discharge. That is, it has been shown that doctors are less likely to prescribe pain medication to people of color and people they perceive as poor.

How can we have a situation in which the ER contributes to opioid use, but doctors are thought to restrict their access to the very patients that tend to use public ERs?[5]

The answer could possibly be due to the fact that, in contrast to prescriptions at discharge, during triage the dispensation of pain medication is ubiquitous and plays a central role in managing the front-room waiting list. In 2001, JCAHO, the major accrediting agency that shapes standards of healthcare, made "pain" its fifth vital sign. In part, ERs were required to ensure, no matter their overcrowding levels, that patients had timely access to pain management. Patients' "right" to have their pain recognized and managed were engrained in these new standards of care. This pushed many large ERs to develop "nurse-initiated" protocols that sped up services to waiting patients, most importantly the delivery of opioids during the wait. In 2016, across all ERs (not just large urban public ERs) opioids given at the point of ER discharge occurred in just 38.4 visits per 1,000 adults, while opioids given during the wait occurred in 53.4 visits per 1,000 adults.[6]

This administration of pain medication during the wait allows triage staff to manage ER overcrowding in two ways. First, pain medication temporarily alters waiting patients' vital signs (the primary means by which staff identify the sickest patients) and thus provides nurses with valid medical reasons for selectively delaying the admission of some patients over others. After receiving pain medication (which temporarily makes patients feel better), some patients leave the ER—an outcome that shrinks the wait list. Second, the administration of pain medication creates the potential for triage staff to invoke the stigma of narcotics addiction and criminality about any patient. Triage staff rationalize delays by explaining that some patients who seek care do so only to obtain narcotics. Thus, the act of seeking healthcare at the front-room entrance to the ER can be understood to be an act of criminality.

The following excerpt describes an event that took place in the observation room and illustrates the processes whereby a patient, on the verge of obtaining a bed because he has significant indicators of chest pain, was moved from urgent to non-urgent. Triage guidelines at this hospital dictate that rapidly changing blood pressure, high heart rates, and suspicious EKGs should be upgraded.

'Yeah, it is true. He fits the criteria for a bed, if that's what you're asking,' said Arthur, the head nurse, after I asked him about a patient who had just been complaining about his wait time. 'But what that guy doesn't understand is that we gave him pain medication. And he's been here for what . . . [looking at the computer screen] six hours. He got reassessed and his vitals have changed, he can wait a while longer at this point. . . . The pain meds are doing what they are supposed to do.'

At that point, the patient came back up to Arthur and, while touching Arthur's forearm, said, 'If I die here, it's your fault.' Arthur, aghast, looked down at his arm and said, 'Sir, you need to take your arm off of me right now, I will have the sheriffs come down here and remove you.' The patient walked away.

Several hours later and after two rounds of bed openings had passed, Arthur called the patient for a re-check of his vital signs. He was nowhere to be found. It was clear he was one of the many patients who left the ER prematurely. 'HA!' said Arthur.

I shot him a perplexed look and said, 'What? He wasn't as serious as he claimed?'

Arthur replied, 'Well [pause] . . . he definitely needed a bed at some point. I had him on deck for about four rounds [a nurses' term for instances when beds become available]. He had a concerning EKG, the other one was okay after, and his sweating and heart rate were a bit high before the pain meds, so he meets the criteria . . . but . . .' Sensing Arthur was reluctant to elaborate, I said, 'It must be tough, there are a few people on this list just like him, right?'

With almost seamless transition, he said, 'Yeah. And the thing is . . . this guy has been here a bunch. You saw that from his record. He's got problems and can't take care of himself: eat right, exercise, and go to the damn clinic. Blaming me if you die here? It's your fault for not putting in the time to get it looked at. I mean, look, he took off . . . probably was here just to get the drugs.'

Although many patients leave the ER after receiving pain medication, many others continue to wait, and this necessitates another method of ignoring qualifications for admission. In the preceding example, in addition to administering pain medication, the nurse casts this patient as a part of the undeserving poor. The patient is worthy of delay because Arthur depicts him as not having done anything to fix his own health problems, which Arthur surmises from the patient's purported unnecessary use of the ER and blaming of Arthur for his own predicament. This stigmatization is buttressed by threats of arrest, ambiguous use of the word "record," and presumed drug addiction. Immediately after the exchange, I asked Arthur to elaborate on his indictment of the patient as a drug addict:

> Arthur replied, 'The thing you have to understand: We have a bunch of drug users and drug-pushers in here. Half the time, these people are complaining and are in here for these simple issues, they are just here for the free supply.'

The application of criminal stigma to patients post hoc obscures the true function of pain medication in the ER. To be clear, qualified patients are delayed and deterred from accessing healthcare through the use of pain medication, and the delaying and deterrence are justified through the use of crime control language.

In Roth's and Jeffery's ethnographies of public ERs in the 1970s, criminal stigma was reserved for a small subset of patients: those brought to the ER by police or for drug overdoses.[7] In the contemporary ER, as documented here, pain medication creates the potential to cast all patients as drug addicts, regardless of their relationship to police or actual criminal drug use, and therefore render them undeserving of care. The rhetoric and narratives around drug peddling and addiction—which are a ubiquitous feature of contemporary crime control language (Simon, 2007)—inform triage staff's shared understanding of their patient population and justifications for continuous delays.

Observation, Missing Medical Information, Criminal Stigma

The previous section described how criminal stigma comes to be applied to general patients on the front-room ER wait list (via the administration of pain medication). We now turn to how increased staff observation of waiting patients uses such an understanding in selecting some patients for beds over others. Specifically, we see how triage staff utilize criminal stigma to solve the critical problem of "missing medical information." As we will see, deployment of this criminal stigma occurs along race and gender lines.

The previously mentioned "observation room" in which the more concerning patients waited was actually an important and costly innovation to expand patient services. The idea was to be able to continuously monitor patients as their conditions changed so that extreme deteriorations in their conditions could be identified. This expanded staffing during the wait included nurse practitioners, a higher grade of medical professional, who, in contrast to registered nurses, have the power to assess patients and offer waiting patients advice about whether they should continue their waits.

We can see how criminal stigma is put to use in these moments of increased staff observation. In order to see this link, we have to understand how uncertainty about patients' medical biographies manifest in triage decision-making. Medical staff are faced with much missing medical information about the patients they are trying to assess. As a result, they often use discretion to admit patients on a "hunch" that missing medical information would confirm an urgent ranking. This use of discretion is, in part, informed by criminal stigma about patients. An association of criminality refers to associating oneself, knowingly or not, with any type of engagement with the criminal justice system or the world of drug use, distribution, and violent crime. Criminality is a complex status, but in triage there is little time for making distinctions between types of crimes. As an illustration, the following excerpt details how one woman moved from a less urgent ranking to being immediately admissible:

> A young woman approached the nursing booth and asked the head nurse, named Melinda, how much longer she would have to wait. Melinda gave her the standard response: 'I'm sorry, ma'am, I know you have been waiting a while, but you're going to have to continue to wait; we try to give beds to the sickest patients.'
>
> As the patient walked away, Frank, another nurse, whispered to Melinda, 'Yeah, her vitals are pretty good. . . . I just reassessed her maybe an hour or two ago.' 'Hmmm,' Melinda responded. "She can't be faking that, her eyes are so blood red . . . she looks miserable, but when you look at her vitals they are perfect.' I see Melinda slowly going over the computer and pondering the patient's record. 'Let's look at her labs,' she says. 'I don't know, can't really upgrade her if she isn't indicating anything. It's weird, I don't think I've seen her here before.'

At this point, Melinda, the head nurse, was unwilling to admit the patient despite the disconnect between visual cues of pain (the red eyes) and normal vitals/lab results. Melinda referenced criminal stigma when she explained the delay with the phrase, "It's weird, I don't think I've seen her here before." In the culture of the triage staff, this phrase invokes the baseline assumption that most waiting patients fake illnesses in order to return to the ER and obtain narcotics. Although most patients have some kind of missing medical information, patients who can dissociate themselves from criminal stigma are admitted on "hunches" that missing information constitutes an urgent health problem. Several hours later, this same patient asked Melinda if she could go outside:

'What for? You really shouldn't go outside if your situation is serious . . .' responded Melinda. 'Solamente queria hablar con mi esposo [I only wanted to talk to my husband],' the woman said. Melinda, with a surprised look on her face, said, 'Your husband is waiting for you out there?' After the patient said yes, Melinda told another nurse to go find the husband and bring him to the waiting room. . . . As the man walked in, with painter trousers on, he immediately struck me as one of the many immigrant construction workers in the area. Melinda leaned toward me so as to hide her comment. 'I didn't know she was married and that he was waiting out there for her this whole time . . . that's so cute . . . [as the woman leaned on her husband's shoulder] . . . he really cares about her. . . . I'm pretty sure something must be up 'cause he wouldn't be waiting if he's got work tomorrow . . . [after a short pause] . . . something must really be wrong.'

A short while later, two beds opened up and the patient was admitted ahead of six other people. I said to Melinda, 'How did you know she wasn't faking the pain? Her vitals were good, right?'

'Yeah, it's true, but I mean, you saw her, right, she looked miserable and when we can't really tell if something is going on, that doesn't mean something ISN'T going on. And the thing is, you don't really fake when the family waits for you like that. I asked them and he was in construction and he does have to work tomorrow. Because I told them that they would be here through the night and they stayed anyways. HE stayed with her . . . so you know . . .'

In this example, the head nurse moved from being willing to ignore the missing information to admitting the patient based on a hunch. This move was made possible once the patient was able to demonstrate her relationship with someone who was perceived as earning a living from non-criminal endeavors.

This excerpt points to how criminal stigma (or, in this case, the absence thereof) is deployed according to the intersection of race and gender. Publicly, the ER is a color-blind environment. While medical professionals are willing to verbalize stigma around criminality and welfare-dependency, they are absolutely unwilling to verbalize stigma about race and gender. Yet, over the course of my fieldwork, it became clear that ethnicity and gender mediate how some patients come to be associated or disassociated with criminal stigma in two main ways.

First, ethnicity is critical in determining how a woman's relationship status associates her with criminal stigma. Specifically, when Latina women indicate that they are in relationships with Latino men (whom triage staff largely consider to be involved in non-criminal employment), triage staff are more willing to pursue missing medical information for those patients. In stark contrast stands the assessment of African American women. When African American women associate themselves with African American men, triage staff are likely to assume that such partnerships exist only to support illegal economic activity (e.g., prostitution or drug use) and staff are thus less likely to admit such patients based on hunches. These assumptions draw on broader stereotypes of African American women and specific stereotypes of black men as criminals. This also suggests the strategic deployment of Latino men as a "model minority."[8]

Second, the presence of children and associated gender roles mediate men's and women's relationship to criminal stigma. When women present to the ER with children, triage staff often assume the children were reared, in part, to increase access to public aid, and, by extension, the ER's opioids. The staff's willingness to fill in missing information for such patients is much lower. Yet, when adult men present to the ER with children, triage staff are more likely to assume they are "good fathers" and unassociated with criminality. In other words, for women, children are a sign of welfare dependence (and, by extension, ER abuse), whereas for men, children provide protection against criminal stigma. These gendered deployments of criminal stigma in the ER reflect how women's relationships to men and children are reconstructed by state actors in frontline institutions.[9] The following excerpt took place in observation just after a woman was brought in by the fire department. She was white and instantly struck me as someone who had spent a significant amount of time on the street. The woman was screaming and yelling while nurses unstrapped her from her gurney and put her into a chair. I was standing next to a triage nurse named Romney who was filling out paperwork during the commotion.

I caught Romney's eyes after one particularly loud outburst from the woman. 'So sad,' I said, nodding my head toward the patient. 'Who, her!?'

Romney said. 'That lady has been in here for drug issues. . . .' 'Oh, yeah?'
I replied. 'Look, I have a long history of alcoholism in my family,' she said.
'My uncle was an alcoholic for 15 years, he used to carry around a gallon of
alcohol just like it was a water jug.'

'WOW. That's a lot,' I said. 'He probably wasn't someone who was easy to
be around.'

She looked up at me over the top of her glasses and I felt a level of trust set
in after my comment. 'My sister was a drug addict . . . ya, she was . . . there's
only so much you can do for them. . . . I almost lost my house trying to help
her . . . but I had to stop . . . I just had to stop.'

'I mean, it's family, you have to try . . . ,' I said.

'Exactly, but they have to want to fix it. It's up to them to put in the work.
You can't just sit back and expect people to help you with your health issues.
My husband is sober from meth for 15 years. I didn't do it. He did it. He's a
teacher now.'

'I bet he still struggles with it every day,' I said, attempting to elicit more
sympathy.

Then, with an almost seamless transition and no pause in her speech,
she said, 'You know, I had a patient who once told me that it was my fault
if they died in here [she glanced at the woman who had just come in on
the gurney], yah, can you believe that? [looking at me, while I expressed
shock]. These people, some of them, they come in year after year and don't
get any work done. They have problems and don't go to the clinics to take
care of them. It's not my fault if you die here. It's your fault for not putting in
time to get looked at, get it taken care of, and if you don't have the money,
don't tell me it takes you 10 years to get the money, 'cause some of them have
been coming here for that long.'

The reason I chose to present this excerpt is to illustrate that criminal stigma
travels in multifarious ways. For the white, single woman, the emphasis is on
class and idleness—her health status is connected to an unwillingness to appear in clinics and labor toward health. White persons are not immune from
criminal stigma; stigma simply happens to them in a different way than it
does for black and brown waiting patients. The conferral of criminal stigma
and its relationship to missing medical information is a complicated process, traveling through the prism of race, class, and gender and only visible
through the watching of admissions unfolding in their appropriate context.
While most patients are thought to be poor, it is those poor patients who

associate their poverty with criminality who are downgraded and delayed and become subject to an element of public waiting room life that many do not know exists. This element is what we turn to next,

Police Observation and Roll Calls

The police unit is a ubiquitous feature of general lobby waiting room life in the public ER. To be clear, by "police unit" I refer only to an official public police unit (not private security guards) paid for by the counties and specifically mandated to patrol hospital grounds. The police unit takes on numerous duties that blend into the provision of medicine and, as we shall see, negatively impact the number of C-list general patients who are willing to wait to receive care in the general waiting room. A non-trivial number of patients remove themselves from the wait list because of this police unit, which no doubt contributes to the 20% "left without being seen" figure.

During my fieldwork, the police unit I came to know talked about its role—and medical staff primarily understood that role—in a way that was politically palatable. Police are often seen and talked about as protecting ER staff from angry patients and occasionally kicking out individuals who are not seeking actual care but attempting to spend the night in the waiting lobbies. To that end, the police are often seen checking the wrist bands of individuals, which tells them if patients are actively on the wait list or not. This is seen as a good service by the unit and the medical staff: persons who are not seeking care should be kicked out to free up space and decrease the chances of conflict in an already stressful situation. As one hospital adminis-trator told me, as we looked on while a police unit was conducting its nightly routine of clearing out the waiting room, "The thing is, there are people in here that shouldn't be. They aren't here for emergencies; they should be at the clinics. If I had their problems, I would never come here."

Indeed, because there are always individuals who attempt to spend the night in public ERs, this service can be bracketed off by the staff from the police unit's more substantial impact on the wait list. The unit has experi-enced "mission creep" and has begun to take on duties that significantly im-pact the provision of medicine. This happens in two ways. First, when the waiting lobby becomes particularly overcrowded—that is, when there are no more seats for new patients—the police unit begins to check the IDs, one by one, of each person waiting in the lobby, occasionally reading those names into walkie-talkies so that officers at remote computers can conduct background checks. On many occasions, I observed waiting patients who, after seeing this activity occurring at one end of the lobby, preemptively left the ER. Field interviews with such ex-patients indicated they left the ER because they did not want the police to discover some arrestable status (i.e., an outstanding warrant, probation violation, or status as an undocumented immigrant).

However, this policing also affects people who have little connection with criminal or undocumented statuses: that is, members of the general public who are also pressured to stop seeking healthcare at the front-room entrance. To understand this important point, it is vital to understand the connection between reassessment and policing.

As previously described, reassessment is the process by which nurses are mandated to re-check waiting patients' vital signs at regular intervals. Hospital policy dictates that if patients do not respond when their names are called for reassessment two or more times, they can be removed from the wait list. If patients return after missing their name call, they can be forced to re-register and begin the waiting process again. Nursing staff consider this job to be the least desirable because it rarely results in the upgrading of patients' conditions and usually leads to confrontations with frustrated patients.

When nurses are in charge of reassessment, they are reluctant to expunge patients from the wait list. Depending on whether a patient has received a good moral evaluation, nurses will strike a patient from the list after two, three, or four chances. Moreover, nurses will go out of their way to look for patients in the bathrooms, hallways, or even outside the hospital before expunging them.

Police buttress the link between reassessment and expulsion in the following two ways. First, they use policing tactics to pressure individuals to physically leave the ER when nurses remove them from the wait list. Absent such tactics, patients can sometimes plead their way back onto the wait list when dealing directly with the nurses. Second, when overcrowding reaches critical levels and the wait list swells, police take over the work of reassessment directly. During such instances, a police unit calls out the name of every C-list patient waiting in the front-room lobby. When police are in charge of calling out names, reassessments occur more frequently. The calls are made from one location, and it takes about five seconds to read each name three times. Patients inevitably miss their call. Police see the buttressing of reassessment as one of the primary ways they "keep the waiting line in check." As one officer described it to me:

'Sometimes the nurses give them a little leeway. We just make sure it happens. . . . These people need to be in this room if they are really sick . . . if they are off, out of the ER, god knows what they are up to.

If the nurses do this, a lot of times the people will come crawling back and start hassling them. . . . Saying they were here the whole time. But if we do it, the people are gonna be less likely to challenge what we say. . . . Lots of times if the person is really challenging us, we will just get on the radio and call the guys down [other officers]. We can just surround the suspect, stare him down, pressure, and they will remove themselves. We know how to deal with people that are disrespectful, that's what we do for a living.'

Another officer described his role as follows:

'The hospital has rules about the waiting list. The list would just be endless if we didn't do this. These people come in here week after week, everybody knows they don't really need to be here. And the conditions, the overcrowding in here, can be dangerous, people lose their cool. And these types of people, this is just a fact, I'm not trying to be a dick, crime is always going to be an issue. You have drug peddlers in here. So it helps with safety as well. If we didn't enforce these rules or, like, make them actually work, these people would really be able to abuse the waiting list.'

Two key points stand out from these excerpts. First, police justify their role in expunging general patients by utilizing the same understanding as the nurses of the criminalized patient. When the police officer says, "If they are off, out of the ER, god knows what they are up to," he is demonstrating the shared idea that some patients are not really sick and are perpetrating crime. Patients, who in this context have nothing to do with the criminal justice system, are redefined as suspects. When these patient–suspects attempt to pressure police for re-enlistment onto the wait list, the police respond with arrest tactics to ensure expulsion. When perceiving a threat of arrest, jailing, and a criminal record, even the most resilient patients will leave the public ER. Second, the officers conjoin their traditional roles of ensuring public safety with the mandate to solve the organizational conundrums of overcrowding. When the officer prefaces his crime control statement with "the hospital has rules about the waiting list. The list would just be endless if we didn't do this," the officer indicates his understanding that policing works, in part, to solve overcrowding problems in the front-room waiting lobby.

We should pause, however, to be clear about the true function of this policing. This is not a police unit dedicated to the capture of absconders or individuals who have evaded community supervision. Nor is it a unit mandated with the express purpose of arresting undocumented individuals. Its mandate is to patrol hospital grounds and keep staff and patients safe. This distinction is important, because it means that actual policing practices have developed in a way that primarily works to kick people out of the overcrowded ERs, rather than evolving in a way that arrests more people. I know this because the unit's capacity and resources are limited for actually systematically arresting individuals: doing so requires them to call on the regular police to come and pick someone up and take them to the jail. The unit ironically must pick and choose when they attempt to call the police, making sure that their target is someone a responder would find worthy of making a detour to the hospital for. Thus, the true function of ER policing is not to arrest general patients, but to diffuse the patient wait list.

Rushing Healthcare to Inmates and Arrestees

The frequency with which police and jailers bring individuals involved with criminal justice to the back-room entrance of the public ER significantly affects the front-room waiting line. In essence, ever-present inmates and arrestees receive precedence for the limited beds, thereby crowding the patients waiting in the general wait rooms. This finding is counterintuitive, as we tend to think that the "mark" of the criminal justice system makes it less likely that one would be provided with medical services.[10]

This is not a set policy; it is not written down as administrative code or dictated in a memorandum of understanding with law enforcement agencies. The official preference is always to admit the sickest patients first. The preference for criminal justice wards is something detectable only through watching admissions unfold in real time. When a bed becomes available, a short conversation commences between the head triage nurses in the back room and the front room. They check to make sure there is not an exceptionally needy B-list patient the hospital cannot afford to have continue their wait. If such a patient exists, the inmate or arrestee can be made to continue to wait in a very small area, in a patrol car or ambulance escorted by police, or in the jail bus. The preference for inmates is a social fact generated by the workgroup to solve the routine problems of too many inmates and arrestees.

This preference has a different manifestation for the arrestee and inmate. That is, it matters whether such a patient arrives via police car or arrives via a bus from the jail. I will discuss each in turn.

Triage staff at the back-room entrance justify favoring police arrivals over general patients because they believe that the escorting public safety officials cannot be made to wait. Many of the police arrivals present ailments that would afford the patient a C-list ranking in the front room and a likely 10-hour, or longer, wait. In contrast, when fire departments and ambulance officials bring patients not involved with criminal justice to the back-room entrance, they simply drop them off, and these patients then enter the normal triage process through the front-room entrance. Police, however, cannot relinquish custody of patients brought or escorted to the ER. My discussions with officers at the back-room entrance of the ER revealed that police bring individuals to the hospital for two general reasons. First, public safety officials are legally obligated to provide treatment for any "serious illness or injury" an inmate has suffered during custody.[11] Second, police now often work with mental health task forces or medical providers (such as ambulance teams), or have their own training in medical knowledge. The decision to bring an arrested person or witness to the ER is a conversation that happens between those parties outside the ER and has been studied elsewhere.[12] The following excerpt describes the admission of a police arrival:

> Two police officers were talking with a young man strapped and handcuffed to a gurney, kind of joking with him in a way. 'You make good money. I know you have a better load than I do,' said the police officer to the man. 'We know you're hustling, we've seen you on that corner before, don't lie.'
>
> At this, I assumed the man was one of many brought here for possession of narcotics. He struck me as aloof in a way that instantly made me think he was high on drugs, and I could tell the officers were trying to get him to admit to selling. . . .
>
> 'We gotta get you off the streets, man . . . you keep hurtin' people, your family . . . let's just take you out of there . . .' said the other officer to the man.
>
> After a brief silence (I was very scared to say anything), I managed to ask, 'Why is he here, guys?'

The policeman looked up at me in surprise, looked over to the back-room charge nurse, who nodded to him, and then said, 'He's here 'cause he's high, I mean, he's drunk, too, so I doubt anything is wrong with him per se . . . we just HAVE to take him here.'

'So it's, like, what protocol to bring him down here?' I asked.

'Well, it's not so much that, I mean that's true, but that is kind of up to our judgment. A lot of these guys are high when we take them in, you know, like we can pretty much find stuff people are doing illegal just by talking to them . . . and we're trying to crack down on that area.'

Shortly after this conversation, a nurse escorted the police officers to a bed, where they would sit with the man for the next few hours. As soon as they left, I walked over to the back-room charge nurse to ask him about the admission, "So do the cops ever have to like wait around a bunch? It's kind of surprising a bed was open so quickly . . . right?" The nurse replied,

'Look, there is a reason they have a charge nurse back here in the ambulance entrance and one in the front . . . these cops are coming in all the time with drug guys, sometimes the alcoholics, but mainly the drugs. I have a relationship with those guys, a working relationship. I know what they go through. It's hard out there. It's a courtesy to them. . . . I mean, legally they can't just drop that guy off here . . . 'cause normally if that guy walked through the doors, right, he would be waiting a LONG time. There's no way we can have those cops waiting in the ER for 12 hours when they know nothing's wrong with the guy . . . it would basically kill the police . . . it's just a thing they have to do.'

It is important to note that the back-room entrance has a very limited waiting area. There is space for only two or three gurneys, and every arrival is accompanied by a multitude of law enforcement officials. Thus, in contrast to the front-room waiting lobby, there is very limited space that patients can be delayed into. This is an important fact; as we saw in a previous section, it is the existence of the expanded waiting room that makes it likely that many patients will remove themselves from the wait. At the back-room entrance, there is no such process by which individuals involved with criminal justice can be informally pushed off the waiting list.

The processes favoring inmate arrivals from the jail have distinctive features. Discussion with longtime ER staff indicated that during the past decade, the frequency of jail arrivals to this ER began to exceed the amount of space reserved for inmates. The 15 to 20 beds in this ER's jail ward—the beds in the ER specifically devoted to in-custody patients—are perpetually filled. This is a key routine problem for triage staff, because it means that inmate arrivals must take up beds in the general areas of the ER—beds that might otherwise go to patients from the front-room entrance.

The hospital does not want to admit every inmate from the jail and pushes to receive those cases that can be more easily resolved and quickly sent back to the jail. The jail, on the other hand, wants to send the more complicated cases to the public hospital—the ones they hope will free up limited jail space for longer periods of time. This wider tension manifests itself in a particular routine problem encountered by medical practitioners: whether or not an inmate has an ailment that requires referral to a specialist and a longer stay in the hospital. Knowledge of the patient as an inmate shapes the way that medical knowledge is used to solve that routine problem. Consider the following example:

> I was standing next to a doctor and nurse as the doctor held up an X-ray outside of a patient's room. I could see that the patient was an inmate because of his handcuffs and jumpsuit and the deputies milling about outside the room.
>
> 'He's bleeding from the colon . . . not sure . . ." said the doctor. I spoke up in hopes of getting the doctor to elaborate: 'Is it serious?'
>
> 'Could be anything, really. . . Could be cancer, too.'
>
> 'What's the cause of that?' I said. Shrugging his shoulders matter-of-factly, the doctor said, 'Could be from severe alcohol use or. . . .' He cut himself off and moved away, ignoring me. I suspected he didn't feel too comfortable talking to me about his thinking. I looked at the nurse, and she said, 'We look at the color of the stool . . . '
>
> A while later, I saw the doctor talking to the patient. I moved outside the room and could overhear them. 'How long has the bleeding been going on?' The patient shrugged his shoulders, showing little interest in engaging with the doctor. There was a brief silence. The doctor looked over his shoulder in my direction and then closed the curtain to create a kind of barrier between us.
>
> A couple of days later, I followed up with the nurse and the doctor. After reminding them of the situation, I asked what ended up happening to the patient. It was explained to me that the inmate had self-inflicted bleeding

in his anus with a foreign object. The doctor expressed that he was proud that he had coaxed this admission out of the patient. The nurse said, 'Yes, because it could have been much more involved.'

'More involved? What do you mean?' I asked.

"Well, we could rule out the need for an endoscopy,' said the nurse. 'Right,' the doctor quickly interjected. 'If he was smart, he would have kept his mouth shut and he could have gotten to spend the night in the hospital. . . . A lot of these guys do things to get out.'

'Honestly, I don't blame them,' said the nurse, with the doctor and myself nodding in agreement.

While this is an example of an inmate who was treated correctly for his ailment, it is instructive. The patient is on the border between needing an invasive and time-consuming test—spending the night in the hospital and preparing for a procedure that requires being put under general anesthesia. It is the knowledge of this patient's social conditions (i.e., that he is an inmate in the jail) that allowed the doctor to more quickly resolve the case and discharge him out of the hospital. It is likely that the doctors in the jail pushed to have this patient sent to the ER because his case was potentially a longer and more complicated one.[13]

But this interplay between the social condition of "inmate" and medical uncertainty has costs that are underappreciated without the use of participant-observation. When staff emphasize the context of jail in a patient's background, they inadvertently pigeonhole the patient's medical life into singular ailments, ignoring other ongoing health problems about which inmates often complain. It is true that inmates do create medical events to get out of the jail, but they also do so in order to get into the public hospital—a place where they might have a better chance of having other ongoing health issues dealt with. This was consistent with our understanding of the inmate in Part I of this book: that inmates receive legally adequate but limited healthcare. In the hospital, many inmates attempt to get the care they think they need, and this practice can also be viewed as a kind of health advocacy.

Conclusion

Going back to the 1970s, social scientists have studied ER staff's ideas about undeserving patients, especially the timeless figure of the "Gomer" (get out of my ER) patient. In short, it is well known that ER professionals strongly disfavor "non-urgent" patients (who, presumably, can be treated in outpatient settings). Indeed, medical journals are replete with attempts to understand the motivations of non-urgent patients who supposedly choose to use the ER as a source of primary care.[14]

In the modern public ER, however, we have passed many rules, created many regulatory bodies, and added staff supervision to prevent bias against patients. The rules of JCAHO and EMTALA have been set up so that staff do not skirt their duties and presume to know which presenting problems are serious. In the world of modern triage, everyone is supposed to be seen by a doctor.

The modern ER is thus grappling with a particular tension: the growth in rules to protect patients' rights during their wait and the austerity that has limited the size of ERs. As we have seen, this results in the two routine problems that confront medical staff on a daily basis: the parallel problems of too many B-list patients and the technical inability to ever admit any C-list patients.

We saw how it was the expansion of four kinds of increased patient services during the wait that resolved these two routine problems. The first is the widespread provision of pain medication during the wait. This provision has two effects. On the one hand, it provides triage staff technical reasons to delay admission—by altering vital signs—to qualified patients who would otherwise be entitled to scarce beds. On the other hand, it works to develop a belief among triage staff that, in general, most waiting patients are seeking care less because they are truly urgently sick, and more because they are seeking to abuse opioid drugs.

Second, increasing staff observations of waiting patients creates more opportunities to put this baseline understanding of waiting patients—that they are potentially criminal drug abusers—to work. That is, increasing staff to observe and protect patients during their long wait has the effect of reconstructing the medical biographies—along raced and gendered lines—of waiting patients from qualified to less qualified for admission.

Third, because waiting rooms are so overcrowded, law enforcement must be funded in order to keep those rooms safe and orderly. As we saw, law enforcement officers rarely arrest patients, but inadvertently restrict access by increasing the amount of times that patients are called to be reassessed for important vital signs checks. Again, the provision of medicine—the effort to reassess patients in case their condition worsens during long waits—results in the restriction of access.

Finally, we see another kind of restriction for the general public: the provision of medicine to local arrestees and inmates of the criminal justice system. That is, the expansion of medicine to wards of the criminal justice system— the very dynamic studied in Part I of this book—crowds out general waiting patients.

All of these provisions of medicine work to delay qualified patients seeking care in the front room. Without these four restrictions, the hospital would be unable to resolve the problems associated with an always full B-list and C-list. There is no technical way to diffuse C-list patients from the general waiting room lobbies—patients who, technically, are never supposed to receive beds ahead of B-list patients—than to pressure them to leave the ER. We now turn to explaining this dynamic: Why would a public ER restrict access to healthcare in these ways? Can it solely be explained by the retrenchment-criminalization thesis?

4

Building a Public Hospital That Everyone Knows Is Too Small

We need to account for three things about the restriction of medicine in our emergency room (ER) ethnography. First, what are the origins of the use of opioids to manage patients on long wait lists? Second, what are the origins of increased observation—including both those of medical professionals and those of police—of waiting patients during their long waits? Third, how did these extensions of medical services during the wait come to be associated with criminal stigma? These are the developments that restrict care in the modern, highly regulated public ER.

In order to answer these questions, we can return to the history of Los Angeles County. Consider an important meeting of the Board of Supervisors on April 27, 2003. This meeting was the culmination of several in which hundreds of protestors packed the board room to oppose a 100-bed cut to the County's largest public hospital, Los Angeles County + University of Southern California Medical Center (LAC + USC) and the decision to privatize another hospital (Rancho Los Amigos).

Protestors lined the walls and aisles, held signs, and were disrupting the meeting with chants of "Don't close Rancho! Don't close Rancho!" Sheriff's deputies were asked to calm the crowd several times. Annelle Grajeda, a representative from the local nurses' union, was the first of dozens to offer public testimony. Grajeda first addressed the proposed cuts: "According to an expert in emergency medicine who's visited the hospital over the past two months, overcrowding in the ER is the worst in the nation. This continues to result in tragic, preventable fatalities as patients die in the ER while they're waiting for days to receive care due to lack of available beds. . . . Under these conditions, severe downsizing at LAC + USC would be disastrous. Don't close beds at LAC + USC."

The crowd roared in approval. Next, Grajeda turned her testimony to large social movement that had organized to oppose the cuts:

Redistributing the Poor. Armando Lara-Millán, Oxford University Press (2021). © Armando Lara-Millán.
DOI: 10.1093/oso/9780197507902.003.0005

For the past 37 days on the campus of Rancho, a courageous and determined group of patients . . . family members, employees, and community
supporters have held a round-the-clock vigil at the Ranch. A tent encamp-
ment and support center for this healthcare institution. Patients with disabilities have elected to make this sacrifice to call attention to just how
much would be lost if we were to . . . allow the closure of Rancho.[1]

That patients' rights advocates would oppose these closures was predictable.
What was not predictable was what Grajeda said next:

On Friday, Judge Florence Marie Cooper issued a tentative order granting
a plaintiff's motion for a preliminary injunction to block the closure
of Rancho, and I quote, "until such time as DHS [Department of Health
Services] can assure the court that Rancho's patients will continue to receive comparable inpatient or outpatient medical services and that they will
receive such services in a timely manner and to the same extent as members
of the general population with insurance." Judge Cooper concludes, "It
is abundantly clear to the court that the harm to the plaintiffs, if Rancho
closes, far outweighs the harm to the county if it stays open."[2]

To be clear, in response to a lawsuit raised by this social movement, a federal judge blocked the county from implementing these healthcare cuts. This
ruling would thereafter shape the county's healthcare policy: the order specifically barred the county from making healthcare cuts if those cuts were
solely due to budget shortfall. Even facing severe austerity, the county would
need to uphold its constitutional duty to provide indigent healthcare.

While existing scholarship would predict that mere "retrenchment-
criminalization" results in the kind of restriction we saw in our ER ethnography, Grajeda's testimony points us elsewhere. It was specifically the
confluence of fiscal austerity and legal demand around patients' rights that
would result in the kinds of restriction uncovered in the previous chapter. At
each step of this history, legal demand to protect patient's rights cannot be
disentangled from fiscal austerity to the point that, at times, public officials
would use legal demand to help accomplish cutbacks.

This chapter takes us through three parts. We first detail the decision to rebuild LAC + USC from a 1,200-bed hospital to a 600-bed facility. We see how
by re-emphasizing the patient population as less urgently sick (primarily,

made up of immigrants and homeless persons who inappropriately used the ER) the county was able to obtain billions of dollars in new revenue from the federal government in order to stabilize its budget and rebuild the facility. Second, we examine how legal demand prevented the privatization of Rancho Los Amigos Hospital but led to the subsequent closure of the Martin Luther King (MLK) Jr. Hospital. Instead of blaming budget cutbacks, officials would use legal demand from health regulators concerns about patient safety to eventuate the closure of MLK. Finally, we see how after the closures and downsizing, it was these legal and regulatory forces to protect patients that pushed the county to develop waiting line management techniques of the kind seen in our ethnography. In the end, a system developed in which no matter how downsized inpatient capacity became and no matter how large patient demand became, the county could claim it was providing adequate healthcare.

Downsizing the Flagship Public Hospital

In 1997, the Board of Supervisors approved a plan to significantly downsize LAC + USC. The hospital was built in 1933 with a nearly 3,000-bed capacity. By the early 1990s, the facility had fallen into disrepair and was being threatened with discreditation by state health officials because it did not meet earthquake safety standards. When plans for a replacement were originally drafted in 1992, the county intended to build 1,200 inpatient beds. By the time the replacement plan was finally approved in 1997, the bed count for the replacement facility had fallen to 600 inpatient beds.

As discussed in the Introduction, the years between 1992 and 1997 were a period of immense fiscal crisis. The county faced a $500-million-per-year structural deficit in its health budget. In fact, the chief administrative officer (CAO) had recommended that the county close down LAC + USC entirely, as well as 20 other health clinics. Officials lamented the idea of planning a new hospital at a time when the county was on the brink of fiscal collapse—especially given the context of being unable to open the nearby Twin Towers jail.

Nevertheless, the replacement facility was planned and executed. We look first at how the county found the money to open the hospital. They did so by negotiating with federal officials for what was essentially a bailout. This required broad agreement about federal responsibility for costs associated with illegal immigration—a prime example of redefining a caseload in order to generate revenue from another public agency. We then turn our attention to the sizing of the hospital. Officials were deciding whether to build a 900-bed, 750-bed, 600-bed, or 500-bed facility. Political leaders, bureaucrats, local public health experts, and community advocates all engaged in a heated debate about the appropriate size for the replacement facility.

Federal Funds and the "Undocumented Patient"

In the midst of fiscal crisis, the county was desperate to find a new source of revenue. It would look to the federal government's 1115 Medicaid Demonstration waiver program in order to find it. Typically, states apply to Centers for Medicare & Medicaid Services (CMS) for waivers to the rules that govern the way the federal government reimburses Medicaid-eligible health-care spending; for instance, by covering different categories or patients, different procedures, or changing their reimbursement systems.

Scholars have shown that these waivers have been used for political reasons to funnel federal funding into choice jurisdictions, rather than those specifically in need.[3] In the case of Los Angeles, the waiver was, at the time, conceived and thought of as a financial bailout among county and federal officials. Deep amidst the financial distress caused by the state's appropriation of the county's property taxes in 1992, the idea to pursue direct federal intervention first occurred in a meeting of the county's LAC + USC advisory council, a body organized to plan for the hospital's replacement facility. The following excerpt is taken from the minutes of a meeting in August of 1993:

> Spoke on possible closure of DHS facilities: The Board of Supervisors adopted a County budget that does not include funding for a number of outpatient facilities, four of six comprehensive health centers, and 20 of 41 health centers will be closed. . . . [A] proposal to avoid closure of DHS facilities is to propose to the federal government that a demonstration project for the managed care health plan concept be funded in LA County.[4]

The excerpt shows the link between the county's fiscal crisis, the need to apply for the 1115 federal waiver, and the move toward an emphasis on outpatient settings. The county first pursued the waiver through Democratic Party contacts in the Clinton administration (as Clinton was facing re-election trouble in Los Angeles). In 1995 and 1996, county supervisors and health officials flew to Washington, D.C., nearly a dozen times in order to lobby and negotiate the use of the waiver to fill the county's catastrophic health budget deficit. As the *Los Angeles Times* described one such trip, "The promise of a $364-million rescue package to save Los Angeles County's struggling health care system from collapse moved closer to reality Friday after two days of intense negotiations among federal, state and county officials in the nation's capital."[5]

Understanding what the negotiations entailed are critical. Typically, CMS did not attach strict requirements to state's waivers, but in this case the emergency nature and enormity of the financial aid required the Clinton administration to be able to claim the move would save money in the long term. After Bill Clinton announced the awarding of the "aid" at the end of a Los Angeles campaign tour in September 1995, over the next six months officials at CMS dangled a first-year lump sum payment that would push the county to develop a specific restructuring plan of its health system.[6] That plan was to embark on an unprecedented downsizing of the county's inpatient hospital capacity. The *Times* reported from the negotiations:

> "The county is going to reduce its staffed beds by one third. That is a dramatic number," said one county official involved in the negotiations over the bailout. "And we are characterizing it to the Feds as a minimum number; we'll do better if we can. We are much too heavily weighted toward hospital care." . . . But the one-third figure cited by county officials includes at least 300 beds already eliminated since last summer, when the supervisors approved $150-million in cuts in inpatient services. About 370 more of the estimated 800 beds slated for elimination will count when two county hospitals, Rancho Los Amigos Medical Center and High Desert Hospital, are privatized in the next few years as part of the restructuring effort, health officials said.[7]

Eventually the "bailout" was approved at a level that would resolve the $500-million-per-year structural deficit in the county's health budget. As we shall see, it was this infusion of cash that would drive county officials to downsize their flagship hospital beyond community health needs, seek to privatize two other hospitals before being blocked by a federal court, and close its famed MLK hospital. The county would need to reapply for this arrangement every five years and recommit to downsizing its inpatient system; as Supervisor Yaroslavsky said, "The Clinton administration has made good on its commitment to Los Angeles County. It is up to us to make good on ours."[8]

Before we turn to the execution of this downsizing, we must pause a moment in order to understand the role of the "undocumented patient" in this story. During internal meetings and publicity efforts, county officials depicted the county's indigent patient population as primarily made up of undocumented immigrants. This frame allowed county officials to do two things. First, it allowed them to argue that they were bearing costs (undocumented immigrants' healthcare) of what was a essentially a federal responsibility. Officials argued that it was the federal government's responsibility to pay for the costs of illegal immigration. Second, it allowed local Democratic supervisors to work with their Republican colleagues—who were simply seeking to close the hospitals—to agree on pursuing funding.

A research report the county commissioned in order to apply for the 1115 federal waiver can provide a starting point for understanding the county's emphasis on the undocumented portions of its patient population. The county put together a healthcare task force made up of county medical administrators and healthcare experts from local universities. Within the Board of Supervisors' commission for the report was a specific request to determine the "effect of undocumented persons on the healthcare system."[9] This was an a priori request to have a specific section devoted to the healthcare usage of undocumented persons. Rather than argue that the healthcare costs of undocumented immigration was a reason to cut county systems, the report suggested it was a reason to fund the system more:

> This population benefits most from early interventions designed to promote health and encourage positive health behaviors that can have a lifelong impact. . . . There is evidence that the incidence of diseases such as measles, tuberculosis, hepatitis, and AIDS is significant in this population. Such a significant reservoir of communicable disease should not be allowed to exist beyond the reach of the public health system. County officials should continue to place this issue high on their agenda.[10]

The report was referring to increasing diversity from Asian and Latino immigration. It emphasized the health problems of this population in such a way that it corroborated with the previously discussed goals of the 1115 federal funds. By emphasizing that the "population benefits most from early interventions designed to promote health and encourage positive health behaviors," and noting its high birth rates and incidence of communicable disease, the report was framing their health needs as benefiting best from expanded outpatient care. This linked the 1115 federal funds' mandate to increase outpatient care with a framing of the county's indigent population as less urgently sick precisely because they were immigrants.

In March 1993, Congressman Anthony Beilenson, a Democrat in the US House of Representatives (representing Southern California), wrote to the Board of Supervisors and requested a tour of the county's public hospitals and the opportunity to speak with hospital staff. "He expressed an interest in services provided by the County and the medical center to illegal immigrants related to the recent legislation he has introduced," commented the county's director of the Department of Health Services.[11] Congressman Beilenson held a press conference in front of LAC + USC and spoke about his "five-piece" anti-illegal-immigration legislation. Referring to the "huge burden of illegal immigration," local governments were "buckling under the pressure of providing education, healthcare, and other services because the federal government will not." While his legislation advanced border tightening, social security restrictions, and barring the children of illegal immigrants from citizenship, its focus was on pushing the federal government to pay local governments for the costs of illegal immigration.[12] Supervisor Antonovich, a member of the County Board of Supervisors and staunch anti-illegal-immigrant politician, worked with the congressman to design the legislation and accompanied him on the tour of LAC + USC. Writing in a letter to Supervisor Burke, a fellow member of the County Board of Supervisors, Antonovich stated, "The blame for the 1.5 billion annual cost to serve LA County illegal aliens for law enforcement, health, and welfare . . . must be placed at the doorstep of federal government."[13]

This was a frame with broad appeal. Rather than use concerns over illegal immigration to make a case that healthcare should be defunded, as would be suggested by the retrenchment thesis, county officials used the reframing to help *gain* an infusion of public revenue. Essentially, it allowed healthcare professionals, Democratic Party members, and conservatives to skirt the discussion of whether or not undocumented persons were deserving of care and instead allowed them to agree on the idea that such persons were less urgently sick and ripe for federal funding.

A 750-Bed or 600-Bed Hospital?

The idea that the county would pivot to outpatient settings was the primary driver of the 600-bed replacement for LAC + USC. Yet this 600-bed plan was far below the officially recognized level of demand. The Department of Health Services had commissioned three medical research reports from local academic and private sector sources in order to assess community health needs. The three reports were circulated, all detailing the current needs of the community, demographic projections, and the testimonies of medical personnel, which pointed to the need for a 750-bed hospital. All three reports emphatically stated that 750 beds would meet the bare minimum need even if all additional outpatient services were added. To be clear, this meant that a 600-bed hospital was below what outpatient supporters could possibly imagine.[14]

While to healthcare providers in county research groups "managed care" represented a variety of proposals—primarily that an individual's care would be coordinated by a physician—to county political leaders it became a justification for downsizing inpatient capacity so long as the county compensated with expanded outpatient capacity. This use of the managed care idea relied on the logic that physicians would guide individuals toward early intervention and less-expensive treatment settings. For example, the CAO justified his recommendation of the even-smaller 600-bed plan by "taking into consideration the current trends in the delivery of health services (e.g., managed care) and designing LAC+USC to meet the needs of the operation of current services by the department within existing financial constraints."[15] This quote from the CAO illustrates county leaders' conflation of the managed care framing with the county's need to cut costs due to financial shortfall.[16]

Critical to justifying the even-further-downsized hospital was the idea that hospital patients would be re-routed to healthcare services in the private sector:

> By serving fewer patients on site (i.e., downsizing the medical center), these [resources] will be reinvested in caring for those patients in other settings (e.g., outpatient sites, other DHS facilities, and/or other delivery models (e.g., arrangements with the private sector).[17]

The entire plan rested on the assumption that there existed significant interest within the private medical community to contract with the county for services to indigent patients. It would be private facilities that would provide the bulk of the excess care. Every planning document in the period leading up to the 1997 600-bed decision made reference to these as-yet-to-be-determined agreements. As one report stated, "In addition, studies have shown that there are many patient beds available within community hospitals and that these hospitals are very interested in participating in this unique partnership."[18] During board meetings leading up to the decision in 1997, prominent private-sector hospital leaders testified as to whether or not they would be interested in contracting with the county. All, including representatives from the local private hospital association, expressed verbal interest only, and were unwilling, much to the dismay of county leaders, to sign any contracts before the plan was completed. Indeed, the private sector had spent the past 15 years closing ERs and sending indigent patients to county facilities. A year later, the Department of Health Services was still looking for private facilities willing to contract with the county and resorted to sending out 25,000 letters to private healthcare providers in order to solicit interest in doing so.[19]

Even with a downsized medical facility, a majority of the members of the Board of Supervisors were not convinced of the county's ability to fund a new medical center. From their perspective, it was unfathomable to plan a medical replacement facility at a time when the county was considering closing its existing facility for good. It was only by downsizing the hospital to the 600-bed level that county officials could argue that the operational savings generated from such a significant downsizing would completely offset the cost of new construction. This was an argument that won over the necessary votes.[20]

The link between the downsized LAC + USC and receipt of the 1115 funds is corroborated in the language of the final vote for the new hospital. Supervisors Burke and Yaroslavsky, two Democratic Party politicians, were the swing votes necessary to offset Eastside Supervisor Molina, who advocated for the larger, 750-bed hospital, and conservative Supervisors Antonovich and Dana, who advocated for an even-smaller, 500-bed replacement.[21] Burke and Yaroslavsky offered the following rationale to justify their votes for a 600-bed replacement facility:

Two years ago, we were threatened with a crisis in our health delivery system that came close to dramatically reducing our facilities that are a vital part of the safety net for literally millions of people in LA County. Thanks to the assistance of the federal government and Bill Clinton, we saved our safety net. Three years remain on 1115 waiver and we must meet requirements, including a greater reliance on outpatient care and reduction of hospital beds. We also have a responsibility to ensure that the safety net is not jeopardized by undertaking a capital project of such unrealistic magnitude that we cannot sustain it absent a heavy and continuous subsidy from state and federal funding.

Keeping in mind the managed care statistics . . . it is prudent to approve the 600-bed replacement plan. We also recommended the CAO and DHS initiate a request for proposals from non-profit and other private facilities for the delivery of inpatient and outpatient care.[22]

The preceding excerpt was written into the language of the final approval of the 600-bed LAC + USC hospital. It ties together the receipt of the 1115 federal funds, the county's need to manage its public resource mismatch problem, and the downsizing of LAC + USC.

The Closure of Martin Luther King Jr. Hospital

The downsizing of the LAC + USC hospital was not enough to continue to receive the federal funds. As we saw in the introduction to this chapter, the county would also move to privatize the Rancho Los Amigos hospital—but would fail to do so because of a federal court injunction. The county would abandon these plans and embark on a convoluted plan to close the famed MLK hospital in Watts. The key was that, because the federal court injunction specifically barred the county from making cuts if those cuts were due to budgetary reasons, they would need other reasons for downsizing MLK. As we shall see, by claiming that the facility was being closed due to concerns over patient safety at the behest of healthcare regulators, local leaders could skirt the federal order.[23]

The closure of the 200-bed MLK public hospital occurred in three steps. In 2004, the nine-bed trauma unit was closed. This was met with tremendous opposition from community stakeholders because its storied trauma center was the only such center in the Watts community, which community advocates emphasized as riddled with gang violence.

In 2007, the hospital was reduced from 200 beds to a 48-bed inpatient center. This was met with only some community opposition. In 2008, the facility was closed entirely. The final decision to close was met with very little community opposition, and, in fact, all of the leaders who led the previous opposition to downsizing had come to support the decision to close.

What changed? Each step illustrates the deep relationship between progressive legal actors and austerity that drove transformation in the hospital system. The interplay between these was so coupled that it was difficult for actors in the moment—and for us in retrospect—to disentangle which was the ultimate driving force.

In 2004, after several highly publicized patient deaths and a *Los Angeles Times* exposé, the Department of Health Services recommended that the trauma unit at the MLK hospital be closed. The Department of Health Services and Board members were adamant that the decision was not a budgetary one. This was key, and was the primary point of tension between patient advocates, county officials, and a potential court ruling that would block the closure. The county's justification for the closure was that it was a patient safety issue spurred by concerns on the part of regulators, in the form of threats from CMS and the loss of accreditation from JCAHO. County officials also claimed they were not saving any money from the closure, as they would pay nearby hospitals to take on additional caseloads.

Indeed, the amount of regulatory attention this hospital received was astonishing: in 2004 alone the hospital received nine separate surveys from CMS and JCAHO. These federal and private regulators survey hospitals for patient safety and have the power to accredit hospitals, which provides legitimacy and, in the case of CMS, eligibility for federal government reimbursement. We can think about these regulators as providing a type of legal demand, but one that is distinct from patients' rights advocates. CMS officials sent letters to the Department of Health Services indicating they were considering rescinding the hospital's eligibility for federal funds reimbursement—a death knell for the hospital. For its part, JCAHO conducted five surveys—two unannounced—in response to adverse clinical events and decided on a preliminary repeal of the hospital's accreditation.[24]

The problem for department officials was that although the trauma center was not specifically mentioned in any of the surveys as a problem area, it was a huge drain on hospital resources, so much so that Department of Health Services officials felt that hospital staff were prevented from fixing the other issues listed in the surveys. As one memo stated:

> Outside regulators have not singled out the trauma services for specific criticism, the general problems identified in such areas as document, medical

management, and patient assessment, exist through the facility. The trauma unit is inextricably tied to the rest of the hospital and its resources. Trauma patients are serviced by the same ancillary service departments as patients elsewhere in the hospital and once a patient leaves the trauma unit and is admitted to an inpatient bed, the individual's outcomes are equally dependent upon the consistent delivery of high quality patient care.[25]

Because trauma patients are highly complex and draw many of the hospital's ancillary services, for department officials, closing the unit would allow nursing staff to be placed in more concerning areas of the hospital. "While they constitute only nine percent of the hospital's admissions, the highly acute condition of trauma patients . . . places extraordinary demands on numerous hospital systems. . . . The stresses place greater demands on the hospital and inhibit the correction of the underlying problems in its operation."[26]

As with the effort to stop the closure of the Rancho Los Amigos National Rehabilitation Center described earlier in this chapter, community activists packed the Board of Supervisors' meetings in the weeks leading up to the recommendation to close the MLK trauma center. This was a major problem for county officials, especially Supervisor Burke, whose constituency in South Central Los Angeles was primarily impacted by the closure. As a staunch advocate for the public hospital system, Supervisor Molina was also heavily concerned with the closure.

The key for the county was to convince community opposition that the closure was not a budgetary decision, but rather a closure to ensure patient safety. This was the central contradiction: officials wanted the closure to appear as a victory for progressive efforts. This necessitated focusing the public's attention on regulators' concerns and on efforts of the department to work hard—including to spend money—to address concerns over patient safety. The Department of Health Services (DHS) was adamant that no money was being saved by the closure of the trauma unit, because resources were being redirected to the University of California, Los Angeles (UCLA), and nearby private hospitals to take on the additional patients. In the following exchange between a board member and the DHS director, we can see the need to paint the closure of the trauma center in 2004 as unrelated to budgetary concerns:

SUP. YAROSLAVSKY: Is the recommendation you're making to suspend trauma at King being done for budgetary reasons? That's an allegation that's been made by a number of people, that we're doing this to save money.

DR. THOMAS GARTHWAITE: Absolutely not.

SUP. YAROSLAVSKY: Are we going to save money by closing the trauma down?

DR. THOMAS GARTHWAITE: No, I don't think we'll save money. It may cost us a little more to pay for the patients in the private sector.

SUP. YAROSLAVSKY: So what is the reason you would close the trauma down?

DR. THOMAS GARTHWAITE: I think very clearly to take some of the stress off. This is a hospital where we have to—we have to get the right staff properly trained, in the right places to do their job every day . . . the ultimate question that I have to ask myself is, is this a safe hospital? Is—when you're in a trauma ambulance and you have a choice of two hospitals, one may be a little farther away and one may be a little closer, do you go to the closest one or do you go to the one that's ready to take care of you? And I'm not saying that the trauma center isn't ready to take care of the person that comes in, but this hospital, overall, is stressed. There's no reserve, there's no safety margin. It's like driving your car right on the edge of a cliff. Anything can just push it over, and we—in order to . . . [interjections, crowd anger]

SUP. MOLINA: Again, on the audience, you've been doing really well. There's no need to be disruptive. Please.

The public was not convinced. Patient advocates countered that CMS and JCAHO had never specifically asked the county to close the trauma center. In one open board meeting, public speakers even pushed officials to admit whether CMS had privately suggested to the county to close the trauma center. If the trauma center was not the problem, then why close it?[27]

Officials relented, admitting that no suggestion was ever made, and then had to turn to a different kind of logic of justification. The new logic rested on the inability of the Department of Health Services to hire permanent nursing staff. Essentially, because the hospital was losing accreditation, hospital officials claimed they could not convince potential hires to take nursing jobs at the hospital (nurses feared they would be laid off and forced to look for new jobs). This meant that the department had a scarcity of staff, even if it had the money to pay for adequate staffing, and could claim that resources—in the form of nursing staff—were needed to fix problems elsewhere in the hospital.

This logic was persuasive. The entire issue became centered around the training of medical staff, rather than budget allocation. Here is the exact moment this logic moved the discussion forward:

SUP. YAROSLAVSKY: . . . I don't know where some of the legislators or one of the legislators who said that board members, I read that in a press article, that board members had said that CMS had made us close the trauma center. CMS never asked us to close the trauma center. . . . This is not being done because the federal government has said, "Close the trauma center," it's being done because the government has said, "Fix the hospital and, if you don't fix the hospital, you're going to have to close it because we're going to pull the money from it, and JCAHO is going to pull the accreditation, et cetera." So that's the pressure we're under. . . . Now, I want to say something about this rush business, because that's another thing. I know Ms. Burke feels it was rushed. Dr. Garthwaite, did you come up with this idea last week? The elements of this plan?

DR. THOMAS GARTHWAITE: Well, we've been discussing how to decompress the hospital for at least a couple months, because, as we've noticed, the deterioration in the ability to hire nurses, as we've tried to figure out how we were going to get everyone trained and be able to pass all these accreditation surveys, we've been going through one after another after another of surprise surveys, day after—week-long surveys, weekend surveys, you know, it just became clear we had to do something to slow things down and to be able to make sure everyone's trained and ready for inspections and that the processes were fixed and so forth. . . .

SUP. YAROSLAVSKY: Okay. And I think it's important, because none—nothing like this comes together in four days or three days. . . .[28]

It was this logic of undertrained staff that moved the issue along. We can clearly demonstrate this point. When Los Angeles County officials downsized the hospital from 200 beds to 48 beds, public pressure was appeased with the claim that no budgeted positions would be cut. Instead, department officials planned that existing staff at MLK would be re-interviewed and, if qualified, would be transferred to other public hospitals in the county to be appropriately trained. In the effort to cast the closures as simple staff transfer, officials claimed that this plan of action would actually cost the county an extra $38 million—thus abating fears that the move was budget-related. Staff would be retrained and ultimately moved back into the hospital.

It turned out, however, that after the hospital was downsized, Department of Health Services officials quickly realized they could not operate a 48-bed hospital if they transferred out the nursing staff for retraining. Practically no staff were transferred, and the $38 million in costs was never accrued. This was not a duplicitous maneuver; the board was just as shocked as anyone that the staff were not transferred out. The hospital was, in fact, downsized without the spending of the extra $38 million, and the downsize thus represented a significant cost saving to the county.

Ultimately, it was a self-fulfilling prophecy that the hospital had been downsized, and a final CMS survey in August 2007 had ended the ability of the hospital to receive Medicare and Medicaid reimbursement. I mean this in two senses. First, when the county downsized the hospital to 48 beds, then permanent nursing staff began to look elsewhere for employment, which then forced the county officials to rely on undertrained traveling nurses. These and other temporary staff were difficult to train for the purposes of passing CMS surveys, and department officials suspected that failure was likely. As one supervisor said:

SUP. BURKE: [The surveys] identified a thousand problems. . . . One thing they also said was that they had the capacity to get staff people who could come in who could put these things into effect. That, we never got. They just didn't have it. We ended up with mostly traveling nurses and everybody who came in came in during the week and left and we never saw them again after their contract and we did not get those staff people. But that's water under the bridge.[29]

Ironically, many of these staff failures, if we actually look at the CMS surveys closely, were due to a lack of capacity! For instance, the clinical event that triggered the final failed CMS survey was the staff's inability to appropriately transfer a neurological patient to LAC + USC, which had the facilities to treat such patients. While, indeed, the survey showed that MLK staff failed to check on the patient during the wait for transfer, in reality there was not much the staff could do, as the patient was specifically awaiting transfer to a facility properly equipped to grapple with neurological ailments. MLK's neurological services had fallen victim to the 2004 trauma closures.

Here we see an ambiguous relationship between austerity and progressive law. By looking at the incremental decisions made to downsize the hospital— such as the need to cast the downsizing as a regulatory agency issue rather than a budgetary issue—we see that officials focused on the rationale of staff retraining. But as time progressed, no staff were retrained and the county ultimately saved money—much to the surprise of top county officials. It was the role of the regulatory agencies, which were concerned about patient safety, that allowed the county to justify closure. The comparison with the case of Rancho Los Amigos discussed at the beginning of this chapter is critical. The closure of Rancho Los Amigos was successfully blocked by a federal court because the move was cast primarily as a budgetary decision. In contrast, the closure of the trauma center at MLK was justified by regulatory agency concerns about patient safety. Without the lubrication of patient safety concerns, MLK's closure may have been blocked by a federal court.

Managing the Wait Lists

One piece of the puzzle remains. We have thus seen how legal demand and austerity created a redistribution that resulted in the restricted (but funded) public hospital system. But how were the specific techniques seen in our ER ethnography created out of this process? As we shall see, the use of heavy opioids to manage wait lists, additional medical staffing to watch over waiting patients, and police staffing of waiting rooms all find their origins in this confluence of austerity and progressive law. We trace this history here.

Legal Origins of Opioid Medication

The role of pain medication in the ER waiting room finds its origins in a last-ditch effort to stave off closure of the MLK hospital. CMS's penultimate survey of the hospital in June 2007 included three specific complaints. Department officials responded to these complaints with new administrative and procedural solutions that they hoped would appease CMS officials. As we saw, CMS officials returned two months later, in August, and recommended that the hospital no longer be eligible for federal reimbursement. The solutions the department came up with in the interim would prove durable and would be put into use systemwide—including in the heavily overcrowded LAC + USC waiting room.[30]

In the archival record, we can actually pinpoint the exact cases that triggered CMS concerns about waiting patients' access to pain medication. The key document described a "Patient B" who was found during a CMS visit to the MLK ER. Patient B presented at 10:42 p.m. with a complaint of stomach pain that had been present for two weeks. During the triage interview, a nurse documented that Patient B's pain was in all four quadrants and radiated to the patient's back. The patient also reported multiple incidences of nausea and vomiting, pain that was "severe" with a score of 10 out of 10, and pain that created a burning sensation. The patient's temperature was recorded as 102 and heart rate was recorded as 97. The patient was moaning and had facial grimacing during the initial examination. No medication was provided to alleviate the patient's pain or fever. The patient was given a "Level 3" triage score, which would be similar to the "C" category of lower severity that we saw in our ethnography of the public ER.

Two hours later, the patient was reassessed and given 650 mg of Tylenol. The patient's pain level was described as having decreased to a "seven out of 10." Five hours later (and a total of seven hours since the patient's time of arrival), the patient was reassessed and described as experiencing severe pain and nausea. At 9:30 a.m., 11 hours after presenting to the ER, the patient was finally transferred to surgery to undergo an exploratory procedure. CMS was concerned that, other than the one dose of Tylenol, the patient received no medication to alleviate pain during this 11-hour wait.

Another case describes "Patient D," encountered during a CMS site visit to MLK. The patient was triaged at 11:35 p.m. as having severe pain, an oxygen saturation level of 100%, and a heart rate of 95. He had difficulty breathing at the time of his first examination. The CMS survey pointedly wrote:

> There was no documentation about why he was left in the lobby of the ED. NO pain medication or other pain relieving interventions where provided. There was no re-assessment of the patient until he was taken to a treatment area five hours later.[31]

At 8:40 a.m., the patient was finally administered pain medication. He waited another nine hours (19 hours after presenting for treatment) for his lab results.

The Patient B and Patient D incidents documented in the survey were highly concerning to CMS officials (see Figure 4.1). The problem for department officials is that it is physicians who are able to administer opioid pain medications to patients, but it is registered nurses who staff the triage department. Patients were required to wait many hours to see a doctor in order to receive these opioids. But doctors are expensive, and they cannot be made to staff the triage waiting area—this is the whole reason there is a difference between a patient waiting under the care of nurses and a patient who receives a bed inside an ER staffed by a physician.

> **Immediate Actions – Patient D:**
> - The ED Nurse Manager provided education to all ED RNs on the requirement to notify physicians of all patients waiting to be seen that are experiencing pain, which requires interventions based on the pain policy.
> - A multidisciplinary team of ED physicians and ED nurses reviewed the current triage process. As a result of that review, the triaging process was re-designed to provide for a more timely medical screening examination. This process includes the following:
>   - ○ The triage nurse and registration clerk are co-located so that the triaging process and the registration process can occur simultaneously.
>   - ○ A physician will be available to the triaging area to perform immediate medical screening examinations for patients who are identified as a level 3. Upon completion of the medical screening examination, based on the patient's clinical presentation, tests and treatments (including pain management) will be ordered and carried out.

Figure 4.1 "Statement of Deficiencies and Plan of Correction."
Source: County Online: on file.

Department officials responded by coming up with a new procedural rule. One physician would be made "available" to the triage nurses anytime they felt they needed to administer pain medications. This made triage nurses' access to opiate pain medications easier. As a top Department of Health Services official mundanely described it, "Further training was provided to emergency room nurses to ensure that physicians are contacted if any form of management is needed prior to the medical screening exam taking place."[32]

As we saw in our ethnography in Chapter 3, this practice evolved in such a way as to decrease patients' access to healthcare. Patients who were given pain medication during their wait experienced a stabilization in their vital signs, which provided triage nurses with the justification to delay some qualified patients over others. With longer waits and the stabilization of their pain, some patients also left the wait without being seen. In this way, pain medication directly acted to cull the wait list. Pain medication was also linked to the criminal stigma of narcotics abuse among the patient population, thereby contributing to another level of patient culling.

In other words, the use of pain medication to cull the wait list evolved out of a concern on the part of a regulatory agency about reducing patient suffering. CMS was concerned about a simple fact: If patients were going to have to wait for long periods before being seen by a doctor, they needed to have some access to pain medication during that wait. The department responded by increasing patient access to those resources. This is an addition of funding and spending that works to push patients into reneging from seeking access to healthcare or, as we have seen, the restriction of healthcare through its provision during the wait.

The Restrictive Purpose of Adding Triage Staff

When the county argued that outpatient facilities would compensate for a decline in public hospital capacity, it was relying on the assumption that triage could vet less-urgent patients away from the ER and toward outpatient facilities. Triage was the linchpin of the county's entire downsizing plan. The assumption is coded deeply within every health planning and hospital architecture document leading up to the 1997 LAC + USC replacement plan. A report from the oversight committee supervising the architectural plans of the LAC + USC replacement facility wrote:

> A facility programmed for 600/500-bed sized options will enable more patients to enter the hospital than can be admitted within the planned inpatient capacity. In order to control the flow of patients it may require transfer of patients with suitable diagnoses to other DHS or contract facilities . . .
> . . . the high level of trauma and ER visits anticipated at the facility will require medical center staff to diagnose and stabilize inpatients prior to transferring them to other DHS or private facilities. The new replacement hospital will also serve as the county specialty outpatient referral facility, thus adding to the diagnostic and treatment levels required at the facility. As a result, the expanded diagnostic and treatment capacity of the replacement hospital has been recommended by the committee.[33]

This is an example of the expanded role of triage in the architectural plans of the LAC + USC replacement facility—in this case, the "expanded diagnostic and treatment capacity." Of note is that the report justified the expanded role of triage by admitting it was needed to solve the coming overcrowding crisis caused by the downsized hospital replacement plan. The decision rested on the assumption that officials could always tell who needed institutionaliza- tion and who needed to be referred to abdicated institutionalized space.[34]

Once the facility was finally opened in 2008, increased medical staffing in triage took on the additional role of sending regulatory signals to JCAHO about adequate care. Immediately after the two-day move to the new LAC + USC hospital, it was completely overrun—opening over capacity—just as critics of the plan had predicted. With reports of waiting periods extending beyond state limits for incoming ER patients, the Board of Supervisors—after taking a tour of the new facility and seeing the overcrowding with their own eyes—ordered the hospital to send patients to private hospitals after nine hours of waiting. Yet, as also predicted, there was no money in the county budget to do so. The waiting time would settle at an average of 12 hours in the new hospital (Lin II, 2008).

But if regulatory agencies had caused the closure of MLK over concerns for patient safety, how could those same regulators approve of overcrowding that produced 12-hour wait times? In the years following the opening, the new LAC + USC was no stranger to citations and site visits from JCAHO and CMS.

In the fall of 2010, the county and CMS found a mutual solution. Hospital administrators were able to accomplish a decrease in the "left without being seen" (LWBS) indicator at the LAC + USC ER. In a few months, the indictor dropped from 18% to 3% of waiting patients who left the ER before being seen by a physician. This was a major victory for hospital administration, as the indicator was seen by state and federal regulators as a major sign of pa- tient distress and a consequence of extreme overcrowding.[35]

The origins of this dramatic decrease started with a key site visit from regu- latory agencies in May 2010. At the direction of CMS (in response to a public complaint), the State of California's Department of Public Health conducted a site survey of the LAC + USC ER. After the survey, inspectors focused on a key problem: delays in the ER's ability to provide timely medical screening exams (MSE) to waiting patients. These exams are the same type of vital signs checks discussed in our ethnography. They are the interviews in which triage nurses first examine waiting patients and assign ranks to waiting patients.[36]

In response to the survey, hospital administration took staff from the treatment areas and relocated them to the triage areas in order to perform additional MSEs. To be sure, the number of staff performing MSEs increased. The move was successful. In the first month alone, the average time to MSE decreased from 239 minutes to 75 minutes for C-list-equivalent patients and 57 minutes for all patients. A month after the change was instituted in September 2010, department officials discovered an incidental impact of this change: the LWBS rate fell. Because the transferred staff were nurse practitioners (NP) (in contrast to registered nurses, who typically preformed MSEs), MSEs conducted by these staff were counted as patients having seen a physician. Officials were pleased, as it signaled compliance to regulators.

The problem, however, was that despite these positive signals, patients would still continue to wait 8 to 12 hours on average to actually enter into a treatment bay in the ER after receiving their MSE. That is, even after seeing these nurse practitioners, patients would continue to wait the 8 to 12 hours and, if they left during that time frame, would no longer be included in the LWBS rate. Despite the dramatic change effected in wait time to MSE, the average overall wait time never dropped.

The nurse practitioners' MSEs were essentially the same as those administered by the registered nurses (RNs) (checks of vital signs and rankings of triage), with one exception: nurse practitioners had the power to discharge waiting patients. Nurse practitioners were instructed to find patients who were so non-urgent that they could be referred to clinics or sent home. In essence, patients who left the ER on their own accord were replaced with patients who were rationally discharged by these nurse practitioners. As the head administrator of the hospital framed it:

> But going back to the main topic, what we are trying to address is the medical screening exam and more importantly decompressing our ER as Carol said, the strategy was to move all, as much of the activity in the back room up front. So we have nurse practitioners instead of RNs doing triage and assessment, they're actually either completing the medical screening exam or getting most of it done. The objective is to try to identify the lower level, Level 3 patients that can be discharged from that triage effort. In the peak time, we are going to complement the NPs in the triage area with a physician so we can get some of the decisions. So it's to be very robust and very well-supported.[37]

It is worth recalling that this entire effort allowed department officials to signal compliance with regulator concerns about overcrowding at the hospital. These patients were essentially moved out of the ER before receiving treatment in beds and counted as having been "seen by a physician." As we saw in our ethnography of triage decisions, such demarcations are embedded in the culture of triage that tends toward parsimony. In other words, in response to regulator concern about patient safety and within the context of the hospital that was built too small, officials responded by recasting the patient as non-urgent and eligible for denial.

The fact that the actual wait time to entry into a treatment bay of the ER never declined during this administrative maneuver was not lost on department officials and county politicians. At the end of the emergency reports on the hospital's overcrowding, the department director lamented to the supervisors:

DR. MITCHELL KATZ: . . . We, in terms of our general level of overcrowding, we have about the same-to-slightly-better in terms of statistics. One of the interesting things that we had found is that we are seeing substantially more people than we previously have but we have not been able to impact waiting times. And I think that's a theme that you may well see continue; that is, as you get more and more efficient, you would think that you would shorten wait times, but that's only true if people don't start coming more because they know that they can be seen in a reasonable period of time. And so I think we are both becoming more productive and at the same time I'm not really able to impact the wait times. Thank you.[38]

The administrators at LAC + USC did everything they could to reasonably lower overcrowding at the ER. Streamlining operations in the ER did nothing to change the underlying fact that the hospital was built too small—the average wait time would oscillate between 12 and 8 hours. So long as triage officials could perform MSEs in the right amount of time, the hospital could satiate regulators despite having these 8–12-hour average wait times.[39]

The Origins of Hospital Police

At 12:20 p.m. on February 8, 1993, Damacio Ybarra Torres walked into the waiting lobby of the LAC + USC hospital. For the prior five years, Torres had been living in a $15-per-night Skid Row hotel, where he shared a common toilet and used a tall metal locker for storage. Just before coming to the ER,

Torres left a note in his hotel room, which police would later find. The note said, "I am dying. No one seems to care."[40]

For 10 minutes, Torres paced back and forth in the jam-packed waiting room. Suddenly, he shouted, "Give me something for my pain! Can't you give me something for my pain?" After drawing the attention of triage staff, Torres pulled out a .357 Magnum pistol and shot three triage staff members at point-blank range. "He could have shot anybody he wanted, he wanted to shoot those doctors," said a waiting patient who was witness to the incident. Over the next four hours, Torres barricaded himself in a nearby room with two hostages. As police attempted to negotiate with him, Torres was recorded as saying, "It's their turn to wait. They've made me wait, I'm going to make them wait."[41]

The incident set off a firestorm in the county. For some, it was an indication of the billions of dollars in cuts the Los Angeles County healthcare system had undertaken in recent years. These were cuts to outpatient clinics that many believed created the overcrowding crisis in the ER, which, in turn, facilitated patient frustration over wait times. At the same time, the crisis was also an indication of the uncontrollable propensity for violence among the poor in Los Angeles. Supervisor Mike Antonovich submitted a motion that ordered the county sheriff to determine the need for security improvements and additional police units. Supervisor Gloria Molina submitted a motion that would instruct the Department of Health Services to "evaluate and make recommendations regarding ways to decompress our hospital and comprehensive health center walk-in clinics." Newly elected supervisor Burke created a motion that called both for security guards and to "develop alternatives that will alleviate some of the waiting time at the ER."[42]

"It's like a war zone in there," said a triage staff member quoted in a *Los Angeles Times* headline.[43] "I encounter violent patients on a weekly basis, most days of the week," said a doctor quoted in another article.[44] The month-long indignation was best exemplified by a *Los Angeles Times* write-up:

> The incident is only the most recent example of the rising tide of violence that has spilled over into the nation's urban emergency rooms. "We are an open front door to whatever society has to offer, and some of these patients are not the best people," said Dr. Marshal Morgan, Chief of Emergency Medicine. . . . Bob McCloskey, an official of the county nurses' union said, "They have a lot of unruly patients in those emergency rooms," "They cuss, they spit. Some are high on drugs or drunk and they are hard to control."[45]

A litany of unrepresentative statistics began to frame the incident as part of a wider policy problem. Conflating verbal confrontations (that tend to occur in highly charged, overcrowded ERs) with actual violence, the *Los Angeles Times* wrote the following: "During a six-month period in 1991, officials . . . logged 1,400 incidents of violence or threats. So Monday's tragedy came as no surprise to many County-USC ER workers." Ignoring the highly amorphous and general category of "assaults," the *Times* wrote, "During their careers, two out of three emergency room nurses have reported being assaulted, according to a 1991 survey of 1,200 emergency room nurses." This statistic also presented career figures as if they were indications of recent trends. Not to ignore murder entirely, the *Times* wrote, "In recent years, assailants have killed people at hospitals in San Diego, New York, Washington, Danville, Pa., and Utah."[46]

After the shooting in 1993, supervisors' staff discovered a two-year-old report commissioned by the Department of Health Services. The "Halloran Report," as it was called, was a private consultant's study of violent threats at LAC + USC, with recommendations for improving security. The Board of Supervisors would make use of this report in order to respond to the shooting crisis.[47]

The entire archival record of the county's efforts around the Halloran report is framed by the conflation of patient/nurse confrontations with gang violence. County leaders largely ignored the role of overcrowding in rising patient tensions. In the request for funds to commission a report, the hospital's chief of contract operations wrote, "The medical center is faced with an emergency situation of escalating violent crime being committed on our grounds. . . . Over the past few months, the medical center has been the site of a series of violent life-threatening incidents. In one incident members of a gang shot and seriously wounded a rival gang member visiting a friend who had been shot in a gang-related incident . . . similar incidents have exacerbated an ever-increasing volume of violent crimes."[48]

The following items were presented for discussion at a meeting of the task force in charge of commissioning the Halloran report. Of the many "concepts and ideas which could be used to develop specific actions to curb gang violence at the medical center," some examples include "establishing agreements with local law enforcement agencies to notify the medical center in advance when a patient is being brought in due to gang incidents and looking into training patient care personnel to be able to recognize characteristic of gang members and notify safety police before a problem occurs."[49]

In the report, gang violence was soon conflated with the more widespread issues of patient confrontations, homeless patients, and overcrowding. According to the Halloran report:

> It was observed that transient persons make frequent use of the first-floor cafeteria facilities and restrooms. It was obvious that these persons were not visitors to the hospital or seeking medical assistance. It was also observed that the presence of these transients was causing a great deal of consternation amongst employees and inpatient visitors. It was also noted that several transient-type persons were making what appeared to be a daily visit to the campus area for the collection of discarded aluminum cans from trash containers.
>
> One such person was observed entering the basement area of the general building and engaging in a brief communication with a hospital service employee in what may have been a drug-related activity. The matter was properly reported to police administration . . .
>
> The volume of patients and accompanying visitors seated in the ER waiting area, as well as the triage and pre-admittance areas, frequently exceed the seating capacity and results in persons sitting or standing in the corridors. These conditions are the breeding grounds of disturbances, which are generated by long waiting periods, frayed tempers and exasperation. . . . The inevitable result is a hostile outbreak resulting in safety police officer involvement.[50]

The Halloran report successfully conjoins the ideas of "transient" persons, who in this report are criminal by virtue of using the hospital as shelter and for narcotics distribution, with the violent tendencies of individuals experiencing overcrowded conditions. Overcrowding, of course, could be seen as an indictment of the defunding of the public health system in Los Angeles. Here, it is taken as a precondition to patients' inevitable violent tendencies.

Of the original 98 recommendations to come out of the CAO's report after the shooting, the board funded only 29, most of which were security enhancement recommendations.

For our purposes, there were two other plausible alternative lines of action that help us understand the role of austerity and progressive law. One recommendation was to add inpatient beds to decrease overcrowding. This was a non-starter, as the county was deep in the fiscal crisis of the early 1990s. The other solution on the table was to use temporary trailers to expand the size of the waiting rooms. The logic for this was that by physically decompressing the waiting rooms, patient tension would decrease. This solution was debated fully and was ultimately shot down by the county's lawyer. Officials were concerned that regulatory agencies would view the temporary trailers as problematic for patient safety (as there would be no nurses available to quickly attend to patients with deteriorating conditions).

Thus, it was not simply retrenchment or criminalization that pushed this hospital police force. The specific role in legal demand also shaped its historical formation. The trailer option was the cheaper of all options, much cheaper than funding police forces. Without the fear of regulatory concern over patient rights in those trailers, it proved to be a viable solution.

In favor of these two solutions, as influenced by the Halloran report, the Department of Health Services recommended that the county train and fund a "gang suppression unit." The department's request to the County Board of Supervisors for funding of the unit stated as follows: "Due to the increase in gang-related incidents, it has been necessary to establish a gang intervention/suppression unit."[51] The county tripled the number of around-the-clock police officers, including eight more officers in the ER at LAC + USC (Tobar 1993). While it was not identified as such in the *Los Angeles Times*, the expanded gang suppression unit at the hospital would be charged with "interfacing with ward staff," "mak[ing] visual evaluations of patients," "identify[ing] characteristics of gang members," and "implement[ing] a 24-hr accounting of who is entering and exiting the medical center."[52] The unit was given the discretion to develop a policy of collecting visitor information, including addresses and names, to distribute color-coded badges (indicating authorized areas), and to create what was described as a "neighborhood watch program" on hospital grounds that would "allow for information of criminal misconduct to be reported through an organized system of volunteers."[53]

In total, we can see that these three waiting line management techniques— opioid administration, expanded medical observation, and permanent police observation—were all born out of the history of legal demand and austerity. The retrenchment-criminalization thesis fails to fully explain these developments. While a lack of funds and a criminalized understanding of the patient population certainly formed the background of these policies, it was the specific confluence with legal demand around patients' rights that provided this particular form. The use of opioids and increased medical staff observation of waiting patients (which worked to superficially lower the "left without being seen rate") were all born out of regulatory concern for the immense waiting times that had been caused by downsizing the redistributive effort to obtain federal funds. Even the police unit at the hospital, so clearly linked to a criminalization of the patient population, is linked to legal demand: as we saw, the county refused the even cheaper alternative of expanding wait rooms due to legal concerns. Again, in conversation with our ethnographic account, we can see how these three developments actually evolved out of the abatement effort to resolve the crisis of austerity and legal demand.

Conclusion

In the Introduction to this book, we tried to explain the restriction of medicine in large public hospitals with the "retrenchment-criminalization" thesis. The thesis presumed that social service institutions, like public hospitals, have faced severe fiscal retrenchment for the past 40 years, and this led these institutions to develop methods of deterring people from accessing their services. Many connected this with the emergence of criminalized rhetoric about the people who used these institutions—using the understanding that the urban poor are less poor and more criminal in order to police, drug test, and make them ineligible for resources.

We saw, however, that public spending on healthcare in the United States, even when controlled for rising medical prices, has actually persisted in the 1980s, 1990s, and the first decade of the 2000s—exactly when we might expect retrenchment. Public hospital funding in large cities in particular was made stronger, with laws passed to make sure they could maintain their heavy burden of uncompensated care. These funding mechanisms—1115 waiver and Disproportionate Share Hospital (DSH) programs—were even saved from conservative attempts to turn the entire system into a block grant.

The history presented in this chapter fits exactly this countervailing dynamic. The public healthcare system in Los Angeles did face a major problem of fiscal austerity in the mid-1990s, but this alone cannot explain the development of restriction. In the face of this retrenchment, public officials shifted from thinking about their patients as urgently sick to perceiving them as less urgently sick immigrants and homeless persons. By doing so, they were able to capture funds from the federal government in order to resolve their fiscal crisis. This was an infusion of cash—one that fits the trend of growing public healthcare costs—through the redistribution of the poor.

As we saw, this redistribution came with the requirement that the county downsize its inpatient capacity. Legal demand came into play when those downsizing efforts—the cutting of beds at LAC + USC and the privatization of Rancho Los Amigos hospitals—were halted by a social movement and federal court order. Because it has a constitutional duty to provide indigent healthcare, the county could not simply cut services.

In essence, the restrictive dynamics we saw in our ER ethnography— opioid use to management wait lists, increased triage staff observation, and police presence in wait lists—were born out of this iterative dynamic between the need to achieve downsizing (which was linked to the redistribution required to receive federal funds) and the needed legal signals to appease healthcare regulators. JCAHO's and CMS's concern about patients' rights during long waits led directly to the developments we saw in our ethnography. It is only possible to understand these developments—which were extensions of healthcare and public spending—if we see them as linked to the redistribution used to resolve the crisis between law and austerity.

An addendum is needed for those interested in healthcare policy in particular. Some may ask whether downsizing inpatient capacity to rely more on outpatient settings is indicative of restriction at all. Indeed, the federal funding from the Clinton administration examined in this chapter was linked to the nationwide effort to restructure healthcare delivery through what was called the "managed care revolution."[54]

The argument that more outpatient services are a good public policy choice is not what is at stake here. When the Board of Supervisors voted in 1997 on the plan to rebuild LAC + USC, they relied on the "managed care revolution" to rationalize the sizing of the hospital. They chose to build the hospital with 600 beds; yet, as we saw, every study commissioned measured the minimum demand for the community at the level of 750 beds. Critically, these studies all made the 750-bed minimum estimate on the basis that managed care assumptions would be met; that is, only if the county linked its healthcare users with more preventive care and contracted out to private facilities could the community tolerate 750 beds.

In other words, this was not a public policy choice to provide better health-care, nor was it simple retrenchment; this was an effort to keep a dying public hospital system in the midst of crisis between the law and fiscal austerity. This is the complicated story of how a hospital gets built too small. It required a deep interplay of progressive legal actors, austerity, and the search for new revenue.

Conclusion

Toward the Administrative Disappearing of Social Suffering

There exist people who, had they been jailed under some other policy machination, would have been released from jail and lived other lives. These are the formerly incarcerated who have lost their right to youth. There are realities of people with disease, chronic illness, and premature death in their families because public officials chose one policy solution over another. These are all moments in people's lives—moments of suffering—that are erased when the state declares public problems resolved.[1]

My hope is that by the end of this chapter we can begin to think less about strengthening or weakening states and begin to think more about the "disappearing" of crisis and its accompanying social suffering. We often view states as, in the first order, seeking to punish their populations, to make war, to redistribute wealth, to gather information about their populations, to help businesses, to protect the rich, to protect the poor, or to carry on any of their other publicly named activities. Such endeavors have led some scholars—usually ethnographers of urban poverty governance—to focus on the state's resiliency, namely institutions that have grown in their power to control people. For others—usually historical sociologists—it has led to a focus on the state's diminishing capacity and its inability to help people. The public shares a similar divergence. It seems obvious to some—usually those on the left—that, at least since the political careers of Ronald Reagan and Margate Thatcher, things like social security, pensions, healthcare for the poor, food stamps, unemployment compensation, and many other initiatives meant to protect citizens from the risks of life and economy have been under persistent attack. To others—usually those on the right—the efforts to create a leaner "nanny state" have completely failed and public spending has only grown in opulence, usually to the detriment of rights and freedoms.[2]

In part, we are of many minds about what the state is doing because we misrecognize a key state activity: the periodic, public resolution of intractable

Redistributing the Poor. Armando Lara-Millán, Oxford University Press (2021). © Armando Lara-Millán.
DOI: 10.1093/oso/9780197507902.003.0006

social problems. Such resolutions appear to us as expansions or contractions in state power and spending, but they defy easy characterization. As we shall see, focusing on state activity as a series of crisis abatements helps us to home in on hidden forms of social suffering. Despite the fact that such crises—for instance, jail and hospital overcrowding—are periodically resolved, important forms of social suffering become erased from the public record. We can begin to apply such logic to other cases and contexts.

Redefining Urban Poverty Governance

In recent years, ethnographies of criminal justice and social service settings have shown dramatic transformations in the way that social control is exerted on the urban poor. Rather than jail individuals who contribute to visible forms of street poverty, police have increasingly been shown to coordinate with sanitation, health, and welfare workers to continuously shuffle such persons between spaces. Criminal courts, in addition to adapting to new "color blind" forms of racism, have also been shown to wield rehabilitation programs to maintain surveillance and control of poor people, rather than to convict and jail them. In the social service domains, Departments of Children and Family Services have increasingly been shown to exert punitive decision-making when removing children or providing resources to domestic violence survivors. Not to be outdone, healthcare providers like ambulance service fleets, pharmacists, and substance abuse/mental health treatment programs have also been shown to merge corporate production demands and crime control logic all in an effort to restrict access to care.[3]

These transformations—including the ones examined in this book—can appear to us as very organized and explained by broad forces such as neoliberalism, racism, or a need to socially control supposedly dangerous populations. Such forces can be combined into what scholars call "urban poverty management." The idea is that public institutions are needed to "manage" the poor and poor people of color, controlling them lest they become a problem to the social order. This has been the raison d'être of an entire generation of scholarship on poverty management; that transformations in the way the state governs are due to the state's interest in deepening social control.

Sociologist turned philosopher Bruno Latour used the term "theoretical acceleration" to describe how sociologists often observe developments in social life and, without tracing them, lean too heavily on broad historical forces to explain them. As such, it is possible that our understanding of poverty governance transformations—especially those we connect to mass imprisonment, deinstitutionalization, or retrenchment-criminalization—are underspecified. Rather than make such a leap, the effort in this book has been to trace the things we find in ethnographic analysis to the actions of the specific decision-makers in the past. This is the point of *historically embedded ethnography*: to observe interesting changes in field sites and to use archival evidence of the specific human action required to make those changes possible.[4]

I shall illustrate what I mean via a summary of this book. In Chapter 1 we delved into the daily life of the jail intake room. A year was spent behind the enclosed spaces of intake, trying to understand the routine problems jailers have in filling up a jail with inmates. We learned in detail how difficult it is for staff to separate out potentially violent "gang members" from the less potentially violent. We also saw the deep uncertainty around who was in need of very scarce medical housing and who could stand to wait for "sick call" in general population housing.

In placing myself in the daily life of the jail workgroup, I found an astonishing solution to the uncertainty created by these problems. Jail staff practiced a culture of viewing the sprawling jail and its resources as a place of health and welfare and one whose resources needed to be protected. On the one hand, this allowed staff to reinterpret attributes of violence in the biographies of inmates as less criminally threatening, thus pushing large swaths of inmates from high-risk scores of eight to medium-risk scores of seven. On the other hand, staff used security threat to determine medical need. When inmates disrupted the intake process, they were subdued by staff, and many times medical staff administered psychotropic drugs, sedatives, and other pharmaceuticals to get inmates through the intake process. This had the effect of assigning such inmates "medical marks" such that their medical complaints would be taken more seriously by intake staff. Other inmates—who did not receive medical marks—were sent to general population, where their medical needs would go ignored.

If we had stopped the study at this juncture it would be easy to understand this development as an expansion of social control with new tools. Indeed, upon medication many of these inmates walk around like zombies—completely unaware and dispossessed of their faculties. This certainly appeared to be the case, as it made the process of jailing easier for jailers and was a new way to subdue the inmate population.

However, as we saw, there are good reasons to be suspicious of linking these developments solely to the broad theories of mass imprisonment and deinstitutionalization; namely, the widespread retrenchment of large urban jail systems. This is why we moved into Chapter 2. We traced what we found in our ethnography of the jail intake room into the archival history of the Los Angeles County jails. What was found was that administrators were not confronting mental healthcare as a crisis in and of itself, but were instead confronting periodic shocks of austerity and legal demand. This pushed jail officials into what I have called *redistributing* the inmate population. The redistribution took the form of recasting the inmate population from primarily violent gang members to less criminally threatening mentally ill, substance abusers, and homeless persons. The pressure to produce medium-security inmates seen in the ethnography was explained by the county's need to generate space that could be sold to other jurisdictions (e.g., INS and state prison system). We see how this quality of "mediumness" came to be associated with medical logic as the county moved to rationalize and make possible a permanent early release system. The system was needed in order to appease federal court overcrowding requirements. The turning of security threats into medical events was born out of legal monitors' concerns over use-of-force statistics and the need to expand jail healthcare within budget limits. Thus, rather than assume the cause of what we found in the ethnography and link this solely to the magic hand of social control, we find its origins in the actions of state officials confronting law and budget retrenchment.

All of these developments also explain what we found in our ethnography of the public ER presented in Chapter 3. We saw the use of crime control language—metaphors of criminal activity and logic of crime deterrence—come to restrict medicine to qualified patients. The mechanisms at work in applying this crime control logic was the widespread conferral of pharmaceuticals during the wait and increases of triage staff and police observation. The use of pharmaceuticals allowed triage staff to obtain valid medical reasons to delay individuals (as vital signs lowered with medication) and gave staff the ability to reinterpret medical biographies with criminal stigma (with idea that patients were not actually sick but were simply seeking drugs).

In our history of the public hospital system, we saw how it was not an effort to control crime but a confluence of austerity and legal demand that drove transformation of the public hospital system. We can see this in three steps. First, in order to pull itself out of deep fiscal disaster, the medical system redistributed the patient population by emphasizing their non-urgent medical conditions, which fit a particular framing of the patients as primarily made up of immigrants and homeless persons. Arguing that the federal government had failed to protect its borders and as a result should provide the county. Second, the new funds came with a requirement that the county downsize its inpatient capacity, but this drew social movement and federal court intervention. Third, the county had to find a way to pursue closures—downsizing LAC + USC and closing MLK hospital—without drawing the ire of the courts. It did so by using health regulatory agencies—who were responsible for patient safety and can be thought of as a kind of legal demand—to resolve this tension. So long as hospitals were declared unsafe by these agencies, the county could close them for reasons other than budget shortfall. In the end, these health regulatory agencies pushed the county to develop waiting line management techniques that we saw in our ethnography: access to pain medication during the wait, increased staff observation to lower waiting time metrics, and increased police presence to avoid other legally risky solutions. All were extensions of public spending to protect patients' rights but appear to us as highly restrictive in form.

It is not that deinstitutionalization, retrenchment-criminalization, and mass imprisonment played no role in these transformations. Certainly, inmates are sicker than they used to be, there is a crime control vision of poor people of color operative among state actors, and the 1980s saw huge growths in jail capacity. But they fail to fully explain the specific phenomena of the expansion of healthcare in jails and its restriction in public hospitals. The theory of redistributing the poor specifically accounts for the widespread retrenchment of jail systems and the persistence of public spending on public healthcare.

We shall see momentarily that this kind of state activity shrouds some kinds of social suffering, but first we must recognize that redistributions are used to resolve crises, not for their expressed political purposes of helping people or exerting social control. On the one hand, officials sometimes are seeking to decrease their responsibility for populations, perhaps because they are losing funding and legitimacy, or because a population has proven difficult to manage. Often, in these situations, policymakers find that scrutiny or accountability over the treatment of a population by a particular agency creates legal problems, bad publicity, or too much administrative uncertainty. On the other hand, there are officials who seek to increase their responsibilities. These officials seek legitimacy for new policy domains or for old ones that have lost it. In these instances, redefinition of particular caseloads, their needs, and appropriate interventions might also come with new sources of public funds. While state leaders may publicly claim they are moving a population to bring their treatment in line with the public's conception of deservingness (e.g., to treat deserving clients with more empathy, or to treat unworthy clients more harshly), privately they may simply be motivated by the desire to give new purpose to failing public agencies or to justify public institutions as ends in themselves.[5]

One instructive example is the case of juvenile offenders during the last three decades of the twentieth century in the California juvenile justice system. The case is characterized by the periodic renegotiation of responsibility for juvenile offenders between state and local governments. The exchange of juveniles always required the garnering of political support, trade-offs between state and local politicians, and, at times, legal action by courts to force different public agencies to take responsibility for the often costly and difficult-to-manage population. At various times, officials at the state level made claims that this group of juveniles was violent and dangerous, and therefore was better housed in state facilities considered to be more secure and built to handle a higher grade of offender. At other times, when overcrowding swelled in state institutions and housing such juveniles proved to be too costly, state officials began to claim they would be better off in county facilities that were closer to their homes and loved ones. Such public proclamations notwithstanding, the private reasons were always the same: political leaders were seeking ways to cut costs or obtain new sources of funding. Occasionally some new funding source for juveniles appeared from federal levels of government, or the public became motivated to approve new taxes, and political leaders would become interested in regaining responsibility for certain classes of juveniles.[6]

We might also apply this framework to the case of unaccompanied children seeking asylum at the U.S.-Mexico border. The long-term and proximal causes are thought to be well known: historical US state and corporate intervention in Central America, as well as more recent extra-state competition for governance and a 2009 right-wing military coup in Honduras. The flow of children escaping violence in these countries doubled in 2014, not only in the United States but to other Latin American countries as well.[7]

US immigration institutions could not simply deny and deport the children. Because of the William Wilberforce Trafficking Victims Protection Reauthorization Act of 2008, officials were bound to provide the refugees with a hearing and place them into care that was "in the best interest of the child" while they awaited those hearings. At first, authorities failed to provide the children with hearings, pushing them through a bureaucratic maze before deporting them. As a result, several legal agencies, including the ACLU, sued. The Obama administration responded by funding hundreds of legal professionals to "expedite" the hearings and the Department of Homeland Security moved to expand facilities to detain the children, including bed space under its own control and lucrative contracts with private corporations.

A redistribution is under way after much public scrutiny, social movement activism, journalist exposés, and inquiries from international human rights agencies showed such housing to be akin to incarceration with inhumane conditions of confinement. As the flow continued and holding facilities became severely overcrowded, authorities began placing some children with sponsors. Little acknowledged is that authorities willingly lost track of thousands of such placements. While concerns were raised, officials downplayed the severity of the problem, arguing that the children were likely simply with trusted family. While that may be true, it is also possible that immigration officials needed to lose track of children due to fiscal and legal pressure around detention centers and hearings, despite the fact that deportation was their expressed goal. Thus, in this moment the state appears as simultaneously weak and oppressive.

More recently, the Department of Health and Human Services began vying for control of the population (and the funding attached to them). The department's officials began testifying before Congress that such children should be placed in "state licensed" facilities. The expressed logic was that such facilities could be held to more humane standards with regular inspections, in a way that detention centers were not. Not to be outdone, NGOs have also been vying for responsibility of the refugees. The continued redistribution of unaccompanied minors will no doubt result in new institutional forms and modalities of social control.[8]

We might also think about direct redistributions between countries, such as the recent explosion in international trafficking of temporary laborers. In these arrangements, one set of state officials essentially agrees to sell the rights to large swaths of people—usually highly contingent workers—and another group of state officials agrees to grant those workers temporary work visas. One example is the delivery of Madagascan workers to various Middle Eastern countries in order to sell their labor to private households. Before a military coup in 2009, Madagascar maintained a productive manufacturing sector, supported by trade agreements facilitated by the International Monetary Fund (IMF) and the United States, which employed a large segment of the Madagascan population. After the coup, these international trade agreements were terminated and Madagascar's unemployment and poverty rates, especially among young women, soared. At a loss for options, the new government in Madagascar facilitated labor agreements with several Middle Eastern countries and thousands of workers, mostly young women, were contracted to employment agencies to work in private homes. Official agreements to exchange this population across international boundaries were only possible once state leaders moved to recast the female workers as more fit for domestic labor than for the manufacturing sector. A legal crisis around the treatment of these women inside their employers' homes has yet to emerge. The negotiation over what to do with contingent workers in Madagascar and other parts of the world continues.[9]

New strategies among police and courts could be linked to the need to, at times, limit the expenditure of jail resources (e.g., Beckett and Herbert 2010; Kohler-Hausmann 2018; Herring 2019; Stuart 2016). Health and welfare agencies may also be responding to, at times, the need to expand services in the wake of legal demand, but in a way that limits the expenditure of resources (e.g., Seim 2017; McKim 2017; Schept 2015; Edwards 2016). Each of these instances shows great transformations in how state actors reformed methods of social control, but whose aims might be linked to limiting the expenditure of resources or the need to meet new demands. While this may be a controversial claim, we ought to examine how the origins of these policies might be linked to crisis abatement, since the need for crisis abatement can also change.

In total, this approach requires focusing on discrete institutional agencies—including both horizontally and vertically disparate agencies and actors—that engage in struggles to recalculate, obtain, or abdicate responsibility for people and the public revenue attached to them. The result is not a coherent population management, in which the movement of people between state agencies is rationally coordinated. Instead, the redistribution of people is a product of distinct agencies acting alone and often in conflict with other state agencies to determine responsibility for different categories of people. This process drives institutional innovation—for instance, by pushing jails to look more like hospitals and hospitals to look more like jails—and projects the illusion that legal requirements have been fulfilled, when, in fact, people have simply been shifted to other sectors of the state or have not been serviced at all.

From Dismantling the State to Disappearing Crisis

In addition to examples of poverty governance, the cases examined in this book are also examples of what historical sociologists call "welfare state resilience." The public hospitals and jails we examined actually constituted additions of funding, institution building, and renewing dying institutions with new mandates amidst widespread retrenchment efforts. The jails expanded their provision of medicine, but did so amidst severe budget curtailments and in such a way that shrouded the needs of many inmates. Public hospitals found ways to renew funding for urban healthcare safety nets amidst the same austerity crisis, but did so in such a way that restricted access to inpatient care and created enormous wait lists. How can we reconcile such contradictions?

Historical sociologists and political scientists have been grappling with an analogous perplexing problem about welfare state institutions: that despite severe political attacks, many important social protections have actually endured. There is overwhelming evidence that—in terms of surface spending levels—very few systems of social protection have experienced fundamental retrenchment (e.g., Pierson 1994, 2001; Esping-Andersen 1999; Huber and Stephens 2001; Korpi and Palme 2001). The American case, in particular, is seen as a quintessential example of welfare state resilience in the face of widespread attack: the mean-tested benefits share of total US social spending increased from 20.1% in the 1980s to 26.8% in 2013 (Campbell 2015).[10]

A cadre of scholars have worked to show that such overall public spending on social programs shrouds deeper "structural retracement." That is, in contrast to highly visible spending on programs, there are longer-term attacks on the public support for social programs, changes in the rules that govern institutions, and the defunding of revenue bases such that social spending will not be supported in the future. Such deeper retrenchment is thought to happen slowly and less visibly through processes called "drift," "conversion," and "layering" (Streeck and Thelen 2005). At times, in an effort to undermine programs through "drift," politicians simply do nothing as institutions fail to keep up with worsening economic conditions (Hacker 2004). In other situations, in an effort we can call "conversion," public officials will redirect old rules or resources to new ends; often, ambiguity in rules will be exploited to push discretion in the direction of retrenchment (Thelen 2003, 2004). Finally, "layering" is a process in which, rather than attack public programs directly, public officials will simply open up other avenues in which citizens can seek out social support, which has the effect of undermining dependence (and support) for existing entitlements (Hacker 2005; Pailer 2005). The classic example is the subsidization of private sector alternatives, such as less effective private health providers in the United States that siphon support for public healthcare (Morgan and Campbell 2011).

Redistributing the poor helps us to clarify the forces that shape public officials' efforts. Instead of only responding to political attempts to scale back public institutions, officials are also grappling with legal demands to add services or respect previously existing rules. Whereas "conversion" is the political use of existing institutional frameworks to restrict services, here we can focus on how legal demands push officials to expand services. Such expansion is similar to "layering," which describes growths in competing systems (usually private partnerships) to undermine existing public options, but legal demand pushes the expansion of services within (not outside) existing institutional frameworks. Redistributions can be programmatic *expansions* to grow and reproduce public institutions.

Acknowledging the role of new legal demands is important because it pushes us to think about what goes on in our public institutions less as resiliency or retrenchment, and more as a "disappearing," which we can describe as the erasure of social suffering that occurs when intractable crisis are temporarily resolved. We should explore what we mean by public resolutions to intractable crises. "Intractable" describes the insurmountable mismatch that officials confront between the number of people legally entitled to services and the availability of state resources; that is, an intractable gap between demand and state resources. We can limit the scope of intractability to the precondition that the supply of needy people and budget resources is beyond jurisdictional control (such as a major change in the class system). A "publicly resolved" situation indicates a practical movement from policy chaos to policy stability or "settledness" (such as when political actors stop working on a problem and produce metrics measuring the matter as settled). In these situations, the state cannot resolve a social problem, but nonetheless develops a significant policy intervention, and subsequently comes to consider the matter resolved.

These crises produce great threats to state institutions. Consider how often we hear of doomsday scenarios in which governments declare that nothing can be done, bankruptcy is afoot, legitimacy seems threatened, and chaos will soon follow. Somehow, despite overwhelming new demands in the midst of budgetary cutbacks, state actors find ways to keep things running and shortly thereafter, the potential for disaster disappears. That state actors routinely solve this tension should be our first clue that something is happening in these moments.

Jail overcrowding and hospital overcrowding are two such intractable problems. They are intractable in the sense that local state government has the legal obligation to deal with them but cannot control the inputs to these problems. The deep poverty that afflicts urban environments (that presumably contributes to many crimes and illness) is beyond its scope. Furthermore, many laws are beyond local control, including the laws that criminalize poor people and those that facilitate health disparities. The demand placed on these institutions is insatiable. There are always more people to jail and more people to hospitalize than can be accommodated. Institutional overcrowding has been a long-term problem for big cities for the past 40 years.

Periodically this long-term problem bubbles up into crises situations. Each crisis was precipitated by some event that made the problem of public concern; for instance, an inmate or a patient was allowed to die and this was seen as related to overcrowding in some way, a riot occurred, or regulators clamped down on bad conditions. Each was met with shock, horror, and predictions of budget default, unprecedented waves of crime and illness, and unyielding litigation. When reading the archival record, it appeared to me that each crisis was seen by officials as the first time they had ever encountered such a severe problem. Each moment was experienced viscerally as a problem whose resolution, to county officials in that moment, appeared to require nothing short of miracles. By pursuing redistribution, the crises became resolved in such a way that they were no longer of public concern, but the long-term problems continue. In the future, these long-term tensions will continue to bubble up into crisis periods and the local state will need to pursue future redistributions.

Even though such resolutions represent expansions of public spending to solve problems, they cannot be fully characterized as resiliency. In essence, this is because it is not the social needs that motivated the original crisis that become resolved, but some other new kind of new social need. To be clear, the original social needs that drove a crisis are transformed into their kinds of needs, needs that can be affordably resolved. In short, as the extent of services to be provided is worked out by legal interlocutors (demand), officials have knowledge about the limits of their budget (resources), as well as about possible metrics that might be used to judge policy resolution. This information can then be used to alter what players view as the problem in the first place. If a new law mandates that an agency provide a service, for instance, that agency will have knowledge about its resources that limit how it can implement the law. This knowledge will allow the agency to attempt to rearticulate what the new law mandated it do in the first place. Thus, what appears to us as resiliency in spending is something else entirely.

There are numerous telltale signs of "disappearing." Redistributions are normally precipitated by the gathering of experts, the convening of public hearings, and consensus building about how best to characterize a problem population and intervene in their lives. Crisis events that gain media attention may compel political leaders and public agencies to convey that they are thinking about old problems in new ways, when, in fact, they are abandoning or capturing populations. Scholars should locate these instances and delve into the archival record surrounding them. Private memos circulated between politicians, administrators, and staff—during crisis periods—often reveal political intent that differs from that which is publicly stated. Scholars might also compare public gatherings and committees of experts to see how the rhetoric and framings of populations change as political leaders address the same challenges in new ways. These moments may reveal political leaders in the process of formulating new content with which to frame a population that they aim to redistribute.

In total, we gain a new way to describe public spending that is neither emblematic of resiliency (Pierson 2001; Esping-Andersen 1999; Huber and Stephens 2001) nor dismantling (Streeck and Thelen 2005; Hacker 2004, 2005; Morgan and Campbell 2011). Scholars who capture persistence in public spending may be missing how social needs have been rearticulated to fit the new context of a resolved crisis. Likewise, scholars who capture retrenchment (even long-term structural retrenchment) may be missing how institutions have shifted to meet other kinds of legal recognized social needs. In both cases, the public institutions have redefined either themselves or the social needs they are meant to grapple with. Such transformation can be described as a disappearing of crisis.

Administrative Disappearing of Social Suffering

What do we gain by focusing on the transformation of demand during crisis? Does it have any real-world consequences? Something happens during such moments that many know, but few know how to describe: the people who were tied to the context of a social problem are erased, their problems and issues are disappeared from officials' descriptions. In this concluding section, I sketch out theoretical terrain for how we might conceptualize and potentially measure the administrative disappearing of social suffering.

Ian Hacking famously wrote about how experts, the human sciences, and institutions are in the business of "making up human kinds." These are categories of people that did not exist before, and because that category now exists, those people begin to embody that category. Hacking's key point was that as officials get to know more about the properties that make up a certain category of people (in the effort "to control, to help, to change, or to emulate them better"), the categories themselves are "moving targets because our investigations interact with the targets themselves, and change them. And since they are changed, they are not quite the same kind of people as before. The target has moved. That is the looping effect. Sometimes our sciences create kinds of people that in a certain sense did not exist before. That is making up people."[11]

This is what happens when a jail redefines its inmate population from violent gang members to less criminally threatening sick people, or when a hospital begins to emphasize the quality of undocumented and less urgently sick homeless people among its patient population. When experts convene, studies are carried out, and statistics are collected, these become instances of "making up human kinds."

What I mean to point out here is that these particular human kinds are tied to a time and place—or what sociologist like to call a context. Here is what I mean. In 2015 an inmate might be emphasized by the state as mentally ill and treated as such, but a person similar to him in the past might have been emphasized as a violent gang member. The social suffering of that comparable person in the past is erased. Erased is the treatment he might have received and how his life might have been impacted by such an intervention.

The version of these persons who existed before—and the social problems that beset the organization in dealing with him—are disappeared. The previous status, tied to an older context, is no longer relevant as a problem.

One (likely overlooked) example from this book will suffice. There was a difference in the way Los Angeles County jail administrators deployed a profitable contract for state prisoners as a solution to the respective crises of 1997 and 2007. It is in exploiting that difference that we can see the administrative disappearing of a people and its associated social suffering. A major component of officials' plan to resolve the jail crisis of 1994–1997 was to fill up empty jail space with California state prisoners (a different government agency that would provide Los Angeles County with essential revenue). As we saw, that empty jail space was created by, in part, releasing thousands of local county inmates into the community on unreasonably large probation caseloads. The release of those inmates was specifically rationalized around the expertise of being able to identify medically needy and less criminally threatening inmates who were suitable for release.

In the crisis of 2004–2007, county officials debated whether to cancel that contract for California state prisoners. Some officials wanted to cancel the contract and kick out the state prisoners so that there would be more space to house local inmates—overcrowding was thought to be a major impetus to the riots that were fueling the new crisis. The problem was that it was not clear to officials whether canceling the contract would leave county with the state prisoners anyway. County officials feared they might lose the revenue the state was paying but would be stuck with the state prisoners anyway. The resolution to the problem was highly contingent and emerged in the following exchange in a 2006 meeting of the Board of Supervisors:

SHERIFF LEE BACA: The CEO and I were somewhat worried that, if we sent them back, we eliminate the money resource and they'd compel us to keep the inmates. I'm pleased to announce to you today, and I just heard this today, that in checking with the California Department of Corrections, they know that they're obligated to take those inmates out of our system. So this is a new piece of information that I learned a half hour ago, before we began . . .

SUPERVISOR YAROSLAVSKY: . . . [I]t wasn't going to work that well because there were two kinds of prisoners, as I recall, state prisoners that we have, some that we are obligated to have, and some that we are taking, but that they have no place to take back, we could end up having those very prisoners without the money . . .

MARC KLUGMAN: I'd like to respond a little bit. I talked to the state. Their position is that these 1,292 beds are part of their bed count per the contract. If they lose the contract, they lose the 1,292 beds. That means that the 1,292 parole violators in the system would be removed . . .

SUPERVISOR YAROSLAVSKY: To where? To where?

MARC KLUGMAN: . . . to state prison. And then the following statement was made to me that they would then parole back to Los Angeles County a larger number of state inmates who are convicted felons . . .

SUPERVISOR YAROSLAVSKY: They would be paroled on the street . . . ? So don't sweat the early release. This is an old George Carlin routine, don't sweat the thunderstorm.

MARC KLUGMAN: . . . [T]his is a statewide problem, it's not a local problem, it's everybody's problem and that's the way that they're addressing it . . .

CAO JANSSEN: I think that's a really important point, because the governor is, you know, they're under a federal court order with respect to the state operations. They have a tremendous capacity problem that we have, it's not unique, so that makes sense, that if they are forced to retake ours, they're going to release somebody else.[12]

The following summarizes the exchange: it was discovered by county officials that state officials would indeed take their inmates back if the county canceled the contract, but it was also discovered that state officials would release other inmates from elsewhere in the California state prison system! In other words, the county resolved its previous crisis of 1997 by contracting to the state to house prisoners at a profit and released thousands of county inmates into the community in order to create space to do so. But in the crisis of 2006, the county canceled that contract to create more space for county inmates, but, in turn, the state released other inmates into the community from elsewhere in its system.

An illusion is produced: in one crisis, the county can claim it is reaching resolution by generating revenue, and in another creating space. In both, thousands of inmates are released into the community. The distinctions or "human kinds" between state and county in this case are distinctions that only matter on paper; something that can be manipulated by officials in order to resolve their problems. County officials realized, for the first time, that these inmates were really just the same group of individuals, with different administrative attributes that could be manipulated toward revenue generation or cost cutting. As a sheriff's official said in 2006, "If you can't skin the cat one way, you can skin it another."[13]

What gets "disappeared" in this case are two groups of people/contexts. Obviously, the state is abdicating authority over the inmates who are sent into the community. But the more concerning are those inmates who were jailed but might have been released under a different arraignment. In the

1997 instance, local inmates were released while state prisoners were jailed. In 2006, local inmates were jailed while state prisoners were released. Those inmates who are jailed endure the suffering and lifelong tole that jailing will wreak on the human psyche.

It is that suffering that is disappeared from the movement of one temporary policy resolution to the next. That status—the inmate who could have been released—gets erased. That empirical reality—that an inmate in 2006 who is sitting in his jail cell can look back at the archival record (or this book) and see that he might have been released had he been jailed in 1997—is disappeared. It is only disappeared because the state has created a redistribution, with no concern about his welfare or his punishment, but in order to resolve its own crisis. *These are instances when the social suffering of huge swaths of people are simply written off on paper.*

If we are going to be able to describe moments of "administrative disappearing" of social suffering, then we need to rid ourselves of our dominant vision of the state: the state as all powerful, growing, and increasing in capacity to gather information about the populace. Essentially, a "Weberian" notion of the state (one that is primarily bureaucratic, extracting entity with a monopoly on coercive power) is used to judge whether its capacity has grown or diminished. This notion has even been extended to symbolic power or the ability of states to name and categorize people and things (Bourdieu 2015). In part, this is due to the influence of Foucault (1975, 1980), who wrote much about the "accumulation of men," in which the emergence of concern about the health and physical well-being of the population was one of the key transformations in the late eighteenth century. Another great influence has been Scott's (1998) interest in how modern states seek to acquire more information and fit people into neatly digestible categories for the purpose of social engineering. Nearly all modern public institutions—including schools, hospitals, prisons, jails, welfare institutions, and, more recently, the collection of "big data"—have been examined as sites of potential growing or diminishing state capacity.[14]

In contrast, when it disappears the state must relinquish some control to make it through crisis situations. We therefore must be equally attentive to how modern states harness what McGoey (2012) called "strategic unknowns" (see also Carruthers and Espeland 1991; Heimer 2012). This is a focus on "the multifaceted ways that ignorance can be harnessed as a resource, enabling knowledge to be deflected, obscured, concealed or magnified in a way that increases the scope of what remains unintelligible" (McGoey 2012, 1).

We might investigate those instances when state officials blame individuals for not accessing available state resources when such officials are reliant on, and budget for, low turnouts. We might also investigate when state actors develop new social control programs but rely on caseloads so large that wards are likely to never create costs. Publicly, these designations allow state officials a way to claim they are continuously intervening in caseloads or safely moving people out of the state's purview, while in practice such designations simply match demand to the exigencies of the budget.

An important caveat: we need to be careful with how we unpack the role of legal demand. Schlanger (2015) points out that when we focus on the role of liberal activists (who no doubt opposed things like over-incarceration) we may risk hamstringing important reform efforts. Likewise, Schoenfield (2018, chapter 8) also points out that while combining Eighth Amendment litigation with discrimination claims under the Americans with Disabilities Act may indeed result in increased carceral resources, such pressure may still be necessary to protect human dignity. Reiter's (2016) suggestion is to couple such legal pressure with continued transparency of administrators, though she warns that legal endogeneity (Edelman 2016) is always a risk.

I believe a certain kind of "history of the present" can be useful for creating a more just future. The idea is that elucidating "a series of troublesome associations and lineages" of the past can "suggest the openness of the future" (Garland 2014, 372). That is, problematizing the present in such a way that reveals the power relations upon which it depends, and the contingent process that brought it into being, disturbs what we previously thought of as immobile, unified, and consistent. These state machinations appear to us as insurmountable, but when we expose their scaffolding—even when that scaffolding is inconvenient—it can help us to carve out novel directions. Recently, social movement actors in Los Angeles have pushed the county to rethink its plans to build a hospital-jail. A new conflict is brewing in which criminal justice authorities may have lost control of its medical redistribution, with the logic now being used to simply close facilities entirely.[15]

The claim in this book is not that legal demand simply refracts impulses to socially control or generate revenue from the bodies of wards, but that it is a core feature of crises. For instance, as recent financial extraction practices have come to light in Ferguson, Missouri, and elsewhere, scholars have increasingly acknowledged that, in addition to punitive impulses, "the underlying question [for state officials] becomes whether an offender is an offender at all or merely a target wearing a dollar sign." This study also points to how public officials additionally see wards as *legal problems*. Packing inmates into any feasible space of jails, unaccompanied minors in detention centers, or letting patients wait untreated for hours in public hospitals is no longer possible with new rules around the rights of these wards. There is no way to explain many institutional forms without understanding how legal demand shapes decision-making.[16]

This suggests something about how we can dismantle unjust state systems. In addition to pursuing legal rules against particular instances of abuse, we ought to be equally attentive to the forces that brought them into being and those that rely on them. Rather than simply adding new rules that mandate new costs, we could seek to create progressive taxation that is specifically tied to the funding of new legal demands. If not, and we simply deprive jurisdictions of particular means of supporting agencies, we risk pushing them into other trickier avenues of profiteering. The rise of profiteering is a major social problem in local governments, and we can be attentive to its complex interplay of punishment, predation, and judicialization.

To conclude, poor people often have a keen sense of our object of analysis— that is, no matter how many times policy elites preach reform, the status quo seems to get reproduced and their social suffering gets "disappeared." Alongside the expansion of control or protection of special interest groups, we should also investigate the maintenance of the status quo as a key state activity. Intractable problems are key moments in which states must mobilize administrative disappearing to ensure that not much change actually occurs. In our case, the social problems of over-incarceration and under-medicalization of the poor persist, while particularly policy crises are temporarily resolved. Yet individuals continue to cycle between county jail, public hospital, and the community, much as they did previously.

APPENDIX
Historically Embedded Ethnography

A generation of ethnographers have found themselves simultaneously criticized for being too theoretical at the same time that they are criticized for under-theorization. Because their data come from a single place and time, they have been told to "stick to their field sites" and to think twice before making claims about external relevance. Yet, ethnographers still face the expectation that they should be able to help audiences think differently about common problems.

For me, this confusion was due to the different ways I was taught to marshal my ethnographic data. Each of the major frameworks I encountered along my journey emphasized different relationships between field notes, history, theory, and the kinds of external validity claims that were possible. There were four such frameworks. I first ignored history and attempted to use existing theory to give meaning to my field. This is largely due to the influence of Katz (2002) and what I call "theory as interpretation," or the push to generate theories about social forces from "poignant" ethnographic scenes. The second was an initial attempt to use history in a way that predominates our field, which I call the "history as context" approach. Often a historical chapter sets the "context" to help us understand how things came to be in the field site. But the ethnographer still focuses on using field notes to interpret the social forces at play. That is, history is bracketed from theories that are gleaned from field notes. Third, I encountered the extended case method (Burawoy 2003, 2009) which reversed the dynamic and made me feel as if I could use my field notes to say something about broad historical transformations. Fourth, I encountered what Vaughan (1996, 2004), Haney (2002), and Hunter (2012) might call "historical ethnography," which generates theory from archival materials. I did not realize it at the time, but this made me question the kinds of grand theorizing I was doing with the extended case method.

In retrospect, each of these provided me exactly what I needed at the time and in the end added up to the final product. I can best describe my approach as "historically embedded ethnography." At its core, this approach generates theory from the link between archives and field notes, rather than either exclusively. In my view, this connection leads to what third wave historical sociologists call "constitutive arguments"—or claims of external relevance that border between historical origin stories and the characteristics that phenomena take on in present-day life (Pacewicz 2020; Lara-Millán, Sargent, and Kim 2020). I am going to draw on my own research experience as well as recent innovations in third wave historical sociology (Adams, Clemens, and Orloff 2005; Clemens 2007; Pacewicz 2020; Hirshman and Reed 2014) to show how ethnographers can be more precise about their use of history and the kinds of external validity claims they are making. In short, this is the journey of how I moved from pre-research, to the confusion of studying jails and hospitals as examples of urban poverty governance, to using them as clarifications of the phenomenon of welfare state resiliency.

Before we begin, I want to point out two caveats. First, many will see the different versions of ethnography I discuss as complementary. For instance, Burawoy (2003) incorporates what I call "history as context" as well as "historical ethnography" (or "archeological revisits") into his formulation of the extended case method. Small (2009) also incorporates the extended case method into his understanding of how external validity claims should work in ethnography. While there are versions of this account that would emphasize the similarities of these uses of history and theory, here I emphasize the differences that were important in moving my research forward. I present a narrative in which my data encountered each of these ways of using history and how it changed the claims I was making. Second, I want to be clear that the use of history in ethnography I espouse here is an alternative. The other models of using history in ethnography do not produce false accounts, but different kinds of worthwhile theories.

Entering the Field: Studying Up and Embodied Costs

I started this venture inspired in two different ways by Wacquant's (2009) *Punishing the Poor*. First, this was the theoretical framework with which I entered the field, and which shaped what I saw and what I was interested in. Wacquant (2009) had called for future scholars to study the way that different institutions of the state that we normally think of as disconnected—things like jails, police, hospitals, schools, courts, and many others—actually interact and shape the lives of the marginalized. I took this to mean that future scholars, especially those of color, should work to expand on the groundwork he had laid.

It was a powerful call, and I wrote most of my proposal for my project around this idea. I initially sought to study Skid Row in downtown Los Angeles and examine the way that multiple institutions were shaping the lives of the destitute in these few square blocks. The location was interesting to me because it was familiar: I had previously studied the area under Jack Katz and Robert Emerson in their ethnography incubator program at UCLA in 2006. It was there that I first developed the craft of ethnography while studying the way that private security guards and public police controlled public spaces around Skid Row.

Waquant's (2009) book also worked on a personal level. When reading it, I kept thinking about my family. I grew up in a Chicano family, some whom were lucky enough to become upwardly mobile, getting caught up in the ascent of Silicon Valley in one way or another, and some of whom were not so lucky, getting caught up instead in California's vast criminal justice system. Two cousins in particular kept returning to the forefront of my mind. I had grown up admiring them; they were both tall (6'6"), handsome, charismatic, and smarter than anyone I knew. One cousin grew up bouncing around small apartments with his mother in San Francisco. One day, he got into a fight with a 17-year-old on a bus. Because he was 18, black, and on public property, he was arrested and spent time in prison. I never found out why my family did not bail him out those first few days in jail. The other cousin grew up in a mansion in San Jose. At a young age, he apparently got into drugs, partying, and other mayhem. I'm still not sure, but rumor was that his parents got him in touch with institutional help and he lives in that same mansion to this day.

There is no shade here; I love both cousins very much, but it was the comparison that drove my work. It is why I wanted my study to focus on decision-makers, rather than the people who had to endure and suffer the consequences of those decisions. I yearned to know what decisions were being made to shape the lives of these two young men. I did not want to know why people engaged in crime or how they resisted criminalization; that was a story I felt had been told. I wanted to "study up," as some ethnographers call it; I needed to make sense of what was going on with the state.

When I returned to Skid Row in 2009, I found myself somewhat underwhelmed. It felt as if others had told the story already: the people living in Skid Row were caught there because of the criminal justice system and the overwhelming presence of shelters and other social services (Davis 2002). Feeling a bit dejected, I was at home one day when I read an article in the *Los Angeles Times* exposing the practice of "hospital dumping"— in which local public hospitals released homeless patients into Skid Row without any housing and often before they were recovered. The article outlined how the county was trying to fix the problem. Apparently, they had been sued over the practice and were developing institutional links with local shelters so that they could safely release the patients. My mind raced. I wondered how the lawsuits would alter the ecology of the local shelter system and how access to these places would change. Would this lead to housing insecure people seeking care in local emergency departments so that they could actually get access to housing? I also wondered about being released from the local jail, which also felt like a kind of "dumping."

Entering the Hospital

I knew I wanted to study decision-making in a hospital and a jail. Because I was attending school in Chicago and had family in Los Angeles and the Bay Area, I cast my net wide. I made requests to hospital administrators at public medical facilities in nine different urban counties: three counties in Northern California, four in Southern California, and two counties in Midwestern states. I contacted the hospitals' respective public relations offices, asked to be directed to personnel who could respond to a research request, and conveyed my interest in conducting observational research of triage departments.

These initial requests were framed as inductive ethnographic inquiries, ones that would study whatever informal culture existed among triage staff. As many an ethnographic novice learns, this was a mistake. The proposals were rejected outright. In my view, these administrators preferred deductive studies with specific research questions that could be, in their view, studied systematically.

In order to understand how to design a deductive study that medical administrators would be amenable to, I sought to gain experience working in a triage department. I learned of volunteer positions that some emergency rooms made available to the public. I entered into one such program as a student volunteer. The program I joined was framed by administrators as having the goal of helping individuals pursue a career in the healthcare field. Typically, in my view, volunteers tended to be undergraduates with goals of becoming physicians, nurse practitioners, or physician's assistants. Because the volunteer positions were intended as educational opportunities, volunteers were encouraged to assist staff in the emergency room wherever they felt they could learn the most and where hospital staff requested their assistance. Duties typically including pushing hospital beds from one location to another, escorting patients, transporting files, helping to clean patient rooms, and other miscellaneous activities. The positions also came with the specific mandate to befriend hospital staff and inquire about their duties in order to learn about healthcare. While most volunteers competed for access to the trauma area of the emergency room, where doctors and nurses treat the most severe cases, I focused on immersing myself in the world of triage decision-making. I was one of the few volunteers to spend most of my time in the triage unit. Most of the healthcare occurring in this department consisted of the diagnosis of incoming patients, managing patients in the various waiting rooms, and grappling with the high levels of tension between staff and waiting patients. I befriended staff and learned the language of triage nurses: how they talked about common problems they faced, how they defined their work, and why they thought emergency rooms were overcrowded.

This language proved extremely useful in pitching an ethnographic study to other public emergency rooms. During the volunteer experience, it became clear that the overarching concern of triage staff was that most of their patients were, in the view of staff, patients with non-urgent medical problems. These were patients who requested emergency-level care for ailments that were, in staff members' views, better fit for outpatient care settings. Nurses framed the problem of overcrowding as due to non-urgent patients' unwillingness to seek care in outpatient clinics and their choice to instead seek care in the emergency room. In my view, nurses expressed the difficulty in making triage classifications among such non-urgent patients. Using this language, I constructed a research design, which proposed to study and catalog how triage nurses make classifications among non-urgent patients. The same administrators who had rejected my previous attempts to inductively observe triage decisions were now open to the study because I had found their language for talking about the problem of overcrowding. That is, the study already conformed to their definition of the problem: that non-urgent patients were to blame for emergency room overcrowding.

I selected one of the public hospitals that approved my research design and entered the emergency department, identified as a PhD graduate student in medical sociology who was conducting research on how triage staff made triage classifications and admission decisions among non-urgent patients. At first, my access to the triage department was limited. I was allowed to sit with triage nurses as they interviewed incoming patients and gave them triage rankings. I was unable to make many inquiries into the process or move around the various rooms of the triage area. In my view, the major breakthrough in access, what ethnographers describe as being accepted as an insider, came when I began verbalize that I shared in the suspicion of patients who seemed to abuse the hospital with fake injuries. I had learned the correct language of this suspicion during my time as a volunteer and began quipping such phrases as: "I can't believe they won't go to a clinic" or "Haven't we seen that guy here before?" These were phrases often utilized by triage nurses in stressful situations or when they shared stories about patients with one another. The repetition of such phrases and the joining in of stories of over-utilization of the emergency room by frequent patients allowed the nurses to see me as an insider and someone who shared their concerns.

Another breakthrough came when I befriended a group of triage staff similar in age. The group was made up of nearly equal numbers of men and women and ranged in age from 26 to 34. The group was a loosely knit friendship circle who, to varying degrees, spent time with one another outside of the workplace. My age seemed to me important, as it probably accounted for shared interests in how to spend leisure time and engage in venues of popular culture (such as television, movies, and music). Such shared interests proved useful in creating bonds during work breaks or in between seeing patients.

Members of this group vouched for my presence in the triage department and expanded my range of access. I was able to freely move about the triage department, in assessment booths, in waiting lobbies, in reassessment sessions, and in the booth where final admissions decisions were made. It also allowed me to shadow head triage nurses for entire shifts as they learned about waiting patients, deliberated on them, and made final admissions decisions. At some point during the research, most members of the triage department knew me as an insider and welcomed my presence. I often made myself useful to whomever I was shadowing by performing duties I had learned as a volunteer. Triage staff are extremely busy, and they found it very beneficial to always have access to someone who would perform what they considered to be necessary but menial tasks. This included transporting files and patients from one location to another, helping nurses search for patients in waiting rooms, searching for misplaced patient records, cleaning areas, and being sent to find and relay messages between triage staff.

I conducted the fieldwork in the hospital in 8- to 12-hour outings, which coincided with the amount of time it usually took for patients to enter the emergency room and receive a bed and was also nearly the length of triage staff members' work shifts. Over the course of the 13 months, the amount of times per week I conducted observational outings varied greatly. During some periods I conducted three such outings a week, and during others I conducted only one. I simply contacted the shift manager at the beginning of the week and notified him/her of the shifts when I planned to come in. The shift manager saw this as a formality and approved whatever shifts I requested. It was necessary to conduct observations during the morning shift, day shift, night shift, and the graveyard shift. I found the graveyard time period easiest to study because many of the staff I had befriended worked this shift, and because it fit with my other fieldwork commitments.

This schedule also varied because of fatigue. The length of the 8- to 12-hour observational outing was a constant source of tension. At first, I found it difficult to be able to immediately write field notes upon returning from the field. I opted to record my field notes using a voice recorder in private (often in my car) every four hours during observations. These recordings were transcribed into text after the project was completed. I did have access to a notepad during observations, in which I wrote shorthand notes to identify general events that occurred during the four-hour periods between recordings. I used these notes to orient the more detailed voice recordings of my field notes. The excerpts reported in this book are taken from these audio-recorded field notes and should be regarded as paraphrasing of conversations.

On the whole, my observations in the triage department focused on staff decision-making around admissions and their shared meaning-making about those decisions, patients, and the problems they collectively faced. In retrospect, the trouble in gaining access—having to learn the language of the triage staff and their perspective—actually guided the research to focus on staff rather than on patients. The language that triage staff used to talk about emergency room overcrowding largely blamed patients for that overcrowding and, in my view, was largely unsympathetic to patients' perspectives and their often tumultuous lives. As I described earlier, I adopted that language and perspective in order to gain the trust of triage staff members, but in doing so, I was also forced to distance myself from patients. While I was able to record significant interactions and discussions with patients, the focus of the chapter remained on triage staff culture. Moreover, I believe that focusing my observations on staff helped me in gaining IRB (Institutional Review Board) approval for the research.

Entering the Jail

Negotiating access to an intake unit of a county jail, while difficult, was easier than negotiating access to a triage department. I set about seeking access to a county jail that was under a court-ordered population cap and was required to institute early releases in order to meet the requirements of that cap. I, again, cast my net wide and contacted many of the 35 such jails in California.

In the jail I ultimately studied, I initiated contact through the public relations department of the sheriff's office in charge of the jail. I identified myself as a student studying criminology who was interested in writing a paper about the use of risk assessment. I did so on the advice of previous scholars who had done work in custody settings; it was suggested that custody officials are often weary of journalists and civil rights lawyers who wish to discredit jail officials. By identifying myself as a student writing a paper, so I was told, I would appear less threatening to jail officials.

After identifying myself to the public relations department, I requested a tour of the jail's inmate intake unit and asked to speak with intake staff. Receiving the tour was not difficult, as the Sheriff's Department often gave such tours to members of the public. A single lieutenant who worked and managed a shift in the jail intake unit gave me a tour. During the tour, I had the opportunity to speak with a number of staff members, including officers who maintained security in the hallways of the intake unit, risk assessment officers, and medical staff who assessed all incoming inmates.

On the tour, similar to the hospital (though in a much more compressed time span), I discovered language for talking about jail overcrowding that conformed to custody officers' definition of the problem. On the tour I heard the following idea and phrase repeated quite often by the intake staff: custody officers felt they had to protect the jail from inmates who were trying to "game the system." The premise was that many of the inmates were somehow trying to get into the jail in order to benefit from jail resources. While I was a bit shocked by this, I did not hesitate to adopt the perspective in order to gain some level of trust with those who might give me access to study the intake unit.

In a follow-up meeting with the lieutenant who gave me the tour of the jail, I expressed my desire to observe and shadow risk-assessment officers in the jail. My goal was to conduct research on how custody officers made risk-assessment and admissions decisions among inmates who wished to be jailed. I also expressed a desire to help custody officers grapple with jail overcrowding, which, I felt, proved that I was making a connection between the causes of overcrowding and inmates who wished to "game the system." In my view, adopting a perspective that conformed to custody staff's definition of the problem, much like with the nurses in the emergency room, would aid me in gaining the trust of custody staff as I progressed in the research.

The lieutenant and some of his staff supported my desire to study risk-assessment decisions and wanted to help me find the easiest way to do so. They suggested I contact a third-party consultant already under contract with the jail to conduct research, observation, and interviews in the jail. Because this third-party consultant was already approved to conduct observation in the jail, being hired by them would be the easiest way for me to conduct my own observations. I contacted the third-party consultant and told them of my desire to conduct observation of the intake unit. I understood the consultant's goal in the jail to be gathering data on how to make the jail more efficient in moving inmates out of the jail and generating cost savings wherever they could be found. At first, they were unprepared to move forward with a qualitative study of the intake unit, as doing so would require going through the process of hiring someone to design the study. Given my background as a qualitative methodologist, I offered my services to help with this study design. I assume my willingness to work for free was useful to the contractor, who was interested in keeping their own costs as minimal as possible, to move forward with the project. In exchange, I requested that I be allowed to use the data that the research team collected on risk assessment.

Within this wider third-party study, my access was limited to two areas of the intake unit. I was primarily allowed to sit with risk-assessment officers as they interviewed inmates and to sit behind medical professionals as they interviewed incoming inmates. In both settings, I had no contact with inmates and was not allowed to speak with them. These areas were completely barred from inmates as they were behind glass windows. Office staff, medical professionals, and deputies roamed freely within these closed-off spaces as they carted files and transferred information between one another. I was able to speak with these staff members freely when they were not engaged with inmates. This allowed me to comment and ask questions about what was transpiring, including when events occurred outside of the two areas. I developed friendships and a rapport with staff members whom I regularly came into contact with, which made me feel free to ask them about decisions they made and interactions with inmates.

Critical to my findings was that fact that I was allowed to accompany medical staff outside of these closed-off spaces when they were called to treat or assess inmates in holding cells within the intake unit. The intake unit had a large number of holding cells where inmates waited for their assignments in jail cells or other routings. Jail staff determined that, since deputies accompanied such nurses, I could, in their words, "safely" observe interactions in these holding cells. I was not allowed to actually enter these holding cells, which held up to 20 inmates at a time, but I could view interactions between medical staff and inmates through glass windows. This proved useful because I was able to see when medical staff members were called to intervene and what they did with the information they garnered from such interventions when they returned to the medical evaluation area.

In contrast to the long duration of my outings in the triage department, my observations in the jail intake room were only four hours per session. I was allowed to carry a notepad while I conducted observations, but I only wrote short phrases, which reminded me of specific events and the sequence of those events. When I returned home, I took these notes and recounted the happenings of the observational outings in detail into a voice recorder. The notes were transcribed into text after the project was completed. In the first five months of fieldwork, I was at the field site three times a week. I stopped conducting fieldwork for three months due to other professional obligations. Upon return to the intake room, the duration of my observations was much more erratic, with some weeks garnering only one four-hour research session. By this time, the third-party contractor's observation project was in full swing and paid staff members were conducting the work. I was welcomed by intake staff on an informal basis to continue my work, and I used the opportunity to shadow specific staff members, especially medical staff who worked inside the intake center.

In contrast to the hospital, my participation during the ethnography of the jail intake staff was limited to speaking with staff during the course of their decision-making. I asked probing questions about what was happening and why. I often "played dumb"—pretending that I did not know why events where occurring—about processes in order to spark conversation and compare different staff members' explanations. In the emergency room ethnography, I conducted menial tasks in order to build trust with nurses, while in the jail, my activities were limited to sitting, listening, following, and speaking with intake staff. I was never unsupervised and needed to ask whatever staff member I was shadowing at the time if I could move on to another person or location.

It is unclear how this more limited access affected my observations in the jail. It is certainly possible that had I been allowed to observe and move about the intake unit freely I would have been privy to some of the more violent incidents that occurred in the jail. I did see such incidents from afar, from the safety of the two spaces I was allowed to observe from, but if incidents occurred in holding cells not directly in my line of sight,

I did not see them. In my view, this most likely pushed the ethnography to focus on risk assessment and medical diagnosis in the jail rather than other likely topics, such as inmate–deputy violence, mistreatment, or how inmates make it through the harrowing 24-hour-long intake process. Like the emergency room, in order to gain the trust of intake staff, I had to adopt a perspective that was not sympathetic to the plight of inmates, and this, in turn, made it impossible for me to speak with inmates awaiting incarceration.

I also suspect that my presence pushed intake officers to verbalize their inner thinking more than they otherwise would have. That is, I do not think that the conversations between inmates and officers are as explicit in every case as they are reported in this book. Officers get the information they need out of inmates without spending anymore time talking to them than they have to. My presence gave officers an excuse to develop these conversations in more detail and nuance. Finally, in order to increase the confidentiality of these conversations, I also took steps to alter specific mentions of crime or criminal histories to equivalent categories (i.e., turning one kind of misdemeanor crime into another kind of misdemeanor crime).

Huang (2015) writes about the "embodied costs" she took on when studying sex workers and their clients. While not the same, her concept helped to clarify some of the things I was feeling during and after my observations. Gaining access to these institutions and "studying up" required me to adopt the professionals' language, much of which was classicist, racist, and completely unsympathetic to the difficult lives of patients and inmates. Feelings of guilt, self-hate, and others were common as I engaged with this language. I could not help but worry that, like the nurses and jailers in my study, I was using this language to boost my own self-esteem. I kept imagining white scholars assuming that I chose my topic of study simply because I wanted to perform "me-search" and I had family connections to research subjects. The vision of such distractors motivated me to keep up with the decision-makers, turning my gaze on the people with power, and to emphatically declare that I was in fact not studying my cousins. In total, I was proud of the effort I was making to understand how power worked, but I was ashamed that I was, in part, doing it to make myself feel better about my topic of choice. To the present day, I still struggle to understand how this affected my mental health.

The First Attempt to Write: Theory as Interpretation

It was when I could predict with some accuracy the decisions that staff were going to be making about their wards that I felt ready to take my first stab at writing. My understanding of how I should go about doing this was informed by what I would call the "theory as interpretation" paradigm.

Having been taught ethnographic methods under Jack Katz, I set about trying to generate theory from my field notes. Little did I know this was only one way of using ethnographic material, which characterized a kind of "camp" among ethnographers: those who subscribed to "grounded theory," or generating theory inductively out of "poignant" ethnographic scenes. In my previous study, Katz once admonished me for drawing on the rise of global finance in downtown Los Angeles to explain what I was seeing among private security guards and the local homeless population. He implored me to theorize about the data I actually had: the interactions between guards and their policing targets. The goal was to find "poignant" scenes—moments when actors acutely felt larger social forces that changed something about their standpoints, emotions, or actions—in our notes and then use them to develop theory (Katz 2002). Imagine a scene with a nurse breaking down crying because he very much wants to admit a sick patient, but there are no beds available. Such a scene would go a long way in conveying to the reader the twin pressures of bed scarcity and a culture of nurses' concern for patients.

I took this lesson and set about writing a first draft of my hospital observations. This way of theorizing was enormously helpful in gathering scenes that poignantly illustrated bias among staff. The key was that such bias really only emerged when bed scarcity produced the need for discretion. That is, bias against undeserving patients really only mattered when nurses needed to use discretion to make decisions when there were not enough beds.

I presented my first article on the hospital to the Northwestern ethnography workshop under Gary Alan Fine—another important influence—and it was well received. After the workshop ended, Gary shared with me two existing ethnographic pieces (George and Dundes 1978; Roth 1972) on emergency rooms. I was devastated. The pieces had already shown staff bias against undeserving patients in the 1970s! There comes a moment in every scholar's journey in which they encounter a piece of sociology that already illustrates the novel things the thought they had uncovered.

This was an important learning moment for me. I learned that instead of fighting against encountering such pieces, I should be grateful for them because they did leg work that could push me to go deeper. At this juncture, the natural inclination is to try to find differences between my observation and what had been observed in the previously published differences. This practice of encountering an existing body of work and returning to field notes in order to reinterpret them is described nicely by Tavory and Timmermans (2014).

What I found was that criminal stigma was much more rampant as a particular form of bias in my field notes than what was reported by the ethnographies of ERs in the 1970s. In those, it was class and race bias that seemed to be at the forefront of staff culture. Criminal stigma was reserved for a small subset of alcoholics. I also noticed that these ethnographies did not really show *how* such bias affected medical decision-making, just that it existed. I knew I was on to something, and this led to my second attempt at writing.

The Second Attempt to Write: History as Context

Another great influence at Northwestern was my advisor Mary Pattillo and her book *Black Picket Fences* (1999). The book used ethnographic material to take on a public problem: the question of why middle-class Black Americans were behind middle-class white Americans on many social, educational, and economic indicators. The topic was of concern to many because public explanations often drew on racist characterizations of Black culture. The book's answer to this question was twofold. First, a historical explanation was offered of Black home inheritance, coupled with socioeconomic change. The homes that had been bought by older World War II and Baby Boomer generations were being passed down to newer generations of Black Americans who were cut out from educational opportunities that would make them competitive in a changing economy. This meant that many middle-class Black neighborhoods were filled with homeowners who could not afford upkeep of their homes, investment in local institutions, and other quality of life issues. Second, Pattillo's ethnographic fieldwork offered another explanation: compared to white middle-class Americans, middle-class Black Americans have denser ties to economically insecure persons and subpar institutional supports. The first explanation served as contextual background for the second, a theory gleaned from interpreting poignant scenes, oral histories, and interactions among her research subjects.

Taking a cue from this kind of ethnographic writing, I set out to place my two ethnographies into historical context. I drew on the history of mass imprisonment in the United States (Western and Pettit 2010), the rise of policing in urban poor communities (Alexander 2010), and rising crime-control logic in public life (Simon 2007) to understand my observations in the ER. I attributed the differences between the ethnographies of the 1970s (in which bias was more race and class based) to my own (in which the bias was primally criminal stigma), to the changing historical context. I did the same with my jail ethnography. I compared the welfare bias I had documented inside of jails to the "carceralized aid" that Comfort (2007) identified and linked to the rise of mass imprisonment and the decline of public welfare outside of jail. These two efforts to connect my observations to historical context resulted in two publications (Lara-Millán 2014; Lara-Millán and Van Cleve 2017).

I would soon come to realize that this use of history in ethnography was amenable to a particular kind of external validity claim, what I call the "history as context" paradigm. The idea is probably best summarized by Small (2009), in which the ethnographer uses history to show how her field site is a situation in which larger social forces are experienced in the extreme. In this way, the ethnographer is using the history to make a claim about external relevance by saying she has selected a "pointy" case, in which broader trends are keenly visible in the field site. Other contexts in which these broader trends are experienced, even those where they are experienced with less fervor, can be expected to produce some version of the findings documented in extreme case. Key is that it is primarily those empirical findings (field notes) that are used to generate the theories—that is, history is used to set the stage for external relevance of a theory gleaned from field notes.

The Third Attempt to Write: The Extended Case Method

I felt dissatisfied with this use of history. Could I claim that other hospitals used police in the same way? Could I claim that all the jails in the United States used welfare stigma to deny medical care? Using Small's (2009) logic of external validity meant that I was implying my case was an example of a wider distribution of cases. The problem is that this use of history as context delinks historical change from the explanatory theory. The history is reduced to a feature of appropriate "casing," while the explanation is still drawn solely from the poignant ethnographic scenes. I was still creating a theory of criminal stigma and welfare stigma based on what I had observed, but using history to set the stage and make an external validity claim.

Because I had adopted this framework, I felt my work was being misread. I was not trying to prove that all hospitals and jails employed these specific practices (an empirical external validity claim), but instead that they were all trying to align the demand for services with the limited resources available to them. This was a fundamental problem that could be dealt with in many different ways. For instance, if a hospital stopped its practices of using police to scare patients away, it would have to figure out some other way to cull demand because of limited services. This was a theoretical external validity claim.

But how did I know this? In part, because of archival evidence I had begun collecting about Los Angeles County. Entering the archives started as a backup project of sorts.

There were times when I became nervous about gaining access to a hospital and jail and I began looking into the history of Los Angeles' parallel institutions. To my surprise, the county ran the two largest jail and hospital systems in the nation. They were enormous, long-standing, and periodically beset with controversy.

I always knew that my inability to name the institutions I was studying could make it difficult to draw on archives of a specific locality. This was, of course, going to be a trade-off. As others have suggested, it is preferable to be able to name the organizations we study, and we might be surprised by how many organizations are willing to be named (Jerolmack and Murphy 2017). The positives of *not* naming the institutions were largely pragmatic; I offered institutional anonymity quite early in an attempt to solicit access. I relied on the fact that the institutional characteristics I sought to study were so widespread to protect this anonymity.[1] In Southern California alone, there are four different high-population urban counties with overcrowded jails and hospitals (Riverside County, San Bernardino County, Los Angeles County, and Orange County). As mentioned earlier, there were 35 county jails in California in 2012 that, due to inmate overcrowding, were under court-ordered population caps and, as a result, released inmates early. Likewise, severe hospital overcrowding is typical of large public hospitals that have over 500 beds and are located in major metropolitan areas that are populated with over 2.5 million persons. For instance, the flagship public ERs of Los Angeles, Chicago, and New York City have average wait times that fluctuate between 9 and 12 hours. The negatives of this anonymity are, of course, that the sites of my ethnographies are very different from the case I examined in the archives. In my analysis, I tried to mitigate this fact by isolating the processes that the cases had in common; that is, examining specific operations that I saw as important in fieldwork and seeking them out in the archival record of Los Angeles County.

As I began searching for ways to study the county's history, I was amazed to learn that Los Angeles County maintained no official repositories of public files! This was surprising; one would think that more recent history would be widely available compared to histories from centuries past. I kept looking and came to learn that several long-running political leaders of the county had, upon retirement, donated their papers to several research libraries. I was lucky in that these political leaders had careers that spanned multiple decades, and their papers actually covered the entire period from 1978 until 2008. The county itself maintains an online collection that covers the period after 2001 to the present. If anyone is curious, there are donated papers on the county's governance going back to the early 1900s.[2]

The documents in these archives were a treasure trove. They included office memos between the County Board of Supervisors and their advisory staff, communiqués between supervisors and department heads, research reports and studies used to inform policy, meeting minutes, relevant newspaper clippings, press releases, and video recordings of news reports and interviews of county officials. In the period before 2001, the most important set of documents were memos between the supervisors and their advisory staff. Each supervisor has aides charged with coordinating policy with each department. These contain a level of candor not readily found elsewhere, as they were ostensibly private communiqués before their donation. For the period after 2001, the transcripts of the weekly Board of Supervisors (BOS) meetings were most productive. These were meetings between the BOS and relevant officials, during which the members debated and voted on policy. For this research, I examined all transcripts concerning discussions of hospitals, jails, probation, and mental health/substance abuse services, and county budget debates. My knowledge of the meetings was buttressed by research reports and memos that were circulated among officials before each meeting. I used these documents to reference purported facts that were discussed during the meetings.

On the other hand, the process of using the archives was difficult in ways that anyone using archives will recognize. First, what appear to be bounded objects of analysis can quickly proliferate into an unmanageable mess, and it is difficult for the researcher to know what is relevant to the study. When researching the problem of jail overcrowding, for instance, a researcher likely will not have the benefit of discovering a series of boxes neatly labeled "jail overcrowding." One must be able to discern what materials are relevant to the analysis of the social problem of jail overcrowding. Second, many individual documents seem as if they may contain one small part of the key to the puzzle, while simultaneously appearing so trivial that they might not be worth paying attention to. It is rare to find a smoking gun–style document that indisputably reveals the truth. Instead, each document may push the researcher forward in a small way, and collectively they can add up to something greater than their parts. Third, when faced with a large body of documents containing various acts, behaviors, value statements, etc., distinguishing between what actors claim and what they actually believe can become difficult.

I did not know it at the time, but my first attempts to wade through these materials were those of a neophyte. I simply read every single relevant document and took notes on them. This was all adding up to something in my head. I wrote memos about what I was seeing, but I did not yet know how or in what way the documents would become important to me.

At this early juncture, the way the archives affected me was by changing my understanding of what I was viewing in the field. In my reading of the archives, I was beginning to get the sense that the county was not primarily interested in punishing poor people, but rather, in raising revenue, cutting costs, and not being sued by various entities. For instance, as I was beginning to become more interested in the hospital-based police force I was observing, I was able to find files on the creation of such a police force in Los Angeles. While it was clear that politicians created the force in reaction to a violent shooting in the ER, as we saw in Chapter 4, they also chose this action over the option of using trailers to expand waiting room capacity. What was interesting was that they decided against the trailers because they feared litigation from healthcare regulators concerned with patient safety. While I did not know how that piece of information fit into the wider story, it did affect how I viewed and took notes on the officers I was observing. I wanted to know not just how they were intimidating patients, but how their actions interacted with patient safety rules and the issue of hospital overcrowding. I began taking notes on these pragmatic, organizational issues in addition to my notes on social control. This opened up a whole new way of seeing in the field.

Circling back to my conundrum that opened this section, my findings in the archives gave me a "hunch" that what was generalizable about my study was not the particular social control methods I was observing, but the organizational need to resolve the demand for services with limited resources. This was something I was seeing in the history of Los Angeles County, as well as in the day-to-day operations of the jail and the hospital where I was doing my observations. I had a sense that these were abstract conditions—the need to resolve demand with resources—that produced solutions that probably could manifest in various ways (e.g., pharmaceuticals in ERs and jails, police in ERs, welfare stigma in jails). Other jails and hospitals may have chosen different solutions to resolve that same tension.

When I entered the academic job market in 2013, I wrote and presented my study as one about what I was calling "the overwhelmed state." My study had evolved from thinking about history as context—the context of mass incarceration—to seeing connections between my archival history of Los Angeles County and the ethnography I had conducted. At this early juncture, that connection was only a parallel: politicians were in the business of resolving demand with resources, and so were frontline workers.

I did not know quite what to make of these connections when I interviewed for a position in the Sociology Department at UC Berkeley. Little did I know that I was about to encounter a third camp in the ethnographic tradition. On my last day at the campus, I popped into a bookstore and bought Burawoy's (2009) book on the *Extended Case Method*. The book recounted his studies that homed in on how to use ethnography to study historical transformation. The purpose of engaging history in this model was not to simply establish casing parameters for *empirical* external relevance, as with the "history as context" model, but instead to use field notes to make externally relevant *theoretical* claims. In many of his examples, scholars used their field notes to say something about the way theories worked. His writing empowered me to use my case to make claims about the way that states governed; I extended out, writing about how we could view state activity as a "series of people exchanges" (Lara-Millán 2017).

Interlude I: The Confusion of Penal Fields

My next step was to read current studies in the urban poverty governance and prepare a book proposal to circulate to publishers. Just as I had been doing, these ethnographies documented changes in police departments, courthouses, probation or parole settings, prisons, mandated drug rehab programs, schools, welfare offices, and many other settings, and were inspired by Wacquant (2009).

As I learned more about the way the Extended Case Method was being used in my subfield, I began to see some problems. The studies were making use of the broad history of mass incarceration to explain the things they had found; that is, because we know that the incarceration system has increased sevenfold in the past 40 years, it is likely that criminal justice actors use health and welfare systems to expand their reach.

The problem with this story is that it confuses the present-day function of a phenomenon with its historical cause. Scholars were using field notes to see that the wards of the state were being socially controlled in new ways, but were imputing social control as the *cause* of transformation in governance settings. For instance, one might find that nurses are administering heavy pharmaceuticals to inmates in a jail (turning them into near zombies), and that this serves the purpose of controlling and degrading those inmates. But was social control the motivating cause of the turn toward medicine?

The reason this was possible for this scholarship is that researchers were drawing on the broad history of mass imprisonment and used their field data to connect to this broad history. Field notes were interpreted with theory—most often an extension of Foucault's biopower or Bourdieu's symbolic violence—and this was linked to the American state's growing carceral capacity, established from secondary sources. How did we know that mass imprisonment was really shaping the new forms of social control we were discovering in our field data?

The problem for me was that I had still been influenced by those early lessons that Katz (2002) had imparted to me so many years before: your theory has to come from your data.

It was difficult for me to square the idea of using broad history from secondary sources as a good way to explain the transformations I was seeing in my field notes. But I still wanted to "extend" out from my field site to make externally relevant claims.

I knew I needed to use my history better. The first place I turned was an emerging style of research among socio-legal scholars such as Mona Lynch, Heather Schoenfeld, Michael Campbell, Joshua Page, Phillip Goodman, Michelle Phelps, Vanessa Barker, and Kelly Hannah-Moffat. These scholars all take on the very complex problem of explaining variation in the size and scope of mass incarceration. They try to explain the historical origins of differences in prison sizes and prison form, or police or prosecutorial tactics. The core tenet of their program is attending to the dynamic interaction between national, state, and local politics to explain that variation. In short, as Heather Schoenfeld writes, "a socio-political perspective on punishment is attuned to the way that macro-conditions in the social and political environment shape political behavior at the various levels of governance, which in turns shapes the ideologies, actors, and politics that produce and impose the 'penal order.'"[3]

While these insights were incredibly useful, I was now even more confused. Because these histories focused on the fragmented nature of policymaking, new penal forms are often reduced to mere "unintended consequences." The development of new "penal orders" get reduced to the outcome of a multitude of actors struggling in a "field," an outcome which none of the parties could have predicted beforehand. As Goodman, Page, and Phelps (2015) write, "This contestation means that programmatic reforms are never fully implemented as intended; instead they 'braid' various, often contradictory penal rationalities. This constant contestation produces 'messiness' on the ground, which paves the road for the next penal turn."[4]

What to make of this? If the historical studies in this field were filled with unintended consequences, how could these then be used to explain what was going on in our ethnographies of governance institutions? How can we have such a systematic order—the continued and expansive social control of the urban poor—while the causes of that order appear to be so varied, piecemeal, and unintended? Again, it seemed as if the historical causes were delinked from the theories that ethnographers developed to interpret their field notes; they bracketed off the question of unintended consequences in order to proffer a theory of social control.

Interlude II: Reconstructing the Archive

In his writings on the Extended Case Method, Burawoy (2003, 2009) included two pieces of work that gave me a path forward: Haney's (2002) and Vaughan's (1996) "historical ethnographies." He had grouped them under the category of "archeological revisits," in which the scholar went on an ethnographic journey into the past, using archives. This was set alongside other ways ethnographers used history (e.g., history as context, comparing one's field site to an earlier ethnography). Something about that felt off.

I met Haney early on in my graduate career and she always pushed me to dig deeper with my use of history. Her work connected an ethnography of the social effects of welfare cutbacks after Hungary's post-socialist transition to changes that had occurred historically, under the socialist regime. She did this by studying a welfare office's case files, showing that the changes that had occurred under the socialist regime shaped how the office was confronting post-socialism. Here she was generating a theory that linked the historical causes with an interpretive theory of her field notes.

Inspired by this, I returned to the archives. I was fortunate enough to have a postdoc that provided the time and resources to be able to do so. This time around I did two things Vaughan (2004) outlined as critical to her historical ethnography of the *Challenger* disaster. First, I reconstructed a timeline of events from disparate archival sources into a chronological order. Like I did, Vaughan (2004) had access to thousands of documents, interviews, and reports that all, in some small way, gave meaning to each event. But the sources gave meaning to events in different order, magnitudes, and from different vantage points. Actors had their own version of what they thought was going on at the time that it happened, and therefore it is only the historical sociologist that can triangulate and reconstruct that situated chronology. In doing so, we can reconstruct the interactional space in which those historical actors were embedded so that we can truly understand why and how they made the decisions that led to the relevant outcomes.

Second, creating this chronology allowed Vaughan and myself to be reflexive; juxtaposing our own a priori explanations, the explanations that actors in the various sources held, and the explanation that arose from the reconstructed chronology. Vaughan had begun with her own explanation that resource scarcity had caused NASA engineers to tolerate cutting corners. This conflicted with the state's explanation that engineers were deviant and willfully ignored their own safety checking rules. The reconstructed chronology offered another theory: it was conformity to a culture of risk toleration and compartmentalizing information about that risk that produced the disaster. When Vaughan presented her finished theory to the engineers, they were aghast to learn how each department had different understandings of events and that their organizational structure had encouraged them to send weak signals to one another about those viewpoints.

In reconstructing the chronology for my case, I discovered that there were three periods of crisis (i.e., 1992–1997, 2004–2007, and 2009–2011). I organized the historical data according to the specific problems that the actors saw during each crisis, as well as what allowed them to absolve themselves of those problems. Specifically, I was interested in the context of each crisis: the kinds of evidence and rhetoric the actors used, the administrative solutions they drew upon, and why they chose the routes they did. Finally, I compared these three periods to look for similarities and differences in order to produce my analysis.

Most importantly, these crisis moments reflect what Ermakoff (2015, 67) calls "moments of collective indetermination." These are moments when actors are collectively at a loss for knowing what to do next. For Ermakoff, there is a distinction between causally meaningful "positive contingency" and moments of pure chance: under positive contingency, "individual agency" can have "big effects," and a small number of people can create conditions that affect a large number of people. Ermakoff also places emphasis on the emotion of the moment: in uncertain situations, actors tend to "search for behavioral cues from peers" and maintain a "wait-and-see attitude" while seeking to "align with a collective stance." The goal of the sociologist in the archive is to focus on the documents that capture positive contingency—an account of how a group made their way out of mutual uncertainty through interactions with each other, creating conditions that had implications going far beyond the group's boundaries.[5]

Documents that contain "expressions of ambivalence and surprise at one's own action provide post factum clues" to understanding positive contingency and their implications for a historical outcome (Ermakoff 2015, 67). This can help us wade through actor's misrepresentations, clarify actual plausible alternative paths, and understand how actors learn from their own mistakes. In short, this kind of data allows for inductive theorizing from archival evidence (Lara-Millán, Sargent, and Sunmin 2020).

Identifying such moments of positive contingency allowed me to juxtapose the literature's explanation (mass imprisonment) with my working explanation (an overwhelmed state) with the chronology's explanation: that public officials are in the business of publicly resolving crises. Periodically, these crises would threaten the legitimacy of local government. Officials moved from one crisis to the next, drawing in funds, trading in caseloads, and selectively abdicating responsibility. Their actions could not be simplified as the result of either being overwhelmed or looking to punish the urban poor; instead they were working to reconstitute dying institutions.

The Final Writing: Historically Embedded Ethnography

In order to figure out how to write up this new analysis, I returned to another influence of mine at Northwestern: my second chair Ann Shola Orloff's *Remaking Modernity* (Adams, Clemens, and Orloff 2005). The book described a great transformation occurring in the field of historical sociology. Like ethnographers, historical sociologists have had a long debate about the utility of their research for generalizable knowledge. Initially, Mill's method of similarity and difference—e.g., looking for causal factors that explain divergent outcomes among similar cases—was thought to be a main method for producing knowledge that could be transported out of specific contexts (Skocpol and Somers 1980). Although this way of constructing external validity claims justified the existence of historical sociology within the discipline of sociology, such claims were shown to inappropriately impose deterministic causality on the analysis of social phenomena (Lieberson 1991). Namely, such accounts presuppose that the social world is made up of fixed entities whose causal forces do not change with context and, like machines, will always affect outcomes in the same way (Abbott 1988).

Seeking to retain what was useful about historical sociology—that it produced useful accounts of social phenomena—without the unjustifiable claims to deterministic causality, historical sociologists turned to within-case analysis (Clemens 2007). Hirshman and Reed (2014) nicely describe what makes this kind of research so distinctive. They note that previous incarnations of historical sociology essentially studied the way that discrete entities—be they actors, groups, or ideas—exert causal force on other discrete entities. Historicized sociology, in contrast, does not take for granted the discreetness of such entities and instead investigates their "emergence." As they write, "How do all the objects and entities that cause things to happen in the social world come to be what they are, with certain meanings, 'causal powers,' and so on? That is, how do the forces in the social world come to possess a certain form or shape that makes them what they are?" (Hirschman and Reed 2014, 265).

Pacewicz (2020) recently explained how such accounts of historical emergence can help ethnographers clarify the kinds of external validity claims they are making. Essentially, both are often making what he calls "constitutive claims." These are external validity claims that straddle a gray area between historical causation and descriptions of a phenomenon's characteristics. In simple terms, these are claims that "x is a thing with the following properties" (Pacewicz 2020, 9). This logic is helpful for ethnographers because it helps to clarify for audiences the utility of our external validity claims that are neither fully historically causal nor descriptive. Constitutive arguments work to "improve others' intuitions about the phenomenon, including but not exclusively others' causal intuitions about appropriate casing, relevance criteria, and the range of plausible mechanistic accounts" (Pacewicz 2020, 9). I encourage ethnographers to consider using this logic.

It was not until the most recent iteration of this book—some eight years after I left the field—that I realized how this framework clarified what I did and helped me to write my final version of the manuscript. In essence, I argued that the phenomenon of increased medical capacity in jails and its decline in hospitals is actually characterized by crisis abatement between law and austerity; therefore, the transformation of urban poverty governance is a case of welfare state resiliency. This is a constitutive argument that straddles both historical causation about the phenomenon's formation and the functional purpose the phenomenon has taken on.

I want to take this one step further. While Pacewicz (2020) offers an important lesson for ethnographers and the kinds of external validity claims they can make, what if we paired ethnography with archival research? Historically embedded ethnography means to empirically trace what we find in our ethnographic observations to chronological histories we reconstruct from archives and theorize inductively from the relationship between historical cause and functional purpose. The main benefit of this method is that it does not allow us to sit with the gray area between historical causality and the description of the phenomenon's characteristics. Instead, it asks the researcher to disentangle them and show their relationship. As Garland (2014) notes, the characteristics that phenomena acquire may be different than the social forces that brought them into being in the first place.

Linking Ethnographic Observation to Reconstructed History

Recall that a major problem with the use of history in the "extended case method" (Burawoy 2003, 2009)—or rather how it is often employed—is that claims are made based on broad theory, not data. In my view, this is what leads to accusations that ethnographers are being "too theoretical." With historically embedded ethnography, we can use the archive to track down the origins of the specific developments we find in field observation. In both parts of this book, three developments were found through observation. While the actors in our field sites have agency to choose between options, something in history has limited their range of choices. These "lines of opportunity" are choices inherited from the past, structured by decisions made years before. In the historical chapters of this book, we see the origins of these observations in three successive crisis periods. By comparing the similarities and differences between crisis periods in the reconstructed history, we can see that austerity and law were pushing redistribution, which then resulted in these developments. Using the archive to track down specific developments can start us on the path to connecting social control (visible through careful ethnographic observation) to haphazard policymaking (visible in detailed history).

Theorizing from the Tracing

Recall that a problem with "history as context" was that history was often bracketed as a causal force, but theory was generated primarily from ethnographic scenes. This often leads to the accusation of "under-theorization" in ethnography. With historically embedded ethnography, we generate our theory from the way that historical formation relates to the present-day practices we are theorizing. We do not bracket history from our interpretation of the actors in our field notes. For instance, I saw that pharmaceuticalization in the hospital and the jail were linked historically to progressive legal concerns for inmates and patients, and this helped me to understand how this form of social control was a kind of crisis abatement. By doing this tracing, I could speak about wider topics (states, austerity, law) without violating that lesson I learned from Jack Katz so long ago: to stick to my data.

I want to close by drawing our attention to Bruno Latour, a great ethnographer and philosopher who is not often brought into conversations about urban poverty governance. He was very concerned by sociology's acceptance of the idea that there are social forces in the world that are beyond the action of any set of actors. Speaking of Los Angeles, he said "You notice individuals . . . walking or working in downtown Los Angeles; then you look at the huge skyscrapers that tower above them; and then it seems reasonable to say that 'the whole is superior to the parts,' or that there emerge out of individual interactions many things that the individual had not anticipated."[6]

While Latour admits that a building in Los Angeles shapes the social life of the individuals who currently occupy that building, his point is that it was lazy to say that the force that the building exudes cannot be linked to the action of coordinating individuals. Taking his que from Gabriel Tard (in contrast to Durkheim), Latour explained that we just need better data on the people who created the building and how they were linked to the people who currently occupy that building. "You are going to tell me that this kind of information on the building of downtown Los Angeles that I took as my example is totally inaccessible so that my thought experiment is just that, a thought, not an experiment. Maybe, but it is not the same thing to say that because of a lack of information we speak *as if* there was a whole superior to the parts."[7]

Notes

Preface

1. Molly Hennessy-Fiske, "Even Death Is Unaffordable," *Los Angeles Times*, July 21, 2009: https://www.latimes.com/archives/la-xpm-2009-jul-21-me-unclaimed21-story. html. A more recent version can be found in: Stefan Timmermans and Pamela Prickett, "Today Is L.A. County's Crucial Annual Memorial for the Living and the Dead," *Los Angeles Times*, December 5, 2018: https://www.latimes.com/opinion/op-ed/la-oe-timmermansandprickett-county-burials-20181205-story.html.

2. Jada Yuan, "Burials on Hart Island, Where New York's Unclaimed Lie in Mass Graves, Have Risen Fivefold," *Washington Post*, April 16, 2020: https://www.washingtonpost. com/national/hart-island-mass-graves-coronavirus-new-york/2020/04/16/a0c413ee-7f5f-11ea-a3ee-13e1ae0a3571_story.html

3. Cary Aspinwall, Keri Blakinger, Abbie Vansickle, and Christie Thompson, "Coronavirus Transforming Jails across the County," *The Marshall Project*, March 21, 2020: https://www.themarshallproject.org/2020/03/21/coronavirus-transforming-jails-across-the-country; Alene Tchekmedyian, Paige St. John, and Matt Hamilton, "L.A. County Releasing Some Inmates from Jail to Combat Coronavirus," *Los Angeles Times*, March 16, 2020: https://www.latimes.com/california/story/2020-03-16/la-jail-population-arrests-down-amid-coronavirus.

4. Eric Reinhart and Daniel Chen, "Incarceration and Its Disseminations: COVID-19 Pandemic Lessons from Chicago's Cook County Jail," *Health Affairs* 39, no. 8 (2020): https://www.healthaffairs.org/doi/10.1377/hlthaff.2020.00652; Mallory Moench, "San Quentin's Coronavirus Outbreak Strains Marin, Bay Area Hospitals," *San Francisco Chronicle*, July 7, 2000: https://www.sfchronicle.com/health/article/San-Quentin-s-coronavirus-outbreak-strains-Bay-15392385.php; Alex Wigglesworth, Rong-Gong Lin II, Sean Greene, Luke Money, and Phil Willon, "Coronavirus Packs San Bernardino Hospitals," *Los Angeles Times*, June 26, 2020: https://www.latimes.com/california/story/2020-06-26/california-coronavirus-cases-surpass-200-000-as-hospitalizations-mount. On the communities' embodied connection to jail exiting, see: Nicole Gonzalez Van Cleve, *The Waiting Room*, New York: The Marshall Project (2018).

5. As a new Black Lives Matter uprising has pushed the defunding of police onto the public agenda, it will only be a matter of time before carceral agencies return to framing the arrested not as sick COVID patients, but instead as criminals, "looters," and other human kinds in need of jailing.

Introduction

1. Quote from: Tina Daunt, "Ill Inmates Transferred to Twin Towers; Jails: Sheriff's Department, Under Fire from U.S. Officials, Seeks to Improve Care," *Los Angeles Times*, January 11, 1998: https://www.latimes.com/archives/la-xpm-1998-jan-11-me-7315-story.html. See also: Tina Daunt, "Jail's Medical Ward to Move to Twin Towers," *Los Angeles Times*, January 1, 1998: https://www.latimes.com/archives/la-xpm-1998-jan-01-mn-4033-story.html.

2. See: Jeffrey Rabin and Sharon Bernstein, "Supervisors Agree on Downsized Hospital," *Los Angeles Times*, November 13, 1997: https://www.latimes.com/archives/la-xpm-1997-nov-13-me-53345-story.html.

3. On the difficulty of mental health statistics in jails, see: Michael Rembis, "The New Asylums: Madness and Mass Incarceration in the Neoliberal Era," in *Disability Incarcerated: Imprisonment and Disability in the United States and Canada*, edited by Liat Ben-Moshe, Chris Chapman, and Allison C. Carey (New York: Palgrave Macmillan, 2014): pp. 139–159. Most accounts of the topic use the same Department of Justice reports produced in 1999 and 2006. The 2006 study reported that 64% of jail inmates suffer from mental illness, while the 1999 survey—which was based on inmate self-reports—reported that 16% of jail inmates suffered some "serious mental illness." Other figures frequently cited are a 152% increase in the number of persons suffering from mental illness in jails from 1980 to 1992, and a 2011 study stating that 14% of men and 20% of women in jail had experience with "serious psychological distress" in the month before the survey. See: Doris J. James and Lauren E. Glaze, "Mental Health Problems of Prison and Jail Inmates" (Bureau of Justice, 2006); Jennifer Bronson and Marcus Berzofsky, "Indicators of Mental Health Problems Reported by Prisoners and Jail Inmates, 2011–12" (*Bureau of Justice*, 2017): E. Fuller Torrey et al. "The Treatment of Persons with Mental Illness in Prisons and Jails: A State Survey" (Treatment Advocacy Center, 2014). The resources on this topic are endless; three important ones are: Ram Subramanian, Ruth Delaney, Stephen Roberts, and Nancy Fishman, *Incarceration's Front Door: The Misuse of Jail in America* (New York: Vera Institute of Justice, 2015); Risdon N. Slate, Jacqueline K. Buffington-Vollum, and W. Wesley Johnson, *The Criminalization of Mental Illness: Crisis and Opportunity for the Justice System*, 2nd ed. (Durham: Carolina Academic Press, 2013); Patricia Erickson and Steven Erickson, *Crime, Punishment, and Mental Illness: Law and the Behavioral Sciences in Conflict* (New Brunswick, NJ: Rutgers University Press, 2008).

4. Between 1996 and 2006, annual ER visits in the United States increased from 90.3 million to 119.3 million (32%), while the number of ERs dropped by 12%, resulting in a 78% increase in visits per ER between 1995 and 2003. Gary L. Albrecht, David Slobodkin, and Robert J. Rydman, "The Role of Emergency Departments in American Health Care," in *Research in the Sociology of Health Care*, edited by J. J. Kronefield (Greenwich, CT: JAI Press, 1996), pp. 289–318; Andrew Wilper et al., "Waits to See an Emergency Department Physician: U.S. Trends and Predictors, 1997–2004," *Health Affairs* 27 no. 2 (2008): pp. 84–95; Blair D. Gifford, Larry M. Manheim, and Diane

Cowper, "Unforeseen Policy Effects on the Safety Net: Medicaid, Private Hospital Closures and the Use of Local VAMCs," in *Social Inequalities, Health, and Health Care Delivery*, edited by Jacobs Kronenfeld (Bingley: Emerald Group, 2002); Gloria J. Bazzoli et al., "An Update on Safety-Net Hospitals: Coping with the Late 1990s and Early 2000s," *Health Affairs* 24, no. 4 (2005): pp. 1047–56; Marion Lewin and Stuart Altman, *America's Health Care Safety Net: Intact but Endangered* (Washington, DC: National Academies Press, 2000); James Gordon, "The Hospital Emergency Department as a Social Welfare Institution," *Annals of Emergency Medicine* 33, no. 3 (1999): pp. 321–25; Ruth Malone, "Whither the Almshouse? Overutilization and the Role of the Emergency Department," *Journal of Health Politics, Policy and Law* 23, no. 5 (1998): pp. 795–832; Jack Needleman and Michelle Ko, "The Declining Public Hospital Sector," in *The Health Care "Safety Net" in a Post-Reform World*, edited by Mark A. Hall and Sara Rosenbaum (New Brunswick, NJ: Rutgers University Press, 2012); Dennis P. Andrulis and Lisa M. Duchon, "The Changing Landscape of Hospital Capacity in Large Cities and Suburbs: Implications for the Safety Net in Metropolitan America," *Journal of Urban Health* 84, no. 3 (2007): pp. 400–14.

5. Angela Davis, "Foreword," in *Disability Incarcerated: Imprisonment and Disability in the United States and Canada*, edited by Liat Ben-Moshe, Chris Chapman, and Allison C. Carey (New York: Palgrave Macmillan, 2014), vii.

6. Lesley Stahl, "Half of the Inmates Shouldn't Be Here, Says Cook County Sheriff," *CBS News*, May 21, 2017.

7. The historical narrative starts the same in each time. In the 1950s and 1960s, reformers pushed the government to release the mentally ill from state hospitals that were exposed as inhumane and ineffective. The 1963 Community Mental Health Care Act was meant to create community health centers that would replace those asylums and place the mentally ill closer to their communities—without burdening families—where they would receive the support they truly needed. See: Michael Dear and Jennifer R. Wolch, *Landscapes of Despair: From Deinstitutionalization to Homelessness* (Princeton, NJ: Princeton University Press, 1987); E. Fuller Torrey, *The Insanity Offense: How America's Failure to Treat the Seriously Mentally Ill Endangers Its Citizens* (New York: W. W. Norton); Sherry A. Glied and Richard G. Frank, "Better but Not Best: Recent Trends in the Well-Being of the Mentally Ill," *Health Affairs* 28, no. 3 (2009): pp. 637–48; Rembis, "The New Asylums: Madness and Mass Incarceration in the Neoliberal Era"; Slate et al., *The Criminalization of Mental Illness*; Subramanian et al., *Incarceration's Front Door: The Misuse of Jail in America*; Bernard E. Harcourt, "From the Asylum to the Prison: Rethinking the Incarceration Revolution," *Texas Law Review* 84, no. 7 (2006): pp. 1751–86; Fred Markowitz, "Psychiatric Hospital Capacity, Homelessness, and Crime and Arrest Rates." *Criminology* 44, no. 1 (2006): pp. 45–72; Timothy Williams, "Troubled Inmates, and a Psychologist as Warden," *New York Times*, July 30, 2015: https://www.nytimes.com/2015/07/31/us/a-psychologist-as-warden-jail-and-mental-illness-intersect-in-chicago.html; Alisa Roth, *Insane: America's Criminal Treatment of Mental Illness* (New York: Basic Books, 2018); Steve Coll, "The Jail-Health Crisis," *The New Yorker*, February 25, 2019: https://www.newyorker.com/magazine/2019/03/04/the-jail-health-care-crisis.

8. It is important to note that these increases only characterize the largest jails in the biggest MSAs; the situation in rural jails, which have much less resources, continues to be a story of healthcare deficit. The D.C. figure does not include corrections officers sent to guard inmates who receive treatment at local hospitals (as a reference point, the California reported that such costs for one inmate can exceed $2,000 per day). Anecdotal figures from: Kil Huh Alexander Boucher, Frances McGaffey, Matt Mckillop, and Maria Schiff, "Jails: Inadvertent Healthcare Providers: How County Correctional Facilities Are Playing a Role in the Safety Net" (Pew Charitable Trusts, 2018); Phil Schaenman, Elizabeth Davies, Reed Jordan, and Reena Chakraborty, "Opportunities for Cost Savings in Corrections Without Sacrificing Quality: Inmate Healthcare" (Urban Institute, 2013); Cook County Adopted Budget (2016), https:// opendocs.cookcountyil.gov/budget/archive/16-Volume-I-Adopted-Budget.pdf; New York City Independent Budget Office, "New York City by the Numbers" (2020), https://ibo.nyc.ny.us/cgi-park2/2020/09/why-has-the-cost-of-correctional-health-services-increased-in-the-last-decade/; On the incredible rise of expensive psychotropic drugs in US prisons and jails, see: Anthony Hatch, *Silent Cells: The Secret Drugging of Captive America* (Minneapolis: University of Minnesota Press, 2019). Statistics on healthcare costs in state prisons are much more widely available: Kil Huh, Alexander Boucher, Frances McGaffey, Matt Mckillop, and Maria Schiff, "Prison Health Care: Costs and Quality: How and Why States Strive for High-Preforming Systems" (Pew Charitable Trusts, 2017); Benjamin C. Tankersley, "State Spending on Prison Healthcare is Exploding," *Washington Post*, October 30, 2013: https://www.washingtonpost.com/blogs/govbeat/wp/2013/10/30/state-spending-on-prison-health-care-is-exploding-heres-why/); Data on healthcare staffing was taken from the Bureau of Justice Statistic's National Jail Census. The reported figures include "professional and technical" staffing in the largest jail systems and/or jail systems with over 1,500 inmates (in 1988) within the top 50 MSAs (there are multiple county jail systems within each MSA). United States Department of Justice. Office of Justice Programs. Bureau of Justice Statistics. National Jail Census, 1999. Inter-university Consortium for Political and Social Research [distributor], 2009-07-09. https://doi.org/10.3886/ICPSR03318.v3; United States Department of Justice. Office of Justice Programs. Bureau of Justice Statistics. National Jail Census, 1988. [distributor], 2005-11-04. https://doi.org/10.3886/ICPSR09256.v2.

9. See: Khalil Gibran Muhammad, *The Condemnation of Blackness* (Cambridge, MA: Harvard University Press, 2011); Jonathan Simon, *Governing through Crime: How the War on Crime Transformed American Democracy and Created a Culture of Fear* (New York: Oxford University Press, 2007); David Garland, *Mass Imprisonment: Social Causes and Consequences* (New York: Russel Sage, 2001). On public schools, see: Carla Shedd, *Unequal City: Race, Schools, and Perceptions of Injustice* (New York: Russell Sage, 2015); Aaron Kupchik, *Homeroom Security: School Discipline in an Age of Fear* (New York: New York University Press, 2010); Victor Rios, *Punished: Policing the Lives of Black and Latino Boys* (New York: New York University Press, 2011); Pedro A. Noguera, "The Trouble with Black Boys: The Role and Influence of Environmental and Cultural Factors on the Academic Performance

of African American Males," *Urban Education* 38, no. 4 (2003): pp. 431–59; David M. Ramey, "The Social Structure of Criminalized and Medicalized School Discipline," *Sociology of Education* 88, no. 3 (2015): pp. 181–201. On welfare offices, see: Kaaryn S. Gustafson, *Cheating Welfare: Public Assistance and the Criminalization of Poverty* (New York: New York University Press, 2011); Joe Soss, Richard C. Fording, and Sanford F. Schram, *Disciplining the Poor: Neoliberal Paternalism and the Persistent Power of Race* (Chicago: University of Chicago Press, 2011). On criminalization in pharmacies, see: Elizabeth Chiarello, "The War on Drugs Comes to the Pharmacy Counter," *Law and Social Inquiry* 40 (2015): pp. 86–122. For Departments of Children and Family Services, see: Kelley Fong, "Concealment and Constraint: Child Protective Services Fears and Poor Mothers' Institutional Engagement," *Social Forces* 97, no. 4 (2019): pp. 1785–1810; Frank Edwards, "Saving Children, Controlling Families: Punishment, Redistribution, and Child Protection," *American Sociological Review* 81, no. 3 (2016): pp. 575–95.

10. I rely on: Frank Thompson, *Medicaid Politics: Federalism, Policy Durability, and Health Reform* (Washington, DC: Georgetown University Press, 2012); Shanna Rose, *Financing Medicaid: Federalism and the Growth of America's Health Care Safety Net* (Ann Arbor: University of Michigan Press, 2013). Rose places emphasis on the role of governors in Medicaid policy-feedback processes who defied partisan expectations in order to capture enormous federal funds. See also: Michael Gusmano, "Review of Financing Medicaid: Federalism and the Growth of America's Health Care Safety Net by Shanna Rose," *Perspectives on Politics* 13, no. 2 (2015): pp. 545–47.

11. On the political uses of the 1115 waivers see: Thompson, *Medicaid Politics: Federalism, Policy Durability, and Health Reform*; Frank Thompson and Courtney Burke, "Executive Federalism and Medicaid Demonstration Waivers: Implications for Policy and Democratic Process," *Journal of Health Politics, Policy, and Law* 32, no. 6 (2007): pp. 971–1004. During the Clinton years, Medicaid expenditures under the waivers grew by more than 470 percent, to $12.6 billion in 2000. Martin Kitchener, Terence Ng, Nancy Miller, and Charlene Harrington, "Medicaid Home and Community-Based Services: National Program Trends," *Health Affairs* 24, no. 1 (2005): pp. 206–12. While the story of DSH has been of overall decline since its inception in the early 1980s, the funds were shown to have been funneled, for political reasons, to high-priority hospitals even when they are not the most in need. Michael Gusmano and Frank Thompson, "The Safety Net at the Crossroads? Whither Medicaid DSH," in *The Health Care Safety-Net in a Post-Reform World*, edited by Mark A. Hall and Sara Rosenbaum (New Brunswick, NJ: Rutgers University Press, 2012): pp. 153–82; Teresa Coughlin and Stephen Zuckerman, "States' Strategies for Tapping Federal Revenues: Implications and Consequences of Medicaid Maximization," in *Federalism and Health Policy*, edited by John Holahan, Alan Weil, and Joshua Weiner (Washington, DC: Urban Institute Press 2003): pp. 1–34. On public hospitals dependence on these funds, see: Lynne Fagnani and Jennifer Tolbert, *The Dependence of Safety Net Hospitals and Health Systems on the Medicare and Medicaid Disproportionate Share Hospital Payment Programs*, Government Accountability Office, July 19, 2019. Overall, hospital inpatient services account for 14%, disproportionate hospital share

payments for 6%, and other acute care for 39% of all Medicaid spending, while 36% is for long-term care and 6% for drugs; Thompson, *Medicaid Politics: Federalism, Policy Durability, and Health Reform*, p. 68.

12. The factors spurring high incarceration rates are thought to include, deindustrialization, the breakdown of informal social controls, stricter sentencing, the criminalization of narcotics, and the enlargement of prison capacity and law enforcement budgets. See: Elizabeth Hinton, *From the War on Poverty to the War on Crime: The Making of Mass Incarceration in America* (Cambridge, MA: Harvard University Press, 2016); Ruth Gilmore, *Golden Gulag: Prisons, Surplus, Crisis and Opposition in Globalizing California* (Berkeley: University of California Press, 2007); Todd R. Clear, *Imprisoning Communities: How Mass Incarceration Makes Disadvantaged Communities Worse* (New York: Oxford University Press, 2007); Garland, *Mass Imprisonment: Social Causes and Consequences*; Malcom Feeley and Jonathan Simon, "The New Penology: Notes on the Emerging Strategy of Corrections and its Implications," *Criminology* 30, no. 4 (1992): pp. 449–74; on carceralized aid see: Megan Comfort, "Punishment beyond the Legal Offender," *Annual Review of Law and Social Science* 3 (2007): pp. 271–96; Megan Comfort, "When Prison Is a Refuge, America's Messed Up," *The Chronicle of Higher Education*, December 2, 2007: https://www.chronicle.com/article/when-prison-is-a-refuge-americas-messed-up/; Alexandra Natapoff, "Gideon's Servants and the Criminalization of Poverty," *Ohio State Journal of Criminal Law* 44 (2014): pp. 445–64. Researchers have documented "carceralized aid" in a variety of settings. Stuart (2016) found that police are increasingly used as gateways to local rehabilitative services, with police acting to route the homeless away from jail and into mandated treatment; Forrest Stuart, *Down, Out, and Under Arrest: Policing and Everyday Life in Skid Row* (Chicago: University of Chicago Press, 2016). Miller (2014) studied prisoner re-entry services and found that supposedly therapeutic spaces (such as churches and community centers) are increasingly linked to police surveillance; Reuben Miller, "Devolving the Carceral State: Race, Prisoner Reentry, and the Micro-Politics of Urban Poverty Management," *Punishment & Society* 16 no. 3 (2014): pp. 305–35. Kohler-Hausmann (2018) studied the lower courts of New York and found that rather than bargaining over sentence length, lawyers haggled over mandated rehabilitative programs. Programs like drug treatment or therapy were seen by courtroom actors as a way to implement some form of accountability; Kohler-Hausmann, *Misdemeanorland: Criminal Courts and Social Control in an Age of Broken Windows Policing* (Princeton, NJ: Princeton University Press). McKim (2017) studied such programs and found that treatment was increasingly conceptualized through criminal justice rubrics; Allison McKim, *Addicted to Rehab: Race, Gender, and Drugs in the Era of Mass Incarceration* (New Brunswick, NJ: Rutgers University Press, 2017). Perhaps the most poignant example is Schept's (2015) study of new "justice campuses," which aim to integrate welfare and criminal justice into single, one-stop locations for a continuum of state assistance and punishment; Judah Schept, *Progressive Punishment: Job Loss, Jail Growth, and the Neoliberal Logic of Carceral Expansion* (New York: New York University Press, 2015). As Haney (2010) has shown, when criminal justice institutions try to shape people with these tools,

wards are forced to interrogate their inner selves, police their feelings, and express new desires that conform to a vision of proper citizenship; Lynne Haney, *Offending Women: Power, Punishment, and the Regulation of Desire* (Berkeley: University of California Press, 2010).

13. See Joshua Page and Joe Soss, "Criminal Justice Predation and Neoliberal Governance," in *Rethinking Neoliberalism: Resisting the Disciplinary Regime*, edited by Sanford Schram and Marianna Pavlovskaya (New York: Routledge, 2017): pp. 139–59, for a criticism of penal studies' difficulty in grappling with ongoing state retrenchment. Some researchers see austerity as mainly part of a generalized "economic insecurity," stroking populist demands in the 1980s, which then pushed authorities to innovate public financing mechanisms in the service of expansion. See: Michael Campbell, "Politics, Prisons, and Law Enforcement: An Examination of the Emergence of 'Law and Order' Politics in Texas." *Law & Society Review* 45 no. 3 (2011): pp. 631–65; David Garland, *Mass Imprisonment: Social Causes and Consequences* (New York: Russel Sage, 2001); Ruth Gilmore, *Golden Gulag: Prisons, Surplus, Crisis and Opposition in Globalizing California* (Berkeley: University of California Press, 2007). Where on-going retrenchment and cost-saving measures have been considered, they have been cast as signs of growing power (See: Loïc Wacquant, "Four Strategies to Curb Carceral Costs: On Managing Mass Imprisonment in the United States." *Studies in Political Economy* no. 69 (2002): pp. 19–30) or have been made actionable only by the Great Recession (See: Jonathan Simon, "Mass Incarceration: From Social Policy to Social Problem." In *The Oxford Handbook of Sentencing and Corrections*, edited by Joan Petersilia and Kevin R. Reitz (New York: Oxford University Press, 2012): pp 23–52).

14. It is important to note that this reversal in jail expansion was accomplished despite strict new sentencing laws during the 1990s (such as California's "Three Strikes" law), population growth, and more intensive policing practices. See: Kohler-Hausmann, *Misdemeanorland: Criminal Courts and Social Control in an Age of Broken Windows Policing*; Stuart, *Down, Out, and Under Arrest: Policing and Everyday Life in Skid Row*. The idea that these declines were related to lower crime rates is offset by the fact that the jails returned to previous population levels once budget support returned. Within the next top 50 MSAs, the largest counties experienced jail population declines, but at different points. Thirteen other counties began their declines in the early 1990s, including those of Texas's large cities, California's Bay Area, and a few located in the US South. A second group of large counties began their declines in the late 1990s; these include the counties of Miami, Atlanta, Boston, and other mid-tier metropolises. Finally, a larger group of 17 counties began their jail population declines in the first decade of the 2000s (before the Great Recession). Altogether, these counties represent 30% of the nation's total jail population; Vera Institute of Justice, "Incarceration Trends—Vera Institute of Justice," accessed March 1, 2019, http://trends.vera.org/incarceration-rates?data=pretrial. Regarding the jail population declines in the early 1990s, these occurred in the following locations: Chicago (Cook County); New York (New York and Essex counties; Los Angeles (Los Angeles and Orange counties); the Bay Area (Alameda, San Francisco, Santa Clara, and Contra Costa counties); Houston (Harris County); Dallas; Austin (Travis County); San Antonio (Bexar

County); Charlotte (Mecklenburg County); Orlando (Orange County); District of Columbia; San Diego; Cincinnati (Hamilton County); Memphis (Shelby County); and Richmond, VA. In the late 1990s, there were declines in Miami (Miami-Dade County), Detroit (Wayne County), New Orleans, Atlanta (Fulton County), Boston (Suffolk County), Minneapolis (Hennepin County), Cleveland (Cuyahoga County), Nashville (Davidson County), Milwaukee, Birmingham (Jefferson County), Buffalo (Erie County). Early 2000s declines were in Philadelphia, Seattle (King County), Phoenix (Maricopa County), Tampa Bay (Hillsborough County), Columbus (Franklin County), Denver, Baltimore, St. Louis City, Portland (Multnomah County), St. Paul (Ramsey County), Pittsburgh (Allegheny County), Sacramento, Las Vegas (Clark County), Indianapolis (Marion County), Virginia Beach, Jacksonville (Duval County), Oklahoma City, Raleigh (Wake County), and Salt Lake City. Those locales that do not fit this pattern or have no data include Kansas City (Jackson County), Riverside, San Bernardino, Providence County, Louisville (Jefferson County), and Hartford County.

15. Brian D. Johnson and Stephanie M. DiPietro, "The Power of Diversion: Intermediate Sanctions and Sentencing Disparity under Presumptive Guidelines," *Criminology: An Interdisciplinary Journal* 50, no. 3 (2012): pp. 811–50; James Pitts, Hayden Griffin, and W. Wesley Johnson, "Contemporary Prison Overcrowding: Short-Term Fixes to a Perpetual Problem," *Contemporary Justice Review* 17 no. 1 (2014): pp. 124–39; Claire Shubik-Richards and Don Stemen, "Philadelphia's Crowded, Costly Jails: The Search for Safe Solutions" (Pew Charitable Trusts' Philadelphia Research Initiative, 2010); Todd Clear, Michaelfno Reisig, and George Cole, *American Corrections* (Boston: Cengage Learning 2019).

16. Jamie Peck, "Austerity Urbanism," *Cityscape* 16, no. 6 (2012): pp. 626–55.

17. Linda Lobao and Lazarus Adua, "State Rescaling and Local Governments' Austerity Policies across the USA, 2001–2008," *Cambridge Journal of Regions, Economy and Society* 4 no. 1 (2011): pp. 419–35.

18. Edelman was quoted by a news segment: "Weekend Gallery: County Budget," *KTLA 5* (Edmund D. Edelman Papers. The Huntington Library, San Marino, CA, 1953–1994 [bulk 1974–1994]: Box: 12/File: 4 [Hereafter "Edelman Papers: Box/File]) and "Budget 6/11/93," *Ch. 13 Los Angeles News Report*, June 13, 1993 (Edelman Papers: 11/14); see the County CEO's statements: "Potential Impact of Failure of Proposition 172," Sally Reed to BOS, no date (Edmund D. Edelman: 528/2). On Proposition 13, see: Isaac William Martin, *The Permanent Tax Revolt: How the Property Tax Transformed American Politics* (Stanford, CA: Stanford University Press, 2008); Lisa McGirr, *Suburban Warriors: The Origins of the New American Right* (Princeton, NJ: Princeton University Press, 2002).

19. Jeb E. Barnes and Thomas F. Burke, *How Policy Shapes Politics: Rights, Courts, Litigation, and the Struggle over Injury Compensation* (Oxford: Oxford University Press, 2014). What is lost in many analyses of urban poverty governance is what legal historians call the "problem of the democratic state." Essentially, a "Weberian" notion of the state (one that is solely a bureaucratic, extracting entity with a monopoly on coercive power) has been applied to the problem of urban poverty governance.

Any analysis of how the state manages the poor must show how the effort to control, imprison, and silence exists not in spite of democratic institutions, but rather interacts in concert with them. In the view of Sawyer, Novak, and Sparrow (2012) this problem is so pervasive in many studies that it becomes impossible to account for the differences between a democratic state and a totalitarian state; Stephen W. Sawyer, William J. Novak, and James T. Sparrow, "Toward a History of the Democratic State," *The Tocqueville Review/La Revue Tocqueville* XXXIII no. 2 (2012): pp. 7–18.Important exceptions to this dearth is the socio-legal historical scholarship on uneven penal development: Campbell (2011); Lynch (2011); Reiter (2016), Schoenfeld (2010); and Feeley and Rubin (1998). Essentially, in these analysis in order to win over fiscal conservatives who had opposed prison building in the 1970s, penal advocates reframed federal court Eighth Amendment rulings as infringements upon states' rights and penal expansion as a conservative cause (Schoenfeld, 2018). Reiter (2016) demonstrates that the rise of solitary confinement in California prisons was, in part, an unintended consequence of progressive lawsuits against indeterminate sentencing. However, in the researchers' analyses, these moments of legal demand were understood as having been overcome, laying the groundwork for a period of unfettered penal expansion., Mona Lynch "Mass Incarceration, Legal Change, and Locale: Understanding and Remediating American Penal Overindulgence," *Criminology & Public Policy* 10 no. 3 (2011): pp. 673–98; Keramet Reiter, *23/7: Pelican Bay Prison and the Rise of Long-Term Solitary Confinement* (New Have: Yale University Press, 2016); Heather Schoenfeld, "Mass Incarceration and the Paradox of Prison Conditions Litigation." *Law & Society Review,* 44 no. 3 (2010): pp. 731–68; Michael Campbell, "Politics, Prisons, and Law Enforcement: An Examination of the Emergence of 'Law and Order' Politics in Texas." *Law & Society Review* 45 no. 3 (2011): pp. 631–65; Malcom Feeley and Edward Rubin, *Judicial Policy Making and the Modern State: How the Courts Reformed America's Prisons* (Cambridge University Press, 1998).

20. Margo Schlanger has documented the continued presence of federally imposed jail population caps and jail litigation. These have been the primary way that federal courts have maintained constant vigilance around jail conditions. In California alone, there were 35 counties operating under court-imposed population caps before realignment. See: Margo Schlanger, "Civil Rights Injunctions over Time: A Case Study of Jail and Prison Court Orders." *N.Y.U. Law Review* 81 no. 2 (2006): pp. 550–630; Margo Schlanger, "Plata v. Brown and Realignment: Jails, Prisons, Courts, and Politics." *Harvard Civil Rights-Civil Liberties Law Review* 48 no. 1(2013): pp. 165–215; Margo Schlanger, "Trends in Prisoner Litigation, as the PLRA Enters Adulthood." *University of California Irvine Law Review* 5 no. 1(2015): pp. 153–79. My own search of the national jail census indicates that between 1990 and 2006, 34 of the largest counties in the top-50 MSAs at some point were subject to court-imposed jail caps. However, this number understates the presence of legal pressure. A focus on technical court ordered population caps fails to capture informal legal pressure exerted from professional legal agencies and health regulatory agencies. For instance, Detroit's Wayne County answered affirmatively to the national jail census/survey in 1990 and 1998

that they were subject to a population cap, but said in 2006 that the "case closed due to external monitor." Los Angeles County, the subject of this paper, answered negatively to the question in 2006, but as we shall see, continued to abide by and rely on the authority granted by the population cap. It is often legal agencies concerned about inmates' rights that play the role of monitors in the wake of a closed cases. In other words, often it is the threat of legal action that can take the place of formal court orders. Both formal court orders and "the mindset that accompanies them" have prevented local jails from packing as many inmates into existing jails, and "have for two decades led each month to thousands of prisoner releases when jail population runs up against the caps" (Schlanger, "Civil Rights Injunctions over Time, 194). Data on population caps of top 50 MSAs taken from: United States Department of Justice, Bureau of Justice Statistics, *Annual Survey of Jails: Jurisdiction-Level Data, 1990*, Study 9569. Inter-university Consortium for Political and Social Research; United States Department of Justice, Bureau of Justice Statistics, *National Jail Census*, 1999, Study 03318. Inter-university Consortium for Political and Social Research; United States Department of Justice, Bureau of Justice Statistics, *Census of Jail Facilities*, 2006 Study 26602. Inter-university Consortium for Political and Social Research. In regard to the prison, see: (Kitty Calavita and Valerie Jenness. *Appealing to Justice: Prisoner Grievances, Rights, and Carceral Logic* (Berkeley: University of California Press, 2015).

21. On how organizations construct signals to appease legal pressure, see: Lauren B. Edelman, *Working Law: Courts, Corporations, and Symbolic Civil Rights* (Chicago: University of Chicago Press, 2016). If legal advocates press state officials to expand patient rights, provide more services, or cut back on maltreatment, then we need to identify exactly what thresholds, measurement techniques, and ongoing surveillance came to be agreed upon.

22. Carsten Jensen, Georg Wenzelburger, and Reimut Zohlnhöfer, "Dismantling the Welfare State? After Twenty-five years: What Have We Learned and What Should We Learn?" *Journal of European Social Policy* 29, no. 5 (2019): pp. 681–91; Eric Patashnik, "Paul Pierson's Dismantling the Welfare State: A Twentieth Anniversary Reassessment: Introduction," *PS: Political Science & Politics* 48, no. 2 (2015): pp. 267–69; Paul Pierson, *Dismantling the Welfare State? Reagan, Thatcher, and the Politics of Retrenchment* (Cambridge, UK: Cambridge University Press, 1994); Paul Pierson, "Irresistible Forces, Immovable Objects: Post-industrial Welfare State Confront Permanent Austerity," *Journal of European Public Policy* 5, no. 4 (1998): 539–60; Peter Hall, "Social Policy-Making for the Long Term," *PS: Political Science & Politics* 48, no. 2 (2015): pp. 289–91; Suzanne Mettler, "Twenty Years On: Paul Pierson's Dismantling the Welfare State?" *PS: Political Science & Politics* 48, no. 2 (2015): pp. 270–73.

23. Wolfgang Streeck and Kathleen Thelen, *Beyond Continuity: Institutional Change in Advanced Political Economies* (New York: Oxford University Press, 2005); Daniel Béland, "Ideas and Institutional Change in Social Security: Conversion, Layering, and Policy Drift." *Social Science Quarterly* 88, no. 1 (2007): pp. 20–38; Jacob Hacker, "Policy Drift: The Hidden Politics of US Welfare State Retrenchment," in *Beyond Continuity: Institutional Change in Advanced Political Economies*, edited by Wolfgang Streeck and Kathleen Thelen (New York: Oxford University Press, 2005): pp. 20–82;

Carsten Jensen, Georg Wenzelburger, and Reimut Zohlnhöfer, "Dismantling the Welfare State?"

24. On the vast literature on "blame avoidance" or how politicians and agencies skirt political blowback in their efforts to dismantle state institutions, see: Markus Hinterleitner and Fritz Sager, "Anticipatory and Reactive Forms of Blame Avoidance: of Foxes and Lions," *European Political Science Review* 9, no. 4 (2017): pp. 587–606; Christopher Hood, *The Blame Game: Spin, Bureaucracy, and Self-preservation in Government* (Princeton, NJ: Princeton University Press, 2011). The "submerged" and "delegated" states themselves can be thought of as extensions of public spending (often to private purveyors), and, in effect, examples of welfare state resiliency. See: Suzanne Mettler, *The Submerged State: How Invisible Government Policies Undermine American Democracy* (Chicago: University of Chicago Press, 2011); Kimberly J. Morgan and Andrea Louise Campbell, *The Delegated Welfare State: Medicare, Markets, and the Governance of Social Policy* (New York: Oxford University Press, 2011).

Chapter 1

1. John Irwin, *The Jail: Managing the Underclass in American Society* (Berkeley: University of California Press, [1985] 2013), p. 135; Roth, *Insane: America's Criminal Treatment of Mental Illness*; Shubik-Richards and Stemen, "Philadelphia's Crowded, Costly Jails: The Search for Safe Solutions"; Subramanian et al., *Incarceration's Front Door: The Misuse of Jail in America*. For a sociological treatment of racialization in jails see: Michael L. Walker, "Race Making in a Penal Institution," *American Journal of Sociology* 121, no. 4 (2016): pp. 1051–78.

2. Los Angeles County Board of Supervisors Meeting Transcript, December 6, 2005 (hereafter "LA County BOS Meeting Transcript" and date).

3. Ian Hacking, "Kinds of People: Moving Targets," *Proceedings-British Academy* 151 (2007): pp. 285–318.

4. On the interactional basis of classification work between inmates and intake workers: Philip Goodman, "'It's Just Black, White, or Hispanic': An Observational Study of Racializing Moves in California's Segregated Prison Reception Centers," *Law & Society Review* 42, no. 4 (2008): pp. 735–70. On the discretion inherent in risk classification: Kelly Hannah-Moffat, "Criminogenic Needs and the Transformative Risk Subject: Hybridizations of Risk/need in Penality," *Punishment & Society* 7, no. 1 (2005): pp. 29–51.

5. See the special issue on Realignment: Charis Kubrin and Carroll Seron, "The Prospects and Perils of Ending Mass Incarceration in the United States," *The Annals of the American Academy of Political and Social Science* 664, no. 1 (2016): 16–24.

6. Jail alternative early release: Johnson and DiPietro, "The Power of Diversion: Intermediate Sanctions and Sentencing Disparity under Presumptive Guidelines"; Pitts, Griffin, and Johnson, "Contemporary Prison Overcrowding: Short-Term Fixes to a Perpetual Problem"; Shubik-Richards and Stemen, "Philadelphia's Crowded, Costly Jails: The Search for Safe Solutions." For the broad variety of release alternatives: Clear,

Reisig, and Cole, *American Corrections*. Standards can change daily: Lara Hoffman, "Separate but Unequal - When Overcrowded: Sex Discrimination in Jail Early Release Policies," *William & Mary Journal of Women and the Law* 15, no. 3 (2008): pp. 591–632. See also: John Monahan and Jennifer L. Skeem, "The Evolution of Violence Risk Assessment," *CNS Spectrums* 19, no. 5 (2014): 419–24.

7. Wildeman, "Invited Commentary: (Mass) Imprisonment and (Inequities In) Health," *American Journal of Epidemiology* 173, no. 5 (2011): pp. 488–91.

8. This and subsequent field note excerpts taken from author's field notes. See methods appendix.

9. On the cultural trope of the mismanaged life, see Michael B. Katz, *The Undeserving Poor: America's Enduring Confrontation with Poverty: Fully Updated and Revised* (New York: Oxford University Press, 2013).

10. Iddo Tavory, *Summoned: Identification and Religious Life in a Jewish Neighborhood* (Chicago: University of Chicago Press, 2016).

Chapter 2

1. Sherman Block, "Treating Mentally Ill in L.A. County jails," *Los Angeles Times*, January 8, 1983: p. B2.

2. Quoted in Abby Sewell, "L.A. County Supervisors Move Ahead with $2 Billion Jails Plan," *Los Angeles Times*, September 1, 2015: https://www.latimes.com/local/lanow/la-me-ln-supes-jail-vote-20150831-story.html; Details sourced from: "Architectural Program for the Consolidated Correctional Treatment Facility and Mira Loma Detention Center, Los Angeles County Jail Plan Independent Review and Comprehensive Report," *Vanir Construction Management*. April 21, 2014 (County online collection: on file [hereafter, County online]).

3. See note 53.

4. Statement in: "Response to the *Los Angeles Times* Newspaper Series," Sherman Block to LA County BOS, *Sheriff's Department, County of Los Angeles* (1996) (Yvonne Brathwaite Burke Papers (1979–1981 and 1994–2008): University of Southern California Regional History Collection [hereafter "Burke Papers"]: 506/1); More generally, see: Margo Schlanger, "*Plata v. Brown* and Realignment: Jails, Prison, Courts, and Politics."

5. Among others, my understanding of these closures and crises comes from: "Edelman Interview," *Week in Review*, July 9, 1993 (Edelman Papers: 13/7); "Fiscal Year 1993–94 Budget Implementation Issues," Jim Miyano to Edelman, *Edelman office*, April 21, 1993 (Edelman Papers: 532/4); "Proposed Sheriff's Department Budget for Fiscal Year 1995–1996," Sherman Block to BOS, *Sheriff's Department*, May 30, 1995 (Burke Papers: s506/1); "Recommendations to Restore Funding to the Sheriff's Department Including Re-opening of Jail Beds," David Janssen to BOS, *CAO Office*, December 9, 2004 (County online: on file); "Response to a Request for a Sheriff's Department's Custody Master Plan," Leyor Baca to BOS, *Sheriff's Department*, August 5, 2004 (County online: on file); "Restoration of Funding to the Sheriff's Department

Including the Reopening of Jail Beds," Leroy Baca to BOS, Sheriff's Department, February 1, 2005 (Burke Papers: 373/19); "Release of County of LA Budget," April 8, 2005 (Burke Papers: s373/8); BOS meeting transcript: December 14, 2004; April 14, 2009; May 13, 2009' June 20, 2009; April 19, 2011 (County online: on file); "Fiscal Year 2011–12 Recommended County Budget," William Fujioka to BOS. *CEO Office* (County online: on file).

6. "Minutes of the Board of Supervisors," *Los Angeles County*, September 12, 1996 (County online: on file).

7. Along with several peripheral memos and Board of Supervisor meeting minutes (which are cited when relevant), this section relies heavily on the following files: "Proposed Funding Plan to Open and Operate the Twin Towers Custody Facility," David Janssen to BOS, *CAO Office*, October 9, 1996 (Burke Papers: 436/15); "Twin Tower/Custody Study Group Recommendations," Randi to Burke, *Burke Office*, September 9, 1996 (Burke Papers: 436/15); "Approval of Agreement with the U.S. Department of Justice Immigration and Naturalization Service (INS) for Housing INS Detainees and Approve in Substantially Similar Form an . . . Agreement with the State Department of Corrections (CDC) for Housing State Detainees," Sherman Block to BOS, *Sheriff's Department*, January 15, 1997 (Burke Papers: 436/15); "Funding Availability: Twin Towers Operational plan," David Janssen to BOS, *CAO Office*, November 8, 1996 (Burke Papers 436/15); "Proposed Funding Plan to Open Twin Towers," Randi to Burke, Burke Office, October 10, 1996 (Burke Papers: 436/15).

8. We can prove this by looking at the progression of the 1996 jail plan from the originally planned 900 state inmates to the final count of 1,400 state inmates. The willingness to always fill extra county jail space with state prisoners occurs throughout planning memos of this period. "It appears the Federal agencies may not be in a position to implement contract until July 1st 1997 (some 6 months after start of plan). In the interim State inmates will occupy the available contact beds to maintain the revenue projections. . . . In the event that the Federal agencies elect not to contract with the County the State will continue to contract with the County for all available beds"; see: "Funding Availability: Twin Towers Operational plan" (Burke Papers 436/15); Original plan in "Proposed Funding Plan to Open and Operate the Twin Towers Custody Facility" (Burke Papers: 436/15) to final plan: "Approval of Agreement. . . ." (Burke Papers: 436/15). With regard to the explicit nature of the plan, consider the following supervisor motion, "Request the Sheriff, the CAO, and the Auditor-Controller to identify the potential revenue available through Federal reimbursements for incarceration of undocumented criminal aliens in County custody facilities and dedicate the amount to the opening and operation of the Twin Towers Correction Facility," "Minutes of the BOS," *Los Angeles County*, May 28, 1996 (County online: on file).

9. LA County BOS Meeting Transcript, December 6, 2005 (County Online: on file).

10. My understanding of these two jail plans comes from a variety of sources. Consider the debates on this issue from the supervisors in LA County BOS Meetings. Supervisor Antonovich can be heard on the January 17, 2005; Supervisor Molina on January 17, 2005; Yaroslavsky needed the clarification on December 6, 2005; Antonovich again

on December 6, 2005, and Antonovich, February 21, 2006. All from: LA County BOS Meeting Transcript (County Online: on file); Also see: "Jail Housing and Security Plan," Leroy Baca, *Sheriff's Department*, March 21, 2006 (County Online: on file); "Approval of County of Los Angeles Jail Facilities Plan," David Janssen and Leroy Baca, *CAO Office*, August 1, 2006 (County Online: on file); "Report on Development of a Capital Plan for Sheriff Jail Facilities and an Assessment of the Sheriff's Jail Housing and Security Plan," David Janssen, *CAO Office*, March 16, 2006 (County Online: on file).

11. This is despite the fact that their request for an additional high-security beds in their crisis plan was approximately 2,000 beds short of the number of high-security inmates in the system. "Jail Housing and Security Plan" (County Online: on file). Also see: "Jail Housing and Security Plan" (County Online: on file); "Approval of County of Los Angeles Jail Facilities Plan" (County Online: on file); "Report on Development of a Capital Plan for Sheriff Jail Facilities and an Assessment of the Sheriff's Jail Housing and Security Plan" (County Online: on file).

12. Jean Guccione, "L.A. Superior Court Stymies Jail Compromise: Court's Refusal to Change Could Force Inmate Reduction," *Los Angeles Daily Journal*, November 12, 1998; see also: "Jail Overcrowding: ACLU Meeting," Petzke to Edelman, *Edelman Office*, April 19, 1987 (Edelman Papers: 534/10). See the role of the court order in the jail master plan: "Consultant Services Jail Needs Assesment/Master Plan," Stuart to BOS, *Edelman Office*, April 28, 1988 (Edelman Papers, 534/6); "Jail Overcrowding," Lawrence to Edelman, *Edelman Office*, June 16, 1988 (Edelman Papers: 534/2).

13. Quote in: "Untiled Letter," Alban L. Niles to Edelman, *Presiding Judge*, May 3, 1994 (Edelman Papers: 204/9); see also: "Untitled Letter," Laurence D. Rubin to Edelman, *Superior Court of Los Angeles*, May 22, 1989 (Edelman Papers: 534/17). On the initial administrative release response: Ted Rohrlich, "County Ordered to Begin Limits on Jail Crowding," *Los Angeles Times*, October 31, 1987. In 1990, sentenced inmates were being released on 65% of served time. In 1994 and 1995, the percentage dropped to 35%. After the opening of a new jail in 1997, the percentage moved to 45%. In 2005, the level dropped to 10% of sentenced time. It was at 20% just before Realignment in 2011. Beyond just the variable percentage time served, the sheriff was also able to release inmates even earlier, using less publicly acknowledged "credits." An internal memo stated, "Currently when a judge sentences a defendant to County jail, a variety of state mandated credits are computed (good time, work time, etc.). After those credits are deducted from the original sentence, the remaining days reflect actual sentence length. The 35% early release percentage is then applied to this original sentence. Therefore, the time served is approximately 25% of the original sentence imposed by the court." "Response to the *Los Angeles Times* Newspaper Series" (Burke Papers: s506/1); "Release Level Matrix," Block to BOS, *Sheriff's Department*, May 12, 1993 (Edelman Papers: 534/7); "Untitled Letter," Block to Burke, *Sheriff's Department*, June 19, 1995 (Burke Papers: s506/1); see the political gamesmanship over early releases in: "Untitled Letter," Block to BOS, *Sheriff's Department*, June 16, 1995 (Burk Papers: s506/1); Carla Rivera and Lisa Respers, "Sherriff, Board, Swap Charges over Early Release of Inmates." *Los Angeles Times*, March 4, 1995; "Sheriff's

Department's Percentage Release Program," Leroy Baca, *Sheriff's Department*, June 6, 2006 (County Online: on file); See the monthly reports after February 15, 2005, to the present: "Status of the Early Release Program-Monthly Report," Sheriff's Department (County Online: on file); see LA County BOS Meeting Transcripts (County Online: on file) of: December 14, 2004; April 14, 2009; May 13, 2009; June 20, 2009; April 19, 2011.

14. See a renewal of the denial of misdemeanants as linked to the Rutherford ruling in: "untitled letter," Block to Burke, *Sheriff's Department*, June 19, 1995 (Burke Papers: s506/1); also see: "Untitled Letter" (Edelman Papers: 534/17); "Effect of half cent sale tax on early release of prisoners," Lawrence to EDE, August 8, 1990, *Edelman Office* (Edelman Papers: 534/2); "Release Level Matrix" (Edelman Papers: 534/7); this sheriff's instituted OR program at the point of jailing represents a significant development if we compare it to the traditional court-administered OR program. From 1964 to 1990, the court program was responsible for only 64,000 released defendants. In contrast, in the first eight months of the sheriff's OR program, 38,042 inmates were released. In part, this is because the sheriff's administrative adaptation was to release all inmates under a certain bail amount while the court's pretrial service division vetted inmates. See: "Analysis and Report of Superior Court's Own Recognizance Program (OR)," Dixon to BOS, *CAO Office*, July 12, 1990 (Edelman Papers: 206/4).

15. LA County BOS Meeting Transcript, July 16, 2013 (County Online: on file).

16. "Projected Fiscal Impact of the Custody Crisis," Block to BOS, *Sheriff's Department*, May 19, 1989 (Edelman Papers 534/2). See also the memo discussing the Sheriff's letter: "S-1, Consideration of Sheriff Block's letter," Miyano to Edelman, *Edelman Office*, June 1, 1989 (Edelman Papers: 534/7).

17. My claim that the letter fundamentally altered county officials' view of their jail system stems from my analysis of the archival record surrounding the fallout of the letter. See, among many others: "Revived CRASH Committee," Lawrence to Edelman, *Edelman Office*, August 29, 1989 (Edelman Papers: 534/1); "Report and Recommendations Concerning Sheriff's Letter on Projected Fiscal Impact of the Custody Crisis," Clinton and Dixon to BOS, *Office of the County Counsel*, August 7, 1989 (Edelman papers: 534/2); "Agenda Item NO. S-1 for Tuesday June 6th, 1989 Consideration of Sheriff Block's Letter," Miyano to Edelman, *Edelman Office*, June 1, 1989. (Edelman Papers: 534/7);

18. "Item S-2—Reports on Jail Overcrowding as Requested by Supervisor Dana," Miyano to Edelman, *Edelman Office*, December 18, 1989 (Edelman Papers: 534/2).

19. My understanding of the programs comes from a variety of sources. See especially: "Twin Tower/Custody Study Group Recommendations" (Burke Papers: 436/15); "Offender Management Program Enhancement," Thelma Harris to Glen Dragovich, *Probation Department*, September 24, 1996 (Burke Papers: 436/15); "Community-Based Alternatives to Custody Program," Block to BOS, April 17, 1997 (Burke Papers: 436/15); "Proposed Funding Plan to Open and Operate the Twin Towers Custody Facility" (Burke Papers: 436/15); "Report on the Development of a Capital Plan for Sheriff Jail Facilities and an Assessment of the Sheriff Jail Housing and Security Plan," Janssen to BOS, *CAO Office*, March 16 2006 (County Online: on file); "Management Audit of the Sheriff's Department," David Janssen to BOS, *CAO*

Office, November 21, 1996 (Requested from County Public Records Department [Hereafter: County Records]: on file); "A Response to California State Auditor Bureau of State Audits," Jerry Harper to Kurt Sjoberg, Sheriff's Department, November 15, 1996 (County Records: on file).

20. "Twin Tower/Custody Study Group Recommendations" (Burke Papers: 436/15).

21. "Offender Management Program Enhancement" (Burke Papers: 436/15).

22. "Offender Management Program Enhancement" (Burke Papers: 436/15).

23. For the period between 1977 and 1986, see: "Untitled Letter," Reiner to Dixon, *Probation Department*, June 9, 1988 (Edelman Papers: 433/2); for later figures: "LA Probation Department Restructuration: Adult Probation Services," Paul Higa, *Probation Department*, September 7, 1999(Burke Papers: s437/8); Ted Rohrlich, "Intensified Supervision of Probation Found Ineffective: RAND Study Concludes That the Program Does Not Dissuade Felons from Committing Additional Offenses," *Los Angeles Times*, January 31, 1991: https://www.latimes.com/archives/la-xpm-1991-01-31-mn-426-story.html; on the dire situation more generally, see: David Freed, "System Overflows with Flood of Probationers Corrections," *Los Angeles Times*, December 21, 1990: p. A1.

24. Passed in 1999, AB 34 provided a small sum of $10 million from the state for pilot programs in just three counties, of which Los Angeles County received nearly half. The same program was expanded under AB 2034 to $55 million (of which Los Angeles County received over a quarter). The MIOCR demonstration grants included $10 million over four years. See: "AB 34 Orientation," Marvin J. Southard to Jim Allen, *Department of Mental Health*, November 1, 1999 (County Online: on file); "Proposed AB 34 Plan," Marvin Southard to Jim Allen, *Department of Mental Health*, July 19, 2000 (County Online: on file); "AB 2034: What works," *Department of Mental Health*, August 31, 2004 (County Online: on file); "Law Enforcement Mental Health Symposium Keynote Speech Speaking Points," *Burke Office*, June 7, 2000 (Burke Papers 474/5). The 16 agencies can be found in: Martha Burt, John Hedderson, Janine Zweig, Mary Ortiz, Laudan Aron-Turnham, and Sabrina Johnson, "Appendix D: Strategies for Reducing Chronic Street Homelessness Final Report," *The Urban Institute* (2004); Mistique Felton, "Proposition 63, The Mental Health Services Act: A Research Agenda" (Berkeley, CA: The Nicholas C. Petris Center on Health Care Markets and Consumer Welfare, 2006).

25. These demonstration programs were developed by the very same jail mental health taskforce that was reconvened in the wake of the 1997 DOJ inquiry. See: "Minutes of the BOS," *Los Angeles County*, October 20, 1997 (County online: on file); see also: "Mentally Ill Offender Crime Reduction Phase II—Demonstration Grant Program...," Leroy Baca, *Sheriff's Department*, February 18, 1999(County Records: on file); "Mentally Ill Offender Crime Reduction Grant Final Report 2005," retrieved online (also on file): www.fmhac.org/uploads/1/2/4/4/124447122/miocrg_final_report_2005.pdf; the infrastructure created by Proposition 36 was in effect through various funding streams from 2000 until 2011, and Proposition 63 began in 2006 and was still in effect in 2017. "Final Penal Code 1210 (Formerly Proposition 36 . . .)" John Viernes, Jr., to Executive Directors of Offender Treatment Program/

Prop. 36 treatment providers and interested others, *Department of Public Health* (County Online: on file); "Proposition 36 Legislation Recommendations," CCJCC Prop. 36 Legislative Advisory Committee to David Janssen, *CAO Office*, January 1, 2001 (Burke Papers: 470/1); "Prop. 36 status report," Mimur to Burke, Burke Office, February 16, 2001 (Burke Papers: 470/1); "Approval for submission of the Mental Health Services Act Community Services and Support plan to the State Department of Mental Health." Marvin Southard to Board of Supervisors, *Department of Mental Health*, September 29, 2005 (County online: on file); "Mental Health Services Act: The State's Oversight Has Provided Little Assurance of the Act's Effectiveness, and Some Counties Can Improve Measurement of Their Program Performance. Report 2012-122," *California State Auditor* (retrieved online: http://auditor.ca.gov/pdfs/reports/2012-122.pdf, also on file).

26. Figures are from the county's six-year report. See: "Substance Abuse and Crime Prevention Act of 2000: Proposition 36 Fiscal Years 2001–2006," *Department of Public Health*, January 2008 (County Online: on file). County of Los Angeles, January 2008. On file. Concerning dismissals under Prop. 36: "If there are no violations of probation, all fees and fines are paid, and the Court finds reasonable cause to believe that a participant will not abuse controlled substances in the future, the Court can dismiss the case" (p. 3).

27. The County's Prop. 63 plan explicitly references the AB 2034 program as its model for linking individuals to community-based services. See: "Mentally Ill Offender Crime Reduction Grant Final Report 2005" (retrieved online); "Approval for Submission of the Mental Health Services Act Community Services and Support Plan to the State Department of Mental Health" (County online: on file); "Mental Health Services Act: The State's Oversight Has Provided Little Assurance . . ." (retrieved online).

28. Documents specifically attribute the reduction in inmates to this court advocacy role: "The County attributes this success to both the program's intensive treatment and the fact that program staff's representatives, including probation officers, advocated in court for CROMIO's clients, telling the court exactly what services were being provided and thereby providing the court a viable alternative to sending the person to prison"; see: "Mentally Ill Offender Crime Reduction Grant Final Report 2005," p. 77 (retrieved online); see also: "Mentally Ill Offender Crime Reduction Phase II—Demonstration Grant Program . . ." (County Records: on file). Quote from: Martha Burt et al., "Appendix D: Strategies for Reducing Chronic Street Homelessness Final Report," Washington, D.C.: The Urban Institute (2004).

29. "Treatment services for those who have a low level of severity include outpatient services (including a combination of individual, family, and group counseling sessions), self-help group meetings, and supplemental treatment services (which included literacy training, vocational guidance, mental health services, health services, and transitional housing). Treatment services for those participants assessed at mid to high severity levels consist of more intensive services such as day treatment, residential detoxification, residential treatment, and narcotic replacement therapy, as needed, in addition to the range of services provided to lower-level participants" (p. 5), "Substance Abuse and Crime Prevention Act of 2000: Proposition 36 Fiscal

Years 2001–2006" (County Online: on file); see also: "Approval of Substance Abuse and Crime Prevention Act of 2000, fiscal year 2006–07," Bruce Chernoff to BOS, Department of Health Services, April 20, 2006 (County Online: on file).

30. Sherman Block, "Treating Mentally Ill in L.A. County Jails." *Los Angeles Times*, January 8, 1983: p. B2. Another example is that of the original architectural plans for Twin Towers, which included hospital services in each of the towers. After planning personnel discovered that this would make each tower subject to state inspection and added costs from state health inspectors, they decided to create a separate third, smaller, 200-bed medical tower. The move was meant to curb medical costs and limit exposure to health inspectors. "Approval of Revised Medical/Mental Health Program Supplemental Agreement NO 4," Richard Dixon to BOS, *Facilities Management Department*, January 26, 1989 (Edelman Papers: 535/4); "Central Jail Expansion Project," Miyano to Edelman, *Edelman Office*, March 7, 1989 (Edelman Papers: 535/4)

31. Amy Louise Kazmin, "L.A. County Jail Infirmary Substandard, State Finds." *Los Angeles Times*, September 15, 1990: https://www.latimes.com/archives/la-xpm-1990-09-15-mn-168-story.html; Amy Louise Kazmin, "Efforts Told to Improve Jail Hospital." *Los Angeles Times*, September 27, 1990: https://www.latimes.com/archives/la-xpm-1990-09-27-me-1705-story.html. Corroborating the *Los Angeles Times* quotes, an internal memo to the Chief Administrative Office downplayed the threat that these 1990 allegations represented to the County: "it is their contention that many of the reported violations result from differences in interpretation of hospital guidelines that are not necessarily applicable to jail hospitals . . . therefore the facility is not threatened by immediate closure in the near future." "Alleged Substandard Conditions in Men's Central Jail Facility," Richard B. Dixon to BOS, September 25, 1990, *CAO Office* (Edelman Papers: 535/4). For its part, the State Board of Corrections had minimum standards for healthcare in jails, but those standards were only advisory in the 1980s.

32. On the revived task force, see: "Minutes of the BOS," *Los Angeles County*, October 20, 1997 (County online: on file); the sheriff is quoted in: Tina Daunt, "Jail Treatment of Mentally Ill Is Criticized," *Los Angeles Times*, October 16, 1997; even the supervisor furthest to the right, Michael Antonovich, acknowledged in 1997 the need to act on the issue of mental healthcare in jails and introduced a board motion to mitigate the problem. See: "Minutes of the BOS," *Los Angeles County*, September 9, 1997 (County online: on file); "Undersheriff Harper Call," Doris to Burke and Herb, *Burke Office*, March 31, 1997 (Burke Papers: s506/1).

33. The information in this section is garnered from an amalgam of sources. While I cite others as necessary in the following, these were most critical: "Sheriff's Jail Mental Health Enhancements and Custody Automation Plan 1997–1998," David Janssen to BOS, *CAO Office*, April 21, 1998 (County Records: on file); "Jail Health Services Review Panel," Michael Kranther to BOS, *Department of Auditor-Controller*, September 27, 2000 (Burke Papers: s436:11); "A Response to California State Auditor Bureau of State Audits," Jerry Harper to Kurt Sjoberg, *Sheriff's Department*, November 15, 1996 (County Records: on file); "Jail's Medical Ward to Move to Twin Towers," *Los Angeles Times*; "Ill Inmates Transferred to Twin Towers," *Los Angeles*

Times; "Overtime Spending," Sheriff to BOS, *Sheriff's Department*, February 17, 1998 (Burke Papers: s506/1); LA County BOS Meeting Transcript, June 21, 2004 (County Online: on file); LA County BOS Meeting Transcript, March 21, 2004 (County Online: on file); "Report back from the Sheriff and Director of Mental Health regarding the release of mentally ill felons in custody in to the general population," Leroy Baca and Marvin Southard to BOS, Sheriff's Department, February 7, 2012 (County Online: on file).

34. "Untitled Letter" (Burk Papers: s506/1).

35. Quote from LA County BOS Meeting Transcript, June 21, 2004 (County Online: on file). In fact, the original plan to open Twin Towers specifically reduced medical services in the jail: "The program impact will be to limit clinic service for male inmates to 16 hours per day rather than operate on a 24-hour basis as originally proposed and to postpone licensing the medical unit as a Correctional Treatment Center . . . full medical staffing at the original program level phased in as funding permits." See: "Proposed Funding Plan to Open Twin Towers" (Burke Papers: 436/15). Another proposal was even more limiting to medical services: "Cost of operating one tower bare bones, does not include IRC or medical services. Medical services may be provided to inmates through central jail facilities." See: "Twin Tower/Custody Study Group Recommendations" (Burke Papers: 436/15).

36. "Sheriff's Jail Mental Health Enhancements and Custody Automation Plan 1997–1998" (County Records: on file).

37. "Report back from the Sheriff and Director of Mental Health regarding the release of mentally ill felons in custody in to the general population" (County Online: on file).

38. At the time, there were claims that this $8 million affected the ability of mental health providers to provide services to indigent patients out in the community. A letter from the Association of Community Mental Health Agencies (representing more than 40 mental health providers in the Los Angeles County area) complained directly about the loss of the $8 million dollars to the jail. See: "Untitled Letter," Carl C. McRaven, Gloria Nabrit, Elizabeth Pfromm, Robert Johnston, Fern Seizer to Burke, *Association of Community Mental Health Agencies*, June 10, 1997 (Burke Papers: 432/17); "Reconfiguration Plan for Mental Health Services Provided by the Department of Health Services," Robert C. Gates and Areta Crowell to BOS, Department of Mental Health, August 31, 1995 (Burke Papers: 432/17); "Sheriff's Department—Medical Services Bureau Review," Watanabe to BOS, *Department of Auditor-Controller*, July 13, 2012 (County Online: On File); "Report on the Appropriation Adjustment Transferring Funding from Provisional Financing Uses to the Department of Mental Health for Improvements to Jail Mental Health Services," Hamai to BOS, *CEO Office*, May 1, 2015 (County Online: on file).

39. I analyze the use of these telephone funds for inmate healthcare in great detail (Lara-Millán, forthcoming). See: "Letter" Sherman Block to Burke, *Sheriff's Department*, July 22, 1993 (Burke Papers: s506/1); "Pacific Bell Inmate Telephone Contract/Audit Report," Donner to Burke, Pacific Bell, April 9, 1998 (Burke Papers: s506/1); Los Angeles County Grand Jury Final Report 1999–2000 (Burke Papers: s506/1). This effort to generate revenue from telephone contracts in the Inmate Welfare

Fund did not incidentally fund the DOJ response plan, it was explicitly designed to do so. See: "Minutes of the BOS," *Los Angeles County*, October 14, 1997 (County online: on file); "Minutes of the BOS," *Los Angeles County*, October 14, 1997 (County Online: on file); Michael Glen Levitt and Nancy Patton, June 29, 1993, Analysis of SB 904, Committee on Budget and Fiscal Review (California State Archives, on file). Also see: Eric Lichtblau and Josh Meyer, "Sheriff's Budget Is Not as Lean as Billed," *Los Angeles Times*, November 3, 1996: https://www.latimes.com/archives/la-xpm-1996-11-03-mn-60961-story.html.

40. LA County BOS Meeting Transcript, July 16, 2013 (County Online: on file).
41. LA County BOS Meeting Transcript, August 4, 2015 (County Online: on file).
42. "Sheriff's Jail Mental Health Enhancements and Custody Automation Plan 1997–1998" (County Records: on file).
43. "Jail Mental Health Evaluation Teams" (JMET); "Report Back from the Sheriff and Director of Mental Health regarding the release of mentally ill felons in custody in to the general population" (County Online: on file).
44. By 2010, after ongoing DOJ monitoring of its mental health services, these teams had been expanded and more formalized into the "Jail Mental Health Evaluation Teams" (JMET); "Report Back from the Sheriff and Director of Mental Health regarding the release of mentally ill felons in custody in to the general population" (County Online: on file).
45. LA County BOS Meeting Transcript, January 20, 2012 (County Online: on file).
46. As one internal memo stated, "The Department's analysis also revealed that force incidents primarily occurred during movement of inmates with mental illness. The analysis also notes that force was higher at TTCC and CRDF, due to these locations being primary housing of mentally ill inmates," Jail Mental Health Evaluation Teams" (JMET). "Report Back from the Sheriff and Director of Mental Health regarding the release of mentally ill felons in custody in to the general population" (County Online: on file). This is a critical report, as it shows use-of-force incidents alongside statistics that link the issue to mentally ill inmates. And the entire logic of providing services is associated with keeping the mentally ill from being subject to force. We can see this link in how the report discusses the teams: "During evening hours, the custodial staff lacks the availability of JMET, which ultimately leads to an increase in risk of force incidents."

The original progressive legal concern over use-of-force and mentally ill inmates in the jail can be found in the 1997 ACLU report: "Complaints Against the Sheriff's Department on the Rise, Says Report by ACLU of Southern California," Christopher Herrera, *ACLU of Southern California*, September 10, 1997 (Burke Papers: s436:11); Also See: "Report from the Citizens Commission on Jail Violence," *Los Angeles County Citizens Commission on Jail Violence*, September 12, 2012. All of these facets came together to finally solve the last progressive legal challenge to the jail's mental health delivery—the 2014 "Rosas" agreement. The agreement scaled up existing methods, including the JMET teams, hiring processing staff in the intake room, and the jail mental health teams to review cases that could be transitioned into general population. The agreement codified mental health services as a matter of tracking

use-of-force incidents: it hired staff to monitor, track grievances, conduct compli-
ance reviews, and mental health incident review teams. See: "Report on Appropriate
Adjustment Transferring Funding from Provisional Financing Uses to the DMH
for Improvement to Jail Mental Health Services CEO, Los Angeles County," Sachi
Hamai to BOS, *CEO Office*, May 1, 2015 (County Online: on file); "Appropriate
Adjustment Transferring Funding from Provisional Financing Uses to LA County
Sheriff's Department and Department of Mental Health," Jim McDonnell, Sheriff's
Department, April 28, 2015 (County Online: on file).

47. As of 2019, social movement actors have successfully forced the BOS to rethink its
hospital-jail. They are, in effect, using an abolitionist frame to challenge the Sheriff's
Department's use of the medical frame for the purposes of expansion. The department continues to press forward and the final form of that this redistribution and
its new hospital-jail remains in jeopardy. See: Matt Stiles, "'No More Jails,' Just
Mental Health Centers. Is That a Realistic Policy for L.A. County?" *Los Angeles
Times*, August 26, 2019: https://www.latimes.com/california/story/2019-08-24/
jail-replacement-mental-health-facility-inmate-supervisors-criminal-justice-reform.

48. Consider one description of the new jail, taken from a planning meeting: "Appropriate
inmates for this level have substance and related disorders, criminal activity, psychological disorders, impaired functioning, and are disassociated with mainstream
values." Notice how "criminal activity" is just one symptom among other medical
ailments that make an inmate qualified for housing in this new hospital-jail. With
regard to the diversion program, a new "Office of Diversion and Re-Entry' (ODR)
was created and was, incredibly, placed under the auspices of the Department of
Health. The new office was created to coordinate diversion at every stage of the criminal justice system process, pushing frontline decision-makers to divert offenders
toward medical supervision at arrest, booking, arraignment, plea bargaining, sentencing, incarceration, and probation. LA County BOS Meeting Transcript, May
16, 2014 (County Online: on file). My understanding of this diversion program and
the new hospital-jail comes from reading the meeting transcripts of every Board of
Supervisors meeting in which they were discussed: May 6, 2014; July 15, 2014; July
29, 2014; September 30, 2014; August 6, 2015; August 11, 2015; September 1, 2015;
April 28, 2015, LA County BOS Meeting Transcript (County Online: on file); as
well as every planning and update document associated with those meeting dates.
See especially: "Los Angeles County Consolidated Correctional Treatment Facility
Population Analysis and Community Health Care Continuum," *Health Management
Associates*, August 4, 2015 (County Online: on file); "Architectural Program for the
Consolidated Correctional Treatment Facility . . ." (County Online, on file).

Chapter 3

1. On previous studies of triage departments, see: Barry Schwartz, *Queuing and
Waiting: Studies in the Social Organization of Access and Delay* (Chicago: University
of Chicago Press, 1972); Julius Roth, "Some Contingencies of the Moral Evaluation

and Control of Clientele: The Case of the Hospital Emergency Service," *American Journal of Sociology* 77, no. 5 (March 1972): pp. 839–56; Roger Jeffery, "Normal Rubbish: Deviant Patients in Casualty Departments," *Sociology of Health & Illness* 1, no. 1 (1979): pp. 90–107. Jeffrey Prottas, *People Processing: The Street-Level Bureaucrat in Public Service Bureaucracies* (Lexington, MA: Lexington Books, 1979). On the new pain standards, see: Patricia Berry and June Dahl, "New JCAHO Pain Standards: Implications for Pain Management Nurses," *Pain Management Nursing* 1 no. 1 (2000): pp. 3–12. On the importance of EMTALA see: Shaun Ossei-Owusu, "Code Red: The Essential Yet Neglected Role of Emergency Care in Health Law Reform," *American Journal of Law & Medicine* 43 no. 4 (2017): pp. 344–87.

2. Prottas, *People Processing*.

3. Renee Y. Hsia et al., "Hospital Determinants of Emergency Department Left without Being Seen Rates," *Annals of Emergency Medicine* 58, no. 1 (2011): pp. 24–32; David Baker, Carl Stevens, and Robert Brook, "Patients Who Leave a Public Hospital Emergency Department without Being Seen by a Physician: Causes and Consequences," *JAMA: The Journal of the American Medical Association* 266, no. 8 (1991): pp. 1085–90; Katherine Arendt et al., "The Left-without-Being-Seen Patients: What Would Keep Them from Leaving?," *Annals of Emergency Medicine* 42, no. 3 (2003): pp. 317–23.

4. Demetrios Kyriacou, "Opioid vs Nonopioid Acute Pain Management in the Emergency Department," *JAMA: The Journal of the American Medical Association* 318, no. 17 (2017): pp. 1655–56

5. Knox Todd, Christi Deaton, Anne P. D'Adamo, and Leon Goe, "Ethnicity and Analgesic Practice," *Annals of Emergency Medicine* 35, no. 1 (2000): pp. 11–16; Susan Hinze, Noah J. Webster, Heidi T. Chirayath, and Joshua H. Tamayo-Sarver, "Hurt Running from Police? No Chance of (Pain) Relief: The Social Construction of Deserving Patients in Emergency Departments," in *Research in the Sociology of Health Care*, edited by J. Kronenfeld (Greenwich, CT: Emerald Group, 2009), pp. 235–61.

6. Rui Pinyao and Susan Schappert, "Opioids Prescribed at Discharge or Given during Emergency Department Visits among Adults in the United States," *National Center for Health Statistics Data Brief* 338 (2019). On JCAHO: Berry and Dahl, "New JCAHO Pain Standards"; on the rise of nurse-initiated protocols to grapple with overcrowding, see: Brian Rowe, Cristina Villa-Roel, Xiaoyan Guo, Michael Bullard, Maria Ospina, Benjamin Vandermeer, Grant Innes, Michael Schull, and Brian Holroyd, "The Role of Triage Nurse Ordering on Mitigating Overcrowding in Emergency Departments: A Systematic Review," *Academic Emergency Medicine* 18, no. 12 (2011): pp. 1349–57; One study showed triage pain management protocols increasing the number of patient receiving pain medication from 45% to 70%; David Fossnocht and Eric Swanson, "Use of Triage Pain Protocol in the ED," *American Journal of Emergency Medicine* 25, no. 7 (2007): pp. 791–93. See also: Anne-Maree Kelly, Catherine Barnes, and Caroline Brumby, "Nurse Initiated Narcotic Analgesia Reduces Time to Analgesia for Patients with Acute Pain in the ED," *CJEM* 7, no. 3 (2005): pp. 149–54; Margarete Fry and Anna Holdgate, "Nurse-Initiated Intravenous Morphine in the ED," *Emergency Medicine* 14, no. 3 (2008): pp. 249–54; Kevin Curtis, Horace Henriquies, Gilbert Francuillo,

Cecily Reynolds, and Freeman Suber, "A Fentanyl-based Pain Management Protocol Provides Early Analgesia for Adult Trauma Patients," *Journal of Trauma* 63, no. 4 (2007): pp. 819–26.

7. Roth, "Some Contingencies of the Moral Evaluation and Control of Clientele"; Jeffery, "Normal Rubbish."

8. Patricia Hill Collins, "Gender, Black Feminism, and Black Political Economy," *The Annals of the American Academy of Political and Social Science* 568, no 1. (2000): pp. 41–53; Elijah Anderson, "The Iconic Ghetto," *The Annals of the American Academy of Political and Social Science* 642, no. 1 (2012): pp. 8–24; Stanton Wortham, Katherine Mortimer, and Elaine Allard, "Mexicans as Model Minorities in the New Latino Diaspora," *Anthropology & Education Quarterly* 40, no. 4 (2009): pp. 388–404.

9. Lynne Haney, "Homeboys, Babies, Men in Suits: The State and the Reproduction of Male Dominance," *American Sociological Review* 61, no. 5 (1996): pp. 759–78.

10. See this relationship in: Erick Eiting, Carrie Korn, Erin Wilkes, Glenn Ault, and Sean Henderson, "Reduction in Jail Emergency Department Visits and Closure after Implementation of On-Site Urgent Care," *Journal of Correctional Health Care* 23, no. 1 (2017): pp. 88–92.

11. Radhika Sundararajan, Andrew Minor, William Paolo, and William Chiang, "Police Detainees in the Emergency Department: Who Do We Admit?" *Webmed Central* (2012): pp. 1–8;

12. Linda Teplin and Nancy S. Pruett, "Police as Streetcorner Psychiatrist: Managing the Mentally Ill," *International Journal of Law and Psychiatry* 15, no. 2 (1992): pp. 139–56. Also see: Josh Seim, "The Ambulance: Toward a Labor Theory of Poverty Governance," *American Sociological Review* 82, no. 3 (2017): pp. 451–75.

13. See the sticky situations that police and their wards create for medical professionals in the ER: Morsal Tahaouni and Emory Liscord, "Managing Law Enforcement Presence in the Emergency Department: Highlighting the Need for New Policy Recommendations," *Journal Emergency Medicine* 49, no. 4 (2015): pp. 523–29; Megan Harada, "Policed Patients: How Law Enforcement Personnel Impact Medical Care in the Emergency Department," *UCSF*, n.d.

14. As a recent ER Physician in an op-ed put it: "We joke with colleagues about 'frequent flyers' for pain medications in the emergency department (ED), but we then let those patients convince us to prescribe the opiates we know will not really help them." See: Pamela L. Pentin, "Drug Seeking or Pain Crisis? Responsible Prescribing of Opioids in the Emergency Department," *Virtual Mentor* 15, no. 5 (2013): pp. 410–15. On studies of the 1970s, see: Victoria George and Alan Dundes, "The Gomer: A Figure of American Hospital Folk Speech," *The Journal of American Folklore*, 91, no. 359 (1978): pp. 568–81; Jeffery, "Normal Rubbish"; Terry Mizrahi, "Getting Rid of Patients: Contradictions in the Socialization of Internists to the Doctor-Patient Relationship." *Sociology of Health & Illness* 7, no. 2 (1985): pp. 214–35. On medical journals, see: Anne-Claire Durand, Stéphanie Gentile, Bénédicte Devictor, Sylvie Palazzolo, Pascal Vignally, Patrick Gerbeaux, and Roland Sambuc, "ED Patients: How Nonurgent Are They? Systematic Review of the Emergency Medicine Literature," *American Journal of Emergency Medicine* 29, no. 3 (2011): pp. 333–45; Steven Krug,

"Access and Use of Emergency Services: Inappropriate Use versus Unmet Need," *Clinical Pediatric Emergency Medicine* 1, no. 1 (1999): pp. 35–44.

Chapter 4

1. LA County BOS Meeting Transcript, April 19, 2003 (County Online: on file).
2. LA County BOS Meeting Transcript, April 19, 2003 (County Online: on file).
3. Josh Pacewicz, "The Regulatory Road to Reform: Bureaucratic Activism, Agency Advocacy, and Medicaid Expansion within the Delegated Welfare State," *Politics & Society* 46, no. 4 (2018): pp. 571–601; Michael Gusmano and Frank Thompson, "The Safety Net at the Crossroads? Whither Medicaid DSH," in *The Health Care Safety-Net in a Post-Reform World*, edited by Mark A. Hall and Sara Rosenbaum (New Brunswick: Rutgers University Press, 2012): pp. 153–82.
4. "Meeting Minutes of the LAC + USC Advisory Council," *Los Angeles County*, August 5, 1993 (Edelman Papers: 301/4).
5. See accounts by the *Los Angeles Times* of the county's odyssey to obtain the initial disbursement in 1996 from the Clinton administration and CMS: Jeffrey Rabin, John Broder, and Josh Meyer, "Breakthrough Seen on $364-Million Deal to Rescue County Health System," *Los Angeles Times*, September 22, 1995: https://www.latimes.com/archives/la-xpm-1995-09-22-mn-48685-story.html; Jeffrey Rabin, Josh Meyer, and Jack Cheevers, "Clinton Offers L.A. Aid Plan Based on Community Care," *Los Angeles Times*, September 23, 1995: https://www.latimes.com/archives/la-xpm-1995-09-23-mn-49148-story.html; Douglas Shuit, "Problems Arise over County Bid for U.S. Health Care Bailout," *Los Angeles Times*, January 12, 1996: https://www.latimes.com/archives/la-xpm-1996-01-12-me-23942-story.html; Jeffrey Rabin and Josh Meyer, "U.S. Bailout of County Health System Stalled," *Los Angeles Times*, February 24, 1996: https://www.latimes.com/archives/la-xpm-1996-02-24-mn-39408-story.html; Josh Meyer and Jack Cheevers, "County to Eliminate a Third of Hospital Beds to Get U.S. Bailout," *Los Angeles Times*, February 27, 1996: https://www.latimes.com/archives/la-xpm-1996-02-27-me-40570-story.html; Josh Meyer, "County, U.S. at Odds over Long-Term Overhaul of Health System," *Los Angeles Times*, February 28, 1996: https://www.latimes.com/archives/la-xpm-1996-02-28-me-40941-story.html?_amp=true; Jeffrey Rabin and Josh Meyer, "County's Health Reform Proposal Delivered to U.S." *Los Angeles Times*, March 2, 1996: https://www.latimes.com/archives/la-xpm-1996-03-02-mn-42132-story.html; Editorial Writers Desk, "County Health Care at the Brink; Washington Must Follow Through with the Aid It Promised," *Los Angeles Times*, March 4, 1996: p. 29; James Bornemeier and Josh Meyer, "County Assured of U.S. Bailout, Supervisors Say," *Los Angeles Times*, March 5, 1996: https://www.latimes.com/archives/la-xpm-1996-03-05-me-43196-story.html; Jeffrey Rabin and Jack Cheevers, "County Health System Bailout Gets Final OK," *Los Angeles Times*, April 16, 1996; https://www.latimes.com/archives/la-xpm-1996-04-16-me-59165-story.html; Jeffrey Rabin, "County Health System to Get More U.S. Aid," *Los Angeles Times*, June 15, 1996: https://www.latimes.com/archives/la-xpm-1996-06-15-mn-15231-story.html.

6. Beyond political re-election calculus, CMS and the Clinton administration saw the Los Angeles County deal as a way to use the biggest public hospital system as a demonstration of the possibility of downsizing large inpatient services. As Clinton said, "And that is a national issue. It's not a Los Angeles County issue. If it can be solved here with the restructuring, a lot of people all over America will be learning a lot from what you are doing. And the working families of America will be better served by it." "Clinton Offers L.A. Aid Plan Based on Community Care," Los Angeles Times. Indeed, in 2005 the plan was expanded to five other California counties.

7. "County to Eliminate a Third of Hospital Beds to Get U.S. Bailout," Los Angeles Times, February 27: https://www.latimes.com/archives/la-xpm-1996-02-27-me-40570-story.html.

8. On the waiver as "bailout" see the reports: "Draft of the Final Project Report for the Medicaid Demonstration Project," Thomas Garthwaite to BOS, Department of Health Services, November 22, 2005 (County Online: on file); "1115 Waiver Summary Report: 1995–2005," Thomas Garthwaite to BOS, Department of Health Services, June 13, 2005 (County Online: on file); Stephen Zuckerman and Amy Westpfahl Lutzky, "The Medicaid Demonstration Project in Los Angeles County, 1995–2000: Progress, But Room for Improvement," The Urban Institute (2001); Sharon Long and Stephen Zuckerman, "Urban Health Care in Transition: Challenges Facing Los Angeles County," Health Care Financing Review 20, no. 1 (1998): pp. 45–58; Daniel R. Levinson, "Audit of California's Section 1115 Medicaid Demonstration Project Extension for Los Angeles County," Department of Health and Human Services, October 24, 2006(County online: on file). The initial relief packaged was constructed in the following way: "The five-year financial relief package brought LACDHS approximately $1.2 billion in federal Medicaid funding, with the two largest components of the funding being a supplemental project pool (SPP) and an indigent care match. The SPP is funded equally by federal and local dollars and was established so that the County could receive federal Medicaid funds for providing ambulatory care to indigents. The indigent care match made LACDHS eligible to receive a federal match for services provided to low-income patients in non-hospital settings"; Zuckerman and Lutzky, "The Medicaid Demonstration Project In Los Angeles County". The County's chief administrative officer summarized the use and conditions of 1115 funds in his letter to the BOS as: "The first year of the [1115 funds] provided the county with fiscal relief to preserve vital inpatient and ambulatory care capacity. Concurrently, we began to downsize the inpatient care system and further the process of public–private partnership agreements for clinics. . . . Development of programs to reduce inpatient utilization by patients with ambulatory appropriate conditions . . ."; "Untitled Letter," Mark Finucane to BOS, Department of Health Services, August 26, 1996 (Burke Papers: 125/5).

9. "Minutes of the BOS," Los Angeles County, February 11, 1992 (Edelman Papers: 537/2).

10. "Report" County Taskforce to Determine Unmet Needs of Uninsured/Underinsured and Public–Private Resources (Edelman Papers: 302/1).

11. "Congressional Visit to LAC + USC Medical Center," Robert Gates to BOS, Department of Health Services, March 23, 1993 (Edelman Papers: 302/1).

12. "Press Release: Congressman Beilenson Introduces Legislation to Control Illegal Immigration," *County of Los Angeles*, (Edelman Papers: 302/1).

13. "Untitled Letter," Antonovich to Burke, *Antonovich Office*, December 22, unknown year (Burke Papers: 428/16). The county's negotiations for the 1115 funds are replete with an emphasis on the federal government's responsibility to pay for the cost of illegal immigration. I will mention two examples: In a letter from Supervisor Edelman to federal healthcare officials, Edelman reasoned, "Washington is giving money to California to pay for illegal aliens," and since California was cutting funding to the county, "the County deserved direct funding from the federal government." On April 20, 1993, the director of Los Angeles County's Department of Health Services traveled to Washington, D.C., to testify before the CMS committee in charge of the 1115 health funds. The comments centered on LAC + USC and the county's status as a primary source of healthcare to immigrants in the area (both documents in Edelman Papers: 250/6).

14. The LAC + USC hospital replacement facility was originally planned as a 900-bed facility with a 300-bed annex to be located in a nearby suburb of Los Angeles, for a total of 1,200 beds. In 1992, the facility was downsized from the initial 1,200-bed replacement plan to a 950-bed replacement plan. The County Department of Health Services initiated this alternative plan in 1992 "because of the worsening economic climate and anticipated limited access to capital included general obligation bonds," wrote the CAO. See: "LAC/USC Medical Center Replacement Project," Moreno to Edelman, *Edelman Office*, December 22, 1992 (Edelman Papers: 302/4); "Alternative Health Facilities Replacement and Improvement Plan," CEO to Tatum, October 16, 1992 (Burke Papers: s351). The three county reports establishing the 750-bed minimum standard are: Robert Tranquada and H. Zaretsky, "County of Los Angeles Health Facilities Improvement and Replacement Plan," *Department of Health Services*, Los Angeles County (1996); Harvey Rose, *Report on the Los Angeles County–USC Replacement Project*, Harvey M. Rose Accounting Group (1995); Lewin-VHI, *LA Model*, prepared for Department of Health Services, Los Angeles County (1997).

15. "Alternative Health Facilities Replacement and Improvement Plan" (Burke Papers: s351).

16. While the usefulness of the managed care plans to justify downsizing the hospital can be found in county health documents throughout this decision-making process, important example are: "Alternative Facilities Replacement and Improvement Plan," Burke to Tatum, Burke Office, October 20, 1992 (Burke Papers: s351); "Responses to Questions Regarding the LAC-USC Replacement Project" DHS to Holifield, *Burke Office*, November 3, 1997 (Burke Papers: 125/5); "Minutes of the LAC + USC Advisory Council," Raul Caro, *Department of Health Services*, August 5, 1993 (Edelman Papers: 301:4); "LAC-USC Medical Center Replacement Project," Mark Finucane to Janssen, *Department of Health Services*, July 2, 1998 (Burke Papers: 125/5); "Architectural Program: Harbor-UCLA Medical Center," Jenkins, Gales, and Martinez, *Department of Health Services* (Burke Papers: s351).

17. "Operational Savings Analysis and SB 1732 Funds," Dixon to BOS, *CAO Office*, June 8, 1992 (Edelman Papers: 301/5).

18. "At the Center: Special Edition," Fernando Vizcarra, *Department of Health Services* (Edelman Papers: 301/4).

19. "Activity Report," Finucane to BOS, *Department of Health Services*, October 9, 1998 (Burke Papers: 125/5). My understanding of the debate around this decision is partially based on the county's video recording Los Angeles BOS Meeting DVD, November 12, 1997 (County Records: on file); See private sector perspective at the time: Brian Johnston and Jim Lott, "Perspective on the Medical Center: County-USC Price Tag Is a Bargain," *Los Angeles Times*, October 30, 1997.

20. See: "LAC-USC Medical Center Replacement/Action Items," Moreno to Bob, *Edelman's Office*, June 24, 1994 (Edelman Papers: 303/1); "LAC-USC Medical Center Replacement Project Operational Savings Analysis," Gates to BOS, *Department of Health Services*, May 24, 1993 (Edelman Papers: 303/1). Indeed, in 1992, the only foreseeable funding for the LAC + USC replacement facility was the recently passed SB 1732, which would fund less than 10% of the planned facility. The project also benefited from the Northridge Earthquake, which struck and damaged the existing facility and allowed the county to claim FEMA emergency funds to use toward a replacement facility.

21. "Motion: Build 600-Bed Hospital with Flexible-Use Annex," Supervisor Gloria Molina, *County of Los Angeles*, September 15, 1998 (Burke Papers: 125/5); "Motion: Support Building a 600-Bed 'Shell,'" Supervisor Michael Antonovich, *County of Los Angeles*, September 15, 1998 (Burke Papers: 125/5); "Motion: Build Hospital with Cap of 600 Beds," Supervisors Burke and Yaroslavsky, *County of Los Angeles*, November 12, 1997 (Burke Papers: 125/5); Los Angeles BOS Meeting DVD, November 12, 1997 (County Records: on file).

22. "Build Hospital with Cap of 600 Beds" (Burke Papers: 125/5); Burke would eventually recognize the scientific communities' steadfast projection that a 750-bed replacement was necessary, even with managed care and privatization assumptions. She drafted a motion calling for a 150-bed expansion one year later. See: "Motion: Build 600-Bed Hospital with Potential 150-Bed Annex," Supervisor Yvonne Burke, County of Los Angeles, September 15, 1998 (Burke Papers: 125/5).

23. This section is based on my understanding the following County LA County BOS Meeting Transcripts: June 18, 2007; June 19, 2007; June 26, 2007; July 17, 2007; August 13, 2007; August 18, 2007 (County Online: on file); "Recommended Adjustments to the 2007–08 Proposed County Budget," David Janssen to BOS, *CEO Office*, June 18, 2007 (County Online: on file); "Corrective Action Plan for Immediate Jeopardy," Chernoff to BOS, *Department of Health Services*, June 19, 2007 (County Online: on file); "MLK-Harbor Hospital Contingency Planning Overview," Chernoff to BOS, *Department of Health Services*, June 22, 2007 (County Online: on file); "Progress Report on Actions Related to Martin Luther King, Jr.–Harbor Hospital Contingency Plan," David Janssen to BOS, *CEO Office*, July 13, 2007 (County Online: on file) "Martin Luther King, JR.–Harbor Hospital Closure Implementation Plan," Chernoff to BOS, *Department of Health Services*, August 13, 2007 (County Online: on file); "Proposed Reductions of Trauma Services at Martin Luther King, Jr/Charles R. Drew Medical Center," Thomas Garthwaite and Fred Leaf to BOS, *Department of Health*

Services (County Online: on file); In addition to the privatization of Rancho, the 2003 Court order also prevented the closure of an additional 100 beds at LAC + USC. This may be confusing, as the 1997 vote to downsize LAC + USC from 1,200 planned beds to 600 would still go forward upon completion in 2008. What happened in 2003 was that the board was trying to bring the old hospital, still in use, in line with the size of the replacement, which was still under construction.

24. "Letter to CMS Regarding Readiness for CMS Survey at MLK-Harbor Hospital," Chernoff to BOS, *Department of Health Services*, July 9, 2007 (County Online: on file); "Attached CMS Plan of Correction Documents for MLK, Jr.–Harbor," Chernoff to BOS, *Department of Health Services*, July 10, 2007 (County Online: on file); "Statement of Deficiencies and Plan of Correction," Department of Health and Human Services, Centers for Medicare & Medicaid Services OMB No. 0938-0391, June 12, 2007 (County Online: on file).

25. "Proposed Reductions of Trauma Services at Martin Luther King, Jr/Charles R. Drew Medical Center" (County Online: on file).

26. "Proposed Reductions of Trauma Services at Martin Luther King, Jr/Charles R. Drew Medical Center" (County Online: on file).

27. LA County BOS Meeting Transcript, September 21, 2004 (County Online: on file).

28. LA County BOS Meeting Transcript, September 21, 2004 (County Online: on file).

29. LA County BOS Meeting Transcript, June 19, 2007 (County Online: on file).

30. "Corrective Action Plan for Immediate Jeopardy" (County Online: on file); "Statement of Deficiencies and Plan of Correction" (County Online: on file).

31. "Statement of Deficiencies and Plan of Correction" (County Online: on file).

32. 6 LA County BOS Meeting Transcript, June 19, 2007 (County Online: on file); "Corrective Action Plan for Immediate Jeopardy" (County Online: on file). In the triage department I observed, the practice of procuring pain medication during the wait was even easier. Registered nurses simply provided written documentation at the end of their shift for physicians to sign off. It was commonly known that physicians approved any request, as triage nurses had become well versed in the administration of these opiates.

33. "LAC-USC Medical Center Replacement Project" (Burke Papers: 125/5). Another example: "The design of the triage, which could serve as the link between urgent care and the emergency room department, will be critically important . . . will screen and direct non-emergency patients to urgent care clinic or adult inpatient facility. . . . At present the ER also provides non-emergency care to the patients not covered by any insurance. This has resulted in waiting period as long as 18 hours and approx. 8,000 patients did not wait to receive ER care in 1990/91 due to the long waiting periods. It will have an observation unit with at least 12-hour observation, which should preclude unnecessary hospitalization. . . . The ER and urgent care clinics should be collocated so that the walk-in patients can be triaged and directed to the appropriate area . . ."; "Architectural Program: Harbor-UCLA Medical Center" (Burke Papers: s351).

34. "FY 1994–95 Bans Authority for Health Facilities Replacement and Improvement Plan," Gates to BOS, *Department of Health Services*, February 8, 1995 (Edelman Papers: s351).

35. For this section, I rely on an examination of 81 reports on the "key indicators of progress from the transition to the new facility" that were released by the Department of
Health Services between 2009 and 2014 (County Online: on file). I also examined
every instance of these reports being discussed in the Board of Supervisors hearings.
The critical movements of discussion and administrative changes occurred in the Fall
2010 LA County BOS Meeting Transcripts (County Online: on file).

36. "Centers for Medicare and Medicaid Services Survey of LAC + USC Hospital," John
Schunhoff, *Department of Health Services*, September 3, 2010 (County online: on file).

37. LA County BOS Meeting Transcripts, September 28, 2010 (County Online: on file).

38. LA County BOS Meeting Transcripts, August 9, 2012 (County Online: on file).

39. Alongside the move of nurse practitioners into triage, administrators dedicated a
14-bed pod in the ER to seeing non-urgent patients ahead of more concerning B-
level patients. This essentially turned a portion of the ER into a walk-in urgent care
clinic. "In the back, in the back area, what we're going to do is convert—plan is to
convert one of the pods, east pod, into a direct patient care pod, meaning that we
have a residency program, that particular pod of 14 beds is going to be dedicated
just for direct patient care. We believe that this will expedite some of the discharges
and will do a lot to decompress the ER, hopefully that will reduce the amount of
time we're in black"; LA County BOS Meeting Transcripts, September 28, 2010
(County Online: on file).

40. Scott   Harris,   "In   Suspect's   Room-Paltry   Belongings,   Ominous   Notes
Investigation: Police Say They Found Writings that Show Premeditation," *Los Angeles
Times*, February 10, 1993: https://www.latimes.com/archives/la-xpm-1993-02-10-
mn-1358-story.html.

41. John Mitchell and Shawn Hubler, "Patient at County-USC Shoots 3 Doctors, Gives
Up in Standoff Violence: One Victim Is Reportedly Near Death and Two Are Listed
as Critical." *Los Angeles Times*, February 9, 1993: https://www.latimes.com/archives/
la-xpm-1993-02-09-mn-1090-story.html.

42. "Minutes of the BOS," *Los Angeles County*, February 9, 1993 (Edelman Papers: 301/4).

43. Douglas Shuit, "Hospitals' Walk-in Powder Kegs Violence and Threats are Common
in Los Angeles County's Emergency Rooms, Where Patients Endure Endless Delays."
Los Angeles Times, February 10, 1993: https://www.latimes.com/archives/la-xpm-
1993-02-10-mn-1331-story.html

44. "County Hospital Shooting," *Daily News*, unknown date (Edelman Papers:).

45. John Mitchell and Shawn Hubler, "Patient at County-USC Shoots 3 Doctors, Gives
Up in Standoff Violence."

46. Douglas Shuit, "Hospitals' Walk-in Powder Kegs Violence and Threats Are Common
in Los Angeles County's Emergency Rooms, Where Patients Endure Endless
Delays." The real story, of course, is that most "incidents" counted in statistics were
confrontations between frustrated patients and frustrated nursing staff in the context
of an overcrowded ER. A county memo revealed the following facts: "Of the 3,465
incidents at LAC-USC, 2,912 were denoted as 'confrontational situations,' while 234
were thefts, 36 were assaults and 14 were 'sexual (non-rape).'" See: "Letter," Kimberly
Kyle to Gates, *Local 660 SEUI/AFL-CIO*, 1993 (Edelman Papers: 302/2).

47. Evidence of the county leaders' discovery, investigation, and eventual use of the "Halloran report" can be found in memos attached to the cache of documents surrounding LAC + USC's effort to contract with Halloran in Box 302, File 3, of the Edelman Papers. See, for example: "Letter," Jerry Buckingham to Block (Edelman Papers: 302/3).

48. "Sole Source Emergency Purchase Order to Hire Security Operations Consultant Donald J. Halloran," Elliot Johnson to Harold Crank, *LAC + USC*, April 2, 1991 (Edelman Papers: 302/3).

49. "Meeting Minutes," *LAC-USC Medical Center Security Task Force*, January 21, 1991 (Edelman Papers: 302/3); "Meeting Minutes," *LAC-USC Medical Center Security Task Force*, February 12, 1991 (Edelman Papers: 302/3).

50. "Evaluation and Recommendations Security Operations LAC-USC County Medical Center," David Halloran, 1991 (Edelman Papers: 302/3).

51. "Medical Center Safety Police 1992–93 Budget Request," unknown author, 1992 (Edelman Papers: 302/3); "Status of Halloran Consulting Report," Gates to BOS, *Department of Health Services*, March 5, 1993 (Edelman Papers: 302/3).

52. "Security Task Force Recommendations," John McClurg, *LAC + USC*, March 19, 1991 (Edelman Papers: 302/3).

53. "Status of Halloran Consulting Report" (Edelman Papers: 302/3).

54. Stephen Shortell, Robin Gillies, and Kelly Devers, "Reinventing the American Hospital," *The Milbank Quarterly* 73, no. 2 (1995): 131–60; Chloe Bird, Peter Conrad, and Allen Fremont, "Medical Sociology at the Millennium," in *Handbook of Medical Sociology*, edited by Chloe Bird, Peter Conrad, and Allen Fremont, 5th ed. (Englewood Cliffs, NJ: Prentice Hall, 2000): pp. 1–10.

Chapter 5

1. I am grateful to the insight of Valeria Luiselli on lost children at the border. John Washington, "'How Do You Address Disappearance?': A Q&A with Valeria Luiselli," *The Nation*, April 1, 2019: https://www.thenation.com/article/archive/valeria-luiselli-interview-lost-children-archive/.

2. The idea that ambivalence can be reconciled by viewing the state as a growing "right hand" (comprising organizations such as police, courts, jails, prisons, and the military) and a weakening "left hand" (comprising organizations such as welfare agencies, unemployment offices, child protective services, social security benefits, and hospitals) falls short. As we shall see, the urban poverty governance literature remains quite ambivalent about the exact definition of "weak" and "strong." See, for example: Joe Soss, Richard C. Fording, and Sanford F. Schram, *Disciplining the Poor: Neoliberal Paternalism and the Persistent Power of Race* (Chicago: University of Chicago Press, 2011).

3. The scholarship on various transformations in urban governance institutions is vast. On changes in policing see: Stuart, *Down, Out, and Under Arrest: Policing and Everyday Life in Skid Row*; Chris Herring, "Complaint-Oriented Policing: Regulating

Homelessness in Public Space," *American Sociological Review* 84, no. 5 (2019): pp. 769–800; Sarah Brayne, "Big Data Surveillance: The Case of Policing," *American Sociological Review* 82, no. 5 (2017): pp. 977–1008; Katherine Beckett and Steve Herbert, *Banished: The New Social Control in Urban America* (New York: Oxford University Press, 2010). On color blind racism in courts, see: Nicole Gonzalez Van Cleve, *Crook County: Racism and Injustice in America's Largest Criminal Court* (Palo Alto, CA: Stanford University Press, 2016). On transformations away from convictions in criminal courts, see: Kohler-Hausmann, *Misdemeanorland: Criminal Courts and Social Control in an Age of Broken Windows Policing*; Alexandra Natapoff, "Gideon's Servants and the Criminalization of Poverty." On changes in correctional settings, see: Haney, *Offending Women: Power, Punishment, and the Regulation of Desire*; Schept, *Progressive Punishment: Job Loss, Jail Growth, and the Neoliberal Logic of Carceral Expansion*. On medical arenas, see: Seim, "The Ambulance: Toward a Labor Theory of Poverty Governance"; McKim, *Addicted to Rehab: Race, Gender, and Drugs in the Era of Mass Incarceration*; Chiarello, "The War on Drugs Comes to the Pharmacy Counter"; for Departments of Children and Family Services, see: Fong, "Concealment and Constraint"; Edwards, "Saving Children, Controlling Families."

4. This is what Latour meant by "keeping the social flat": that the actions we observe people taking in the present day can be empirically traced to the actions of individuals outside of their contexts; Bruno Latour, *Reassembling the Social: An Introduction to Actor-Network-Theory* (New York: Oxford University Press, 2007); Latour, "Network Theory | Networks, Societies, Spheres: Reflections of an Actor-Network Theorist," *International Journal of Communication Systems* 5 (April 8, 2011): pp. 796–810.

5. As Becker described public officials: "On the one hand, he must demonstrate to others that the problem still exists: the rules he is supposed to enforce have some point, because infractions occur. On the other hand, he must show that his attempts at enforcement are effective and worthwhile, that the evil he is supposed to deal with is in fact being dealt with adequately"; Howard Becker, *Outsiders: Studies in the Sociology of Deviance* (New York: Free Press, 1963), p. 127.

6. This analysis comes from my reading of archival materials surrounding the fight to open Los Angeles County's MacLaren Center—a holding/clearing-house facility for probation, foster care, and abused juveniles—with county, state, and federal funds, and the decision to close the facility in 2003. The relevant materials can be found in the following boxes and files of Edelman Papers: 127/5–143/5 (especially 140/2–141/1); 351/5–351/8; 678/13–679/4; and 1024/4–1025/2. See also John R. Sutton, *Stubborn Children: Controlling Delinquency in the United States, 1640–1981* (Berkeley: University of California Press, 1988).

7. Michelle Goldberg, "Yes, Mr. President, the Border Kids Are Refugees," *The Nation*, July 16, 2004: https://www.thenation.com/article/archive/our-refugee-crisis/; Óscar Martínez, "Why the Children Fleeing Central American Will Not Stop Coming," *The Nation*, July 30, 2014: https://www.thenation.com/article/archive/why-children-fleeing-central-america-will-not-stop-coming/.

8. My understanding of this crisis is reliant on: Greg Kaufmann, "What's the Best Way to Actually Care for Unaccompanied Migrant Children?" *The Nation*, October 10,

2019: https://www.thenation.com/article/archive/migrant-children-shelter-dc/; Ron Nixon, "U.S. Loses Track of Another 1,500 Migrant Children, Investigators Find," *New York Times*, September 18, 2018: https://www.nytimes.com/2018/09/18/us/politics/us-migrant-children-whereabouts-.html; Michelle Chen, "Whirlwind Deportations Are Depriving Thousands of Migrants of Their Rights—And Some, of Their Lives," *The Nation*, December 17, 2014: https://www.thenation.com/article/archive/whirlwind-deportations-are-depriving-thousands-migrants-their-rights-and-some-their-live/; Steven Hsieh, "Human Rights Groups Blast Obama's Plan to Open New Immigrant Family Detention Centers," *The Nation*, June 20, 2014. https://www.thenation.com/article/archive/human-rights-groups-blast-obamas-plan-open-new-immigrant-family-detention-centers/; John Washington, "The Amount of Money Being Made Ripping Migrant Families Apart Is Staggering," *The Nation*, October 28, 2019. https://www.thenation.com/article/archive/immigration-ice-family-separation/; Hayes, "U.S. Department of Health and Human Services Before the Subcommittee on Oversight and Investigations Committee on Energy and Commerce United States House of Representatives," September 19, 2019. Also see chapter 2 in: Patrisia Macías-Rojas, *From Deportation to Prison: The Politics of Immigration in Post-Civil Rights America* (New York: New York University Press, 2016).

9. My understanding of the trafficking of Madagascar's workers is taken from Aaron Ross, "Why Are Thousands of Malagasy Women Being Trafficked to Abusive Jobs in the Middle East?" *The Nation*, April 15, 2014: https://www.thenation.com/article/archive/why-are-thousands-malagasy-women-being-trafficked-abusive-jobs-middle-east/. Another recent explosion of officially organized trafficking is the case of the fracking oil boom in Texas. See SanJuhi Verma, "Black Gold, Brown Labor: The Legalization of Indentured Work Through the Transnational Migration Industry," PhD diss., Department of Sociology, University of Chicago (2012).

10. At the core of this idea is Pierson's (1998) work on path dependence in public institutions. Essentially, as institutions age, they begin to take on an inertia of their own that makes them increasingly difficult to dismantle. For one, any politician attempting to dismantle welfare institutions has to contend with pushback from important constituencies who have grown used to entitlements (in our case it would be groups representing local governments and public hospitals). Moreover, past policy decisions meant to enhance the trajectory of these institutions constrain opportunities for retrenchment-minded politicians. Paul Pierson, "Irresistible Forces, Immovable Objects: Post-industrial Welfare State Confront Permanent Austerity," *Journal of European Public Policy* 5, no. 4 (1998): pp. 539–60.

11. Hacking, "Kinds of People: Moving Targets," p. 293.

12. LA County BOS Meeting Transcript, July 11, 2006 (County Online: on file); Also see: LA County BOS Meeting Transcript, August 1, 2006 (County Online: on file).

13. LA County BOS Meeting Transcript, June 3, 2006 (County Online: on file).

14. Michel Foucault, "The Politics of Health in the Eighteenth Century," in *Michel Foucault: Power/Knowledge: Selected Interviews and Other Writings 1972–1977*, edited by Colin Gordon (Brighton: Harvester Press, 1980); James Scott, *Seeing like a State: How Certain Schemes to Improve the Human Condition Have Failed* (New

Haven, CT: Yale University Press, 1998); Mara Loveman, "The Modern State and the Primitive Accumulation of Symbolic Power," *American Journal of Sociology* 110, no. 6 (2005): pp. 1651–83; Pierre Bourdieu, *On the State: Lectures at the Collège de France, 1989–1992*, edited by Patrick Champagne, Remi Lenoir, Franck Poupeau, and Marie-Christine Riviere (Cambridge: Polity, 2015).

15. Elizabeth Marcellino, "LA County Supervisors Scrap $1.7 Billion Contract to Replace Jail: 'It's time to do the right thing," *Los Angeles Daily News*, August 13, 2019: https://www.dailynews.com/2019/08/13/la-county-supervisors-scrap-1-7-bill-contract-to-replace-jail-its-time-to-do-the-right-thing/. Also see: note 85.

16. This resonates with findings on the role of progressive litigation on early penal development. See: Lynch "Mass Incarceration, Legal Change, and Locale: Understanding and Remediating American Penal Overindulgence"; Reiter, *23/7: Pelican Bay Prison and the Rise of Long-Term Solitary Confinement*; Schoenfeld, "Mass Incarceration and the Paradox of Prison Conditions Litigation." In order to win over fiscal conservatives who opposed prison building in the 1970s, penal advocates reframed federal court Eighth Amendment rulings as infringements on state's rights and penal expansion as a conservative cause (Schoenfeld 2010). Reiter (2016) demonstrates that the rise of solitary confinement in California prisons was, in part, an unintended consequence of progressive lawsuits against indeterminate sentencing.

Appendix

1. Andrulis and Duchon, "The Changing Landscape of Hospital Capacity in Large Cities and Suburbs: Implications for the Safety Net in Metropolitan America"; United States Congress Senate Committee, *Hospital Emergency Departments: Crowded Conditions Vary among Hospitals and Communities: Report to the Ranking Minority Member, Committee on Finance, US Senate* (General Accounting Office, 2003). Ray Quintanilla and *Tribune* staff, "Uncertainty Stalks Hospitals," *Chicago Tribune*, October 13, 2006: www.chicagotribune.com/news/ct-xpm-2006-10-13-0610130258-story.htm l+&cd=1&hl=en&ct=clnk&gl=us; Southern California Public Radio, "LA County Hospital Services Faces $204M Deficit," Southern California Public Radio, May 18, 2010; Elaine Rabin, Keith Kocher, Mark McClelland, Jesse Pines, Ula Hwang, Niels Rathlev, Brent Asplin, N. Seth Trueger, and Ellen Weber, "Solutions to Emergency Department 'Boarding' and Crowding Are Underused and May Need to Be Legislated," *Health Affairs* 31, no. 8 (2012): pp. 1757–66.

2. The bulk of my archival material comes from the following holdings. The Huntington Library, located in Pasadena, CA, holds the donated papers of two retired members of the Los Angeles County Board of Supervisors: the "Papers of Edmund D. Edelman, 1953–1994 (bulk 1974–1994)" and the "Papers of Kenneth Hahn 1953–1993." Both are held by the Huntington Library, San Marino, CA. The third holding is the donated papers of another retired member of the Board of Supervisors at the University of Southern California Regional History Collection: the Yvonne Brathwaite Burke Papers (1979–1981 and 1994–2008). I also make use of the county's own

online collection, which covers the period from 2000 until 2011, and selected video recordings of Board of Supervisor meetings that I requested from the county directly.

3. Heather Schoenfeld, "A Research Agenda on Reform: Penal Policy and Politics across the States," *The Annals of the American Academy of Political and Social Science* 664, no. 1 (2016): p. 159; Michael C. Campbell and Heather Schoenfeld, "The Transformation of America's Penal Order: A Historicized Political Sociology of Punishment," *The American Journal of Sociology* 118, no. 5 (2013): pp. 1375–1423; Philip Goodman, Joshua Page, and Michelle Phelps, "The Long Struggle: An Agonistic Perspective on Penal Development," *Theoretical Criminology* 19, no. 3 (2015): pp. 315–35; Vanessa Barker, *The Politics of Imprisonment: How the Democratic Process Shapes the Way America Punishes Offenders* (New York: Oxford University Press, 2009); Joshua Page, *The Toughest Beat: Politics, Punishment, and the Prison Officers Union in California* (New York: Oxford University Press, 2013); Mona Lynch, *Sunbelt Justice: Arizona and the Transformation of American Punishment* (Palo Alto, CA: Stanford University Press, 2009).

4. Phillip Goodman, Joshua Page, and Michelle Phelps, "The Long Struggle: An Agonistic Perspective on Penal Development," *Theoretical Criminology* 19 no. 3 (2015): p. 316.

5. Erving Goffman (1967) basically described these moments and their importance in his essay "where the action is." Moments when individuals' risk something, have no idea what the outcome of the interaction will be, and come to innovate practices and cultural forms. Goffman, *Interaction Ritual: Essays in Face-to-Face Behavior* (New York: The Free Press, 1967).

6. Latour, "Network Theory | Networks, Societies, Spheres," p. 10.

7. Latour, "Network Theory | Networks, Societies, Spheres," p. 14.

References

Abbott, Andrew. 1988. "Transcending General Linear Reality." *Sociological Theory* 6 (2): pp. 169–86.

Adams, Julia, Elisabeth Clemens, Ann Shola Orloff. 2005. *Remaking Modernity: Politics, History, and Sociology.* Durham, NC: Duke University Press.

Albrecht, Gary, David Slobodkin, and Robert J. Rydman. 1996. "The Role of Emergency Departments in American Health Care." In *Research in the Sociology of Health Care*, edited by J. J. Kronefield, pp. 289–318. Greenwich, CT: JAI Press.

Alexander, Michelle. 2010. *The New Jim Crow: Mass Incarceration in the Age of Colorblindness.* New York: The New Press.

Anderson, Elijah. 2012. "The Iconic Ghetto." *The Annals of the American Academy of Political and Social Science* 642 (1): pp. 8–24.

Andrulis, Dennis P., and Lisa M. Duchon. 2007. "The Changing Landscape of Hospital Capacity in Large Cities and Suburbs: Implications for the Safety Net in Metropolitan America." *Journal of Urban Health* 84 (3): pp. 400–14.

Arendt, Katherine W., Annie T. Sadosty, Amy L. Weaver, Christopher R. Brent, and Eric T. Boie. 2003. "The Left-without-Being-Seen Patients: What Would Keep Them from Leaving?" *Annals of Emergency Medicine* 42 (3): pp. 317–23.

Baker, David, Carl Stevens, and Robert Brook. 1991. "Patients Who Leave a Public Hospital Emergency Department without Being Seen by a Physician: Causes and Consequences." *JAMA: The Journal of the American Medical Association* 266 (8): pp. 1085–90.

Barker, Vanessa. 2009. *The Politics of Imprisonment: How the Democratic Process Shapes the Way America Punishes Offenders.* New York: Oxford University Press.

Barnes, Jeb, and Thomas F. Burke. 2014. *How Policy Shapes Politics: Rights, Courts, Litigation, and the Struggle over Injury Compensation.* New York: Oxford University Press.

Bazzoli, Gloria, Ray Kang, Romana Hasnain-Wynia, and Richard C. Lindrooth. 2005. "An Update on Safety-Net Hospitals: Coping with the Late 1990s and Early 2000s." *Health Affairs* 24 (4): pp. 1047–56.

Becker, Howard. 1963. *Outsiders: Studies in the Sociology of Deviance.* New York: The Free Press.

Beckett, Katherine, and Steve Herbert. 2010. *Banished: The New Social Control in Urban America.* New York: Oxford University Press.

Béland, Daniel. 2007. "Ideas and Institutional Change in Social Security: Conversion, Layering, and Policy Drift." *Social Science Quarterly* 88 (1): pp. 20–38.

Ben-Moshe, Liat, Chris Chapman, and Allison Carey. 2014. *Disability Incarcerated: Imprisonment and Disability in the United States and Canada.* New York: Palgrave Macmillan.

Berry, Patricia, and June Dahl. 2000. "New JCAHO Pain Standards: Implications for Pain Management Nurses." *Pain Management Nursing* 1 (1): pp. 3–12.

Bird, Chloe, Peter Conrad, and Allen Fremont. 2000. "Medical Sociology at the Millennium." In *Handbook of Medical Sociology*, edited by Chloe Bird, Peter Conrad, and Allen Fremont, 5th ed, pp. 1–10. Englewood Cliffs, NJ: Prentice Hall.

Block, Fred, Richard Cloward, Barara Ehrenreich, and Frances Fox Piven. 1987. *The Mean Season: The Attack on the Welfare State*. New York: Pantheon Books.

Block, Sherman. 1983. "Treating Mentally Ill in L.A. County Jails." *Los Angeles Times*, January 8: p. B2

Bornemeier, James, and Josh Meyer. 1996. "County Assured of U.S. Bailout, Supervisors Say." *Los Angeles Times*, March 5. https://www.latimes.com/archives/la-xpm-1996-03-05-me-43196-story.html.

Bourdieu, Pierre. 2015. *On the State: Lectures at the Collège de France, 1989–1992*, edited by Patrick Champagne, Remi Lenoir, Franck Poupeau, and Marie-Christine Riviere. Cambridge: Polity Press.

Brayne, Sarah. 2017. "Big Data Surveillance: The Case of Policing." *American Sociological Review* 82 (5): pp. 977–1008.

Bronson, Jennifer, and Marcus Berzofsky. 2017. *Indicators of Mental Health Problems Reported by Prisoners and Jail Inmates, 2011–12*. U.S. Department of Justice: Bureau of Justice Statistics, pp. 1–16.

Brown, Wendy. 2015. *Undoing the Demos: Neoliberalism's Stealth Revolution*. New York: Zone Books.

Burawoy, Michael. 2003. "Revisits: An Outline of a Theory of Reflexive Ethnography." *American Sociological Review* 68 (5): pp. 645–79.

Burawoy, Michael. 2009. *Extended Case Method: Four Countries, Four Decades, Four Great Transformations, and One Theoretical Tradition*. Berkeley: University of California Press.

Burt, Martha, John Hedderson, Janine Zweig, Mary Ortiz, Laudan Aron-Turnham, and Sabrina Johnson. 2004. "Appendix D: Strategies for Reducing Chronic Street Homelessness Final Report." Washington, D.C.: The Urban Institute.

Calavita, Kitty, and Valerie Jenness. 2015. *Appealing to Justice: Prisoner Grievances, Rights, and Carceral Logic*. Berkeley: University of California Press.

Campbell, Andrea. 2015. "The Durability of Pierson's Theory about the Durability of the Welfare State." *PS: Political Science & Politics* 48 (2): pp. 284–88.

Campbell, Michael. 2011. "Politics, Prisons, and Law Enforcement: An Examination of the Emergence of 'Law and Order' Politics in Texas." *Law & Society Review* 45 (3): pp. 631–65.

Campbell, Michael, and Heather Schoenfeld. 2013. "The Transformation of America's Penal Order: A Historicized Political Sociology of Punishment." *The American Journal of Sociology* 118 (5): pp. 1375–1423.

Chiarello, Elizabeth. 2015. "The War on Drugs Comes to the Pharmacy Counter: Frontline Work in the Shadow of Discrepant Institutional Logics." *Law and Social Inquiry* 40 (1): pp. 86–122.

Chen, Michelle. 2014. "Whirlwind Deportations Are Depriving Thousands of Migrants of Their Rights—And Some, of Their Lives." *The Nation*, December 17. https://www.thenation.com/article/archive/whirlwind-deportations-are-depriving-thousands-migrants-their-rights-and-some-their-live/.

Clear, Todd. 2007. *Imprisoning Communities: How Mass Incarceration Makes Disadvantaged Communities Worse*. New York: Oxford University Press.

Clear, Todd, Michael Reisig, and George Cole. 2019. *American Corrections.* Boston: Cengage Learning.

Clemens, Elisabeth. 2007. "Towards a Historicized Sociology: Theorizing Events, Processes, and Emergence." *Annual Review of Sociology* 33 (1): pp. 527–49.

Coll, Steve. 2019. "The Jail-Health Crisis," *The New Yorker,* February 25. https://www.thenation.com/article/archive/whirlwind-deportations-are-depriving-thousands-migrants-their-rights-and-some-their-live/.

Collins, Patricia Hill. 2000. "Gender, Black Feminism, and Black Political Economy." *The Annals of the American Academy of Political and Social Science* 568 (1): pp. 41–53.

Comfort, Megan. 2007. "Punishment beyond the Legal Offender." *Annual Review of Law and Social Science* 3: pp. 271–96.

Comfort, Megan. 2013. "When Prison Is a Refuge, America's Messed Up." *The Chronicle of Higher Education,* December 2. https://www.chronicle.com/article/when-prison-is-a-refuge-americas-messed-up/.

Coughlin, Terasa, and Stephen Zuckerman. 2002. "States' Strategies for Tapping Federal Revenues: Implications and Consequences of Medicaid Maximization." In *Federalism and Health Policy,* edited by John Holahan, Alan Weil, and Joshua Weiner, pp. 145–78. Washington, DC: Urban Institute.

Crafton, William. 2014. "The Incremental Revolution: Ronald Reagan and Welfare Reform in the 1970s." *Journal of Policy History* 26 (1): pp. 27–47.

Daunt, Tina. 1998a. "Ill Inmates Transferred to Twin Towers; Jails: Sheriff's Department, Under Fire from U.S. Officials, Seeks to Improve Care," *Los Angeles Times,* January 11. https://www.latimes.com/archives/la-xpm-1998-jan-11-me-7315-story.html.

Daunt, Tina. 1998b. "Jail's Medical Ward to Move to Twin Towers," *Los Angeles Times,* January 1. https://www.latimes.com/archives/la-xpm-1998-jan-01-mn-4033-story.html.

Davis, Mike. 2002. *Dead Cities: A Natural History.* New York: New Press.

Dear, Michael, and Jennifer Wolch. 1987. *Landscapes of Despair: From Deinstitutionalization to Homelessness.* Princeton, NJ: Princeton University Press.

Durand, Anne-Claire, Stéphanie Gentile, Bénédicte Devictor, Sylvie Palazzolo, Pascal Vignally, Patrick Gerbeaux, and Roland Sambuc. 2011. "ED Patients: How Nonurgent Are They? Systematic Review of the Emergency Medicine Literature." *American Journal of Emergency Medicine* 29 (3): pp. 333–45.

Edelman, Lauren B. 2016. *Working Law: Courts, Corporations, and Symbolic Civil Rights.* Chicago: University of Chicago Press.

Editorial Writers Desk. 1996. "County Health Care at the Brink: Washington Must Follow Through with the Aid It Promised." *Los Angeles Times,* March 4: p. 29.

Edwards, Frank. 2016. "Saving Children, Controlling Families: Punishment, Redistribution, and Child Protection." *American Sociological Review* 81(3): pp. 575–95.

Eiting, Erick, Carrie Korn, Erin Wilkes, Glenn Ault, and Sean Henderson. 2017. "Reduction in Jail Emergency Department Visits and Closure after Implementation of On-Site Urgent Care." *Journal of Correctional Health Care* 23 (1): pp. 88–92.

Erickson, Patricia, and Steven Erickson. 2008. *Crime, Punishment, and Mental Illness: Law and the Behavioral Sciences in Conflict.* New Brunswick, NJ: Rutgers University Press.

Esping-Andersen, Gosta. 1999. *Social Foundations of Postindustrial Economies.* New York: Oxford University Press.

Fagnani, Lynne, and Jennifer Tolbert. 1999. "The Dependence of Safety Net Hospitals and Health Systems on the Medicare and Medicaid Disproportionate Share Hospital

Payment Programs." *National Association of Public Hospitals & Health Systems*, July 19. https://www.commonwealthfund.org/sites/default/files/documents/___media_files_ publications_fund_report_1999_oct_the_dependence_of_safety_net_hospitals_ and_health_systems_on_the_medicare_and_medicaid_disproportion_fagnani_ dependsafetynethospitals_351_pdf.pdf.

Feely, Malcom, and Jonathan Simon. 1992. "The New Penology: Notes on the Emerging Strategy of Corrections and its Implications." *Criminology* 30 (4): pp. 449–74.

Feeley, Malcom, and Edward L. Rubin. 1998. *Judicial Policy Making and the Modern State: How the Courts Reformed America's Prisons*. Cambridge: Cambridge University Press.

Felton, Mistique, J. Liu, T. Finlayson, N. Adams, R. M. Scheffler, and J. F. Ross. 2006. "Proposition 63, The Mental Health Services Act: A Research Agenda." Berkeley, CA: The Nicholas C. Petris Center on Health Care Markets and Consumer Welfare.

Fong, Kelley. 2019. "Concealment and Constraint: Child Protective Services Fears and Poor Mothers' Institutional Engagement." *Social Forces* 97 (4): pp. 1785–1810.

Fossnocht, David Eric Swanson. 2007. "Use of Triage Pain Protocol in the ED." *American Journal of Emergency Medicine* 25 (7): pp. 791–93.

Foucault, Michel. 1975. *Discipline and Punish: The Birth of the Prison*. London: Penguin Books.

Foucault, Michel. 1980. "The Politics of Health in the Eighteenth Century," In Michel Foucault, *Power/Knowledge: Selected Interviews and Other Writings 1972–1977*, edited by Colin Gordon. Brighton: Harvester Press.

Freed, David. 1990. "System Overflows with Flood of Probationers Corrections." *Los Angeles Times*, December 21: p. A1

Fry, Margarete Anna Holdgate. 2008. "Nurse-Initiated Intravenous Morphine in the ED." *Emergency Medicine* 14 (3): pp. 249–54.

Garland, David. 2001. *Mass Imprisonment: Social Causes and Consequences*. London: Sage Publications.

Garland, David. 2014. "What Is a 'History of the Present'? On Foucault's Genealogies and Their Critical Preconditions." *Punishment & Society* 16 (4): pp. 365–84.

George, Victoria, and Alan Dundes. 1978. "The Gomer: A Figure of American Hospital Folk Speech." *The Journal of American Folklore* 91 (359): pp. 568–81.

Gifford, Blair, Larry M. Manheim, and Diane Cowper. 2002. "Unforeseen Policy Effects on the Safety Net: Medicaid, Private Hospital Closures and the Use of Local VAMCs." In *Social Inequalities, Health and Health Care Delivery*, edited by Jacobs Kronenfeld, pp. 45–55. Bingley, UK: Emerald Group.

Gilmore, Ruth. 2007. *Golden Gulag: Prisons, Surplus, Crisis and Opposition in Globalizing California*. Berkeley: University of California Press.

Glied, Sherry, and Richard G. Frank. 2009. "Better but Not Best: Recent Trends in the Well-Being of the Mentally Ill." *Health Affairs* 28 (3): pp. 637–48.

Goffman, Erving. 1967. *Interaction Ritual: Essays in Face-to-Face Behavior* New York: The Free Press.

Goldberg, Michelle. 2004. "Yes, Mr. President, the Border Kids Are Refugees." *The Nation*, July 16. https://www.thenation.com/article/archive/our-refugee-crisis/.

Goodman, Philip. 2008. "'It's Just Black, White, or Hispanic': An Observational Study of Racializing Moves in California's Segregated Prison Reception Centers." *Law & Society Review* 42 (4): pp. 735–70.

Goodman, Philip, Joshua Page, and Michelle Phelps. 2015. "The Long Struggle: An Agonistic Perspective on Penal Development." *Theoretical Criminology* 19 (3): pp. 315–35.

Gordon, James. 1999. "The Hospital Emergency Department as a Social Welfare Institution." *Annals of Emergency Medicine* 33 (3): pp. 321–25.

Guccione, Jean. 1998. "L.A. Superior Court Stymies Jail Compromise: Court's Refusal to Change Could Force Inmate Reduction." *Los Angeles Daily Journal*, November 12.

Gusmano, Michael. 2015. "Review of Financing Medicaid: Federalism and the Growth of America's Health Care Safety Net by Shanna Rose." *Perspectives on Politics* 13 (2): pp. 46–48.

Gusmano, Michael, and Frank Thompson. 2012. "The Safety Net at the Crossroads? Whither Medicaid DSH." In *The Health Care Safety-Net in a Post-Reform World*, edited by Mark A. Hall and Sara Rosenbaum, pp. 153–82. New Brunswick, NJ: Rutgers University Press.

Gustafson, Kaaryn. 2011. *Cheating Welfare: Public Assistance and the Criminalization of Poverty*. New York: New York University Press.

Hacker, Jacob. 2004. "Privatizing Risk without Privatizing the Welfare State: The Hidden Politics of Social Policy Retrenchment in the United States." *American Political Science Review* 98 (2): pp. 243–60.

Hacker, Jacob. 2005. "Policy Drift: The Hidden Politics of US Welfare State Retrenchment." In *Beyond Continuity: Institutional Change in Advanced Political Economies*, edited by Wolfgang Streeck and Kathleen Thelen, pp. 20–82. New York: Oxford University Press.

Hacking, Ian. 2007. "Kinds of People: Moving Targets." *Proceedings-British Academy* 151: pp. 285–318.

Haney, Lynne. 1996. "Homeboys, Babies, Men in Suits: The State and the Reproduction of Male Dominance." *American Sociological Review* 61 (5): pp. 759–78.

Haney, Lynne. 2002. *Inventing the Needy: Gender and the Politics of Welfare in Hungary*. Berkeley: University of California Press.

Haney, Lynne. 2010. *Offending Women: Power, Punishment, and the Regulation of Desire*. Berkeley: University of California Press.

Hannah-Moffat, Kelly. 2005. "Criminogenic Needs and the Transformative Risk Subject: Hybridizations of Risk/Need in Penality." *Punishment & Society* 7 (1): pp. 29–51.

Harada, Megan. n.d. "Policed Patients: How Law Enforcement Personnel Impact Medical Care in the Emergency Department." M.A. Thesis: University of California San Francisco.

Harcourt, Bernard E. 2006. "From the Asylum to the Prison: Rethinking the Incarceration Revolution." *Texas Law Review* 84 (7): pp. 1751–86.

Hatch, Anthony. 2019. *Silent Cells: The Secret Drugging of Captive America*. Minneapolis: University of Minnesota Press.

Hennessy-Fiske, Molly. 2009. "Even Death Is Unaffordable." *Los Angeles Times*, July 21. https://www.latimes.com/archives/la-xpm-2009-jul-21-me-unclaimed21-story.html.

Herring, Chris. 2019. "Complaint-Oriented Policing: Regulating Homelessness in Public Space." *American Sociological Review* 84 (5): pp. 769–800.

Hinterleitner, Markus, and Fritz Sager. 2017. "Anticipatory and Reactive Forms of Blame Avoidance: Of Foxes and Lions." *European Political Science Review* 9 (4): pp. 587–606.

Hinton, Elizabeth. 2016. *From the War on Poverty to the War on Crime: The Making of Mass Incarceration in America*. Cambridge, MA: Harvard University Press.

Hinze, Susan, Noah J. Webster, Heidi T. Chirayath, and Joshua H. Tamayo-Sarver. 2009. "Hurt Running from Police? No Chance of (Pain) Relief: The Social Construction of Deserving Patients in Emergency Departments." In *Research in the Sociology of*

Health Care, edited by Jennie Jacobsk Ronenfeld, pp. 235–61. Bingley: Emerald Group Publishing.

Hirschfield, Paul, and Alex Piquero. 2010. "Normalization and Legitimation: Modeling Stigmatizing Attitudes Toward Ex-Offenders." *Criminology* 48 (1): pp. 27–55.

Hoang, Kimberly. 2015. *Dealing in Desire: Asian Ascendancy, Western Decline, and the Hidden Currencies of Global Sex Work.* Berkeley: University of California Press.

Hoffman, Lara. 2008. "Separate but Unequal-When Overcrowded: Sex Discrimination in Jail Early Release Policies." *William & Mary Journal of Women and the Law* 15 (3): pp. 591–632.

Hood, Christopher. 2011. *The Blame Game: Spin, Bureaucracy, and Self-preservation in Government.* Princeton, NJ: Princeton University Press.

Hsia, Renee Y., Steven M. Asch, Robert E. Weiss, David Zingmond, Li-Jung Liang, Weijuan Han, Heather McCreath, and Benjamin C. Sun. 2011. "Hospital Determinants of Emergency Department Left without Being Seen Rates." *Annals of Emergency Medicine* 58 (1): pp. 24–32.

Huber, Evelyne, and John D. Stephens. 2001. *Development and Crisis of the Welfare State.* Chicago: University of Chicago Press.

Huh, Kil, Alexander Boucher, Frances McGaffey, Matt McKillop, and Maria Schiff. 2017. "Prison Health Care: Costs and Quality: How and why States Strive for High-Preforming Systems." Pew Charitable Trusts. https://www.pewtrusts.org/-/media/assets/2017/10/sfh_prison_health_care_costs_and_quality_final.pdf.

Huh, Kil Alexander Boucher, Frances McGaffey, Matt McKillop, and Maria Schiff. 2018. "Jails: Inadvertent Healthcare Providers: How County Correctional Facilities Are Playing a Role in the Safety Net." Pew Charitable Trusts.

Hunter, Marcus. 2013. *Black Citymakers: How the Philadelphia Negro Changed Urban America.* New York: Oxford University Press.

Irwin, John. [1985] 2013. *The Jail: Managing the Underclass in American Society.* Berkeley: University of California Press.

James, Doris, and Lauren E. Glaze. 2006. "Mental Health Problems of Prison and Jail Inmates." Bureau of Justice.

Jeffery, Roger. 1979. "Normal Rubbish: Deviant Patients in Casualty Departments." *Sociology of Health & Illness* 1 (1): pp. 90–107.

Jensen, Carsten, Georg Wenzelburger, and Reimut Zohlnhöfer. 2019. "Dismantling the Welfare State? After Twenty-five Years: What Have We Learned and What Should We Learn?" *Journal of European Social Policy* 29 (5): pp. 681–91.

Jerolmack, Colin, and Shamus Khan. 2014. "Talk Is Cheap: Ethnography and the Attitudinal Fallacy." *Sociological Methods & Research* 43 (2): pp. 178–209.

Jerolmack, Colin, and Alexandra Murphy. 2017. "The Ethical Dilemmas and Social Scientific Tradeoffs of Masking in Ethnography." *Sociological Methods and Research* 48 (4): pp. 1–27.

Johnson, Brian, and Stephanie M. DiPietro. 2012. "The Power of Diversion: Intermediate Sanctions and Sentencing Disparity under Presumptive Guidelines." *Criminology* 50 (3): pp. 811–50.

Johnston, Brian, and Jim Lott. 1997. "Perspective on the Medical Center: County-USC Price Tag is a Bargain. *Los Angeles Times*, October 30.

Katz, Michael. 2013. *The Undeserving Poor: America's Enduring Confrontation with Poverty: Fully Updated and Revised.* New York: Oxford University Press.

Kaufmann, Greg. 2019. "What's the Best Way to Actually Care for Unaccompanied Migrant Children?" *The Nation*, October 10. https://www.thenation.com/article/archive/migrant-children-shelter-dc/.

Kelly, Anne-Maree Catherine Barnes, Caroline Brumby. 2005. "Nurse Initiated Narcotic Analgesia Reduces Time to Analgesia for Patients with Acute Pain in the ED." *CJEM* 7 (3): pp. 149–54.

Keramet, Reiter. 2016. *23/7: Pelican Bay Prison and the Rise of Long-Term Solitary Confinement*. New Haven, CT: Yale University Press.

Kitchener, Martin, Terence Ng, Nancy Miller, and Charlene Harrington. 2005. "Medicaid Home and Community-Based Services: National Program Trends." *Health Affairs* 24 (1): pp. 206–12.

Kohler-Hausmann, Issa. 2018. *Misdemeanorland: Criminal Courts and Social Control in an Age of Broken Windows Policing*. Princeton, NJ: Princeton University Press.

Korpi, Walter, and Joakim Palme. 2001. *New Politics and Class Politics in Welfare State Regress: A Comparative Analysis of Retrenchment in 18 Countries 1975–1995*. Stockholm: Swedish Institute for Social Research.

Kubrin, Charis, and Carroll Seron. 2016. "The Prospects and Perils of Ending Mass Incarceration in the United States." *The Annals of the American Academy of Political and Social Science* 664 (1): pp. 16–24.

Kupchik, Aaron. 2010. *Homeroom Security: School Discipline in an Age of Fear*. New York: New York University.

Kyriacou, Demetrios. 2017. "Opioid vs. Nonopioid Acute Pain Management in the Emergency Department." *JAMA: The Journal of the American Medical Association* 318 (17): pp. 1655–56.

Lara-Millán, Armando. 2014. "Public Emergency Room Overcrowding in the Era of Mass Imprisonment." *American Sociological Review* 79 (5): pp. 866–87.

Lara-Millán, Armando. 2017. "States as a Series of People Exchanges." In *The Many Hands of the State: Theorizing Political Authority and Social Control*, edited by Kimberly Morgan and Ann Orloff, pp. 81–102. Cambridge: Cambridge University Press.

Lara-Millán, Armando. 2020. "Theorizing Financial Extraction: The Curious Case of Telephone Profits in the Los Angeles County Jails." Forthcoming at *Punishment & Society*.

Lara-Millán, Armando, and Nicole Gonzalez Van Cleve. 2017. "Interorganizational Utility of Welfare Stigma in the Criminal Justice System." *Criminology* 55 (1): pp. 59–84.

Lara-Millán, Armando, Sunmin Kim, Brian Sargent. 2020. "Theorizing with Archives: Contingency, Mistakes, and Plausible Alternatives." Forthcoming at *Qualitative Sociology*.

Latour, Bruno. 2007. *Reassembling the Social: An Introduction to Actor-Network-Theory*. New York: Oxford University Press.

Latour, Bruno. 2011. "Networks, Societies, Spheres: Reflections of an Actor-Network Theorist." *International Journal of Communication Systems* 5: pp. 796–810.

Lewin, Marion, and Stuart Altman. 2000. *America's Health Care Safety Net: Intact but Endangered*. Washington, DC: National Academies Press.

Lichtblau, Eric, and Josh Meyer. 1996. "Sheriff's Budget Is Not as Lean as Billed." *Los Angeles Times*, November 3. https://www.latimes.com/archives/la-xpm-1996-11-03-mn-60961-story.html.

Lieberson, Stanley. 1991. "Small Ns and Big Conclusions: An Examination of the Reasoning in Comparative Studies Based on a Small Number of Cases." *Social Forces* 70 (2): pp. 307–20.

Lobao, Linda, and Lazarus Adua. 2011. "State Rescaling and Local Governments' Austerity Policies across the USA, 2001–2008." *Cambridge Journal of Regions, Economy and Society* 4 (1): pp. 419–35.

Long, Sharon, and Stephen Zuckerman. 1998. "Urban Health Care in Transition: Challenges facing Los Angeles County." *Health Care Financing Review* 20 (1): pp. 45–58.

Kazmin, Amy Louise. 1990a. "L.A. County Jail Infirmary Substandard, State Finds." *Los Angeles Times*, September 15. https://www.latimes.com/archives/la-xpm-1990-09-15-mn-168-story.html.

Kazmin, Amy Louise. 1990b. "Efforts Told to Improve Jail Hospital." *Los Angeles Times*, September 27. https://www.latimes.com/archives/la-xpm-1990-09-27-me-1705-story.html.

Loveman, Mara. 2005. "The Modern State and the Primitive Accumulation of Symbolic Power." *American Journal of Sociology* 110 (6): pp. 1651–83.

Lynch, Mona. 2009. *Sunbelt Justice: Arizona and the Transformation of American Punishment*. Palo Alto, Ca: Stanford University Press.

Lynch, Mona. 2011. "Mass Incarceration, Legal Change, and Locale: Understanding and Remediating American Penal Overindulgence." *Criminology & Public Policy* 10 (3): pp. 673–98.

Macías-Rojas, Patrisia. 2016. *From Deportation to Prison: The Politics of Immigration in Post-Civil Rights America*. New York: New York University Press.

Malone, Ruth. 1998. "Whither the Almshouse? Overutilization and the Role of the Emergency Department." *Journal of Health Politics, Policy and Law* 23 (5): pp. 795–832.

Marcellino, Elizabeth. 2019. "LA County Supervisors Scrap $1.7 Billion Contract to Replace Jail: 'It's time to do the right thing.'" *Los Angeles Daily News*, August 13. https://www.dailynews.com/2019/08/13/la-county-supervisors-scrap-1-7-bill-contract-to-replace-jail-its-time-to-do-the-right-thing/.

Markowitz, Fred. 2006. "Psychiatric Hospital Capacity, Homelessness, and Crime and Arrest Rates." *Criminology* 44 (1): pp. 45–72.

Martin, Isaac William. 2008. *The Permanent Tax Revolt: How the Property Tax Transformed American Politics*. Palo Alto, CA: Stanford University Press.

Martínez, Óscar. 2014. "Why the Children Fleeing Central American Will Not Stop Coming." *The Nation*, July 30. https://www.thenation.com/article/archive/why-children-fleeing-central-america-will-not-stop-coming/.

McGirr, Lisa. 2002. *Suburban Warriors: The Origins of the New American Right*. Princeton, NJ: Princeton University Press.

McGoey, Linsey. 2012. "Strategic Unknowns: Towards a Sociology of Ignorance." *Economy and Society* 41 (1): pp. 1–16.

McKim, Allison. 2017. *Addicted to Rehab: Race, Gender, and Drugs in the Era of Mass Incarceration*. New Brunswick, NJ: Rutgers University Press.

Mettler, Suzanne. 2011. *The Submerged State: How Invisible Government Policies Undermine American Democracy*. Chicago: University of Chicago Press.

Meyer, Josh. 1996. "County, U.S. at Odds Over Long-Term Overhaul of Health System," *Los Angeles Times*, February 28. https://www.latimes.com/archives/la-xpm-1996-02-28-me-40941-story.html?_amp=true.

Meyer, Josh, and Jack Cheevers. 1996. "County to Eliminate a Third of Hospital Beds to Get U.S. Bailout." *Los Angeles Times*, February 27. https://www.latimes.com/archives/la-xpm-1996-02-27-me-40570-story.html.

Miller, Reuben Jonathan. 2014. "Devolving the Carceral State: Race, Prisoner Reentry, and the Micro-Politics of Urban Poverty Management." *Punishment & Society* 16 (3): pp. 305–35.

Mizrahi, Terry. 1985. "Getting Rid of Patients: Contradictions in the Socialization of Internists to the Doctor-Patient Relationship." *Sociology of Health & Illness* 7 (2): pp. 214–35.

Moench, Mallory. 2020. "San Quentin's Coronavirus Outbreak Strains Marin, Bay Area Hospitals." *San Francisco Chronicle*, July 7. https://www.sfchronicle.com/health/article/San-Quentin-s-coronavirus-outbreak-strains-Bay-15392385.php.

Monahan, John, and Jennifer L. Skeem. 2014. "The Evolution of Violence Risk Assessment." *CNS Spectrums* 19 (5): pp. 419–24.

Morgan, Kimberly J., and Andrea Louise Campbell. 2011. *The Delegated Welfare State: Medicare, Markets, and the Governance of Social Policy*. New York: Oxford University Press.

Morgan, Kimberly J., and Ann Shola Orloff. 2017. *The Many Hands of the State: Theorizing Political Authority and Social Control*. Cambridge: Cambridge University Press.

Muhammad, Khalil Gibran. 2011. *The Condemnation of Blackness*. Cambridge, MA: Harvard University Press.

Natapoff, Alexandra. 2014. "Gideon's Servants and the Criminalization of Poverty." *Ohio State Journal of Criminal Law* 12: pp. 445–64.

Needleman, Jack, and Michelle Ko. 2012. "The Declining Public Hospital Sector." In *The Health Care "Safety Net" in a Post-Reform World*, edited by Mark A. Hall and Sara Rosenbaum, pp. 200–13.New Brunswick, NJ: Rutgers University Press.

Nixon, Ron. 2018. "U.S. Loses Track of Another 1,500 Migrant Children, Investigators Find." *New York Times*, September 18. https://www.nytimes.com/2018/09/18/us/politics/us-migrant-children-whereabouts-.html.

Noguera, Pedro. 2003. "The Trouble with Black Boys: The Role and Influence of Environmental and Cultural Factors on the Academic Performance of African American Males." *Urban Education* 38 (4): pp. 431–59.

O'Connor, John. 1998. "US Social Welfare Policy: The Reagan Record and Legacy." *Journal of Social Policy*. 27 (1): pp. 37–61.

Ossei-Owusu, Shaun. 2017. "Code Red: The Essential Yet Neglected Role of Emergency Care in Health Law Reform." *American Journal of Law & Medicine* 43 (4): pp. 344–87.

Pacewicz, Josh. 2018. "The Regulatory Road to Reform: Bureaucratic Activism, Agency Advocacy, and Medicaid Expansion within the Delegated Welfare State." *Politics & Society* 46 (4): pp. 571–601.

Page, Joshua. 2013. *The Toughest Beat: Politics, Punishment, and the Prison Officers Union in California*. New York: Oxford University Press.

Page, Joshua, and Joe Soss. 2017. "Criminal Justice Predation and Neoliberal Governance." In *Rethinking Neoliberalism: Resisting the Disciplinary Regime*, edited by Sanford Schram and Marianna Pavlovskaya, pp. 139–59. New York: Routledge.

Pailer, Bruno. 2005. "Ambiguous Agreement, Cumulative Change: French Social Policy in the 1990s." In *Beyond Continuity: Institutional Change in Advanced Political Economies*, edited by Wolfgang Streeck and Kathleen Thelen, pp. 127–44. New York: Oxford University Press.

Patashnik, Eric. 2015. "Paul Pierson's Dismantling the Welfare State: A Twentieth Anniversary Reassessment: Introduction." *PS: Political Science & Politics* 48 (2): pp. 267–69.

Pattillo, Mary. 1999. *Black Picket Fences: Privilege and Peril among the Black Middle Class.* Chicago: University of Chicago Press.

Peck, Jamie. 2012. "Austerity Urbanism." *Cityscape* 16 (6): pp. 626–55.

Pierson, Paul. 1994. *Dismantling the Welfare State? Reagan, Thatcher, and the Politics of Retrenchment.* Cambridge: Cambridge University Press.

Pierson, Paul. 1998. "Irresistible Forces, Immovable Objects: Post-industrial Welfare State Confront Permanent Austerity." *Journal of European Public Policy* 5 (4): pp. 539–60.

Pierson, Paul. 2001. *The New Politics of the Welfare State.* New York: Oxford University Press.

Pinyao, Rui, and Susan Schappert. 2019. "Opioids Prescribed at Discharge or Given during Emergency Department Visits among Adults in the United States." *National Center for Health Statistics Data Brief* 338.

Pitts, James, Hayden Griffin, and W. Wesley Johnson. 2014. "Contemporary Prison Overcrowding: Short-Term Fixes to a Perpetual Problem." *Contemporary Justice Review* 17 (1): pp. 124–39.

Prottas, Jeffrey. 1979. *People Processing: The Street-Level Bureaucrat in Public Service Bureaucracies.* Lexington, MA: Lexington Books.

Quintanilla, Ray, and *Tribune* staff reporter. 2006. "Uncertainty Stalks Hospitals." *Chicago Tribune*, October 13. https://www.chicagotribune.com/news/ct-xpm-2006-10-13-0610130258-story.html.

Rabin, Elaine, Keith Kocher, Mark McClelland, Jesse Pines, Ula Hwang, Niels Rathlev, Brent Asplin, N. Seth Trueger, and Ellen Weber. 2012. "Solutions Tt Emergency Department 'Boarding' and Crowding Are Underused and May Need to Be Legislated." *Health Affairs* 31 (8) (August 1): pp. 1757–66.

Rabin, Jeffrey. 1996. "County Health System to Get More U.S. Aid." *Los Angeles Times*, June 15. https://www.latimes.com/archives/la-xpm-1996-06-15-mn-15231-story.html.

Rabin, Jeffrey, and Sharon Bernstein. 1997. "Supervisors Agree on Downsized Hospital." *Los Angeles Times*, November 13. https://www.latimes.com/archives/la-xpm-1997-nov-13-me-53345-story.html.

Rabin, Jeffrey, John Broder, and Josh Meyer. 1995. "Breakthrough Seen on $364-Million Deal to Rescue County Health System." *Los Angeles Times*, September 22. https://www.latimes.com/archives/la-xpm-1995-09-22-mn-48685-story.html.

Rabin, Jeffrey, and Jack Cheevers. 1996. "County Health System Bailout Gets Final OK." *Los Angeles Times*, April 16. https://www.latimes.com/archives/la-xpm-1996-04-16-me-59165-story.html.

Rabin, Jeffrey, and Josh Meyer. 1996a. "County's Health Reform Proposal Delivered to U.S." *Los Angeles Times*, March 2. https://www.latimes.com/archives/la-xpm-1996-03-02-mn-42132-story.html.

Rabin, Jeffrey, and Josh Meyer. 1996b. "U.S. Bailout of County Health System Stalled." *Los Angeles Times*, February 24. https://www.latimes.com/archives/la-xpm-1996-02-24-mn-39408-story.html.

Rabin, Jeffrey, Josh Meyer, and Jack Cheevers. 1995. "Clinton Offers L.A. Aid Plan Based on Community Care." *Los Angeles Times*, September 23. https://www.latimes.com/archives/la-xpm-1995-09-23-mn-49148-story.html.

Ramey, David. 2015. "The Social Structure of Criminalized and Medicalized School Discipline." *Sociology of Education* 88 (3): pp. 181–201.

Reinhart, Eric, and Daniel Chen. 2020. "Incarceration and Its Disseminations: COVID-19 Pandemic Lessons from Chicago's Cook County Jail." *Health Affairs* 39 (8): pp. 1412–18.

Rembis, Michael. 2014. "The New Asylums: Madness and Mass Incarceration in the Neoliberal Era." In *Disability Incarcerated: Imprisonment and Disability in the United States and Canada*, edited by Liat Ben-Moshe, Chris Chapman, and Allison C. Carey, pp. 139–59. New York: Palgrave Macmillan.

Rios, Victor. 2011. *Punished: Policing the Lives of Black and Latino Boys.* New York: New York University Press.

Rivera, Carla, and Lisa Respers. 1995. "Sheriff, Board, Swap Charges over Early Release of Inmates." *Los Angeles Times*, March 4. https://www.latimes.com/archives/la-xpm-1995-03-04-me-38557-story.html.

Rohrlich, Ted. 1987. "County Ordered to Begin Limits on Jail Crowding." *Los Angeles Times*, October 31. https://www.latimes.com/archives/la-xpm-1987-10-31-me-4417-story.html.

Rohrlich, Ted. 1991. "Intensified Supervision of Probation Found Ineffective: RAND Study Concludes That the Program Does Not Dissuade Felons from Committing Additional Offenses." *Los Angeles Times*, January 31. https://www.latimes.com/archives/la-xpm-1991-01-31-mn-426-story.html.

Ross, Aaron. 2014. "Why Are Thousands of Malagasy Women Being Trafficked to Abusive Jobs in the Middle East?" *The Nation*, April 15.

Roth, Alisa. 2018. *Insane: America's Criminal Treatment of Mental Illness.* New York: Basic Books.

Roth, Julius. 1972. "Some Contingencies of the Moral Evaluation and Control of Clientele: The Case of the Hospital Emergency Service." *American Journal of Sociology* 77 (5): pp. 839–56.

Rowe, Brian, Cristina Villa-Roel, Xiaoyan Guo, Michael Bullard, Maria Ospina, Benjamin Vandermeer, Grant Innes, Michael Schull, and Brian Holroyd. 2011. "The Role of Triage Nurse Ordering on Mitigating Overcrowding in Emergency Departments: A Systematic Review." *Academic Emergency Medicine* 18 (12): pp. 1349–57.

Verma, SanJuhi. 2012. "Black Gold, Brown Labor: The Legalization of Indentured Work Through the Transnational Migration Industry." PhD diss., Department of Sociology, University of Chicago.

Sawyer, Stephen, William J. Novak, and James T. Sparrow. 2012. "Toward a History of the Democratic State." *The Tocqueville Review/La Revue Tocqueville* XXXIII (2): pp. 7–18.

Schaenman, Phil, Elizabeth Davies, Reed Jordan, Reena Chakraborty. 2012. "Opportunities for Cost Savings in Corrections Without Sacrificing Quality: Inmate Healthcare." Urban Institute.

Schept, Judah. 2015. *Progressive Punishment: Job Loss, Jail Growth, and the Neoliberal Logic of Carceral Expansion.* New York: New York University Press.

Schlanger, Margo. 2006. "Civil Rights Injunctions over Time: A Case Study of Jail and Prison Court Orders." *N.Y.U. Law Review* 81 (2): pp. 550–630.

Schlanger, Margo. 2013. "Plata v. Brown and Realignment: Jails, Prisons, Courts, and Politics." *Harvard Civil Rights-Civil Liberties Law Review* 48 (1): pp. 165–215.

Schlanger, Margo. 2015. "Trends in Prisoner Litigation, as the PLRA Enters Adulthood." *University of California Irvine Law Review* 5(1): pp. 153–79.

Schoenfeld, Heather. 2010. "Mass Incarceration and the Paradox of Prison Conditions Litigation." *Law & Society Review* 44 (3): pp. 731–68.

Schoenfeld, Heather. 2016. "A Research Agenda on Reform: Penal Policy and Politics across the States." *The Annals of the American Academy of Political and Social Science* 664 (1): pp. 155–74.

Schram, Sanford. 2015. *The Return of Ordinary Capitalism: Neoliberalism, Precarity, Occupy*. New York: Oxford University Press.

Schwartz, Barry. 1972. *Queuing and Waiting: Studies in the Social Organization of Access and Delay*. Chicago: University of Chicago Press.

Scott, James. 1998. *Seeing like a State: How Certain Schemes to Improve the Human Condition Have Failed*. New Haven, CT: Yale University Press.

Seim, Josh. 2017. "The Ambulance: Toward a Labor Theory of Poverty Governance." *American Sociological Review* 82 (3): pp. 451–75.

Sewell, Abby. 2015. "L.A. County Supervisors Move Ahead with $2 Billion Jails Plan." *Los Angeles Times*, September 1. https://www.latimes.com/local/lanow/la-me-ln-supes-jail-vote-20150831-story.html.

Shedd, Carla. 2015. *Unequal City: Race, Schools, and Perceptions of Injustice*. New York: Russell Sage Foundation.

Shortell, Stephen, Robin Gillies, and Kelly Devers. 1995. "Reinventing the American Hospital." *The Milbank Quarterly* 73 (2): pp. 131–60.

Shubik-Richards, Claire, and Don Stemen. 2010. "Philadelphia's Crowded, Costly Jails: The Search for Safe Solutions." Pew Charitable Trusts' Philadelphia Research Initiative.

Shuit, Douglas. 1996. "Problems Arise over County Bid for U.S. Health Care Bailout." *Los Angeles Times*, January 12. https://www.latimes.com/archives/la-xpm-1996-01-12-me-23942-story.html.

Simon, Jonathan. 2007. *Governing through Crime: How the War on Crime Transformed American Democracy and Created a Culture of Fear*. New York: Oxford University Press.

Simon, Jonathan. 2012. "Mass Incarceration: From Social Policy to Social Problem." In *The Oxford Handbook of Sentencing and Corrections*, edited by Joan Petersilia and Kevin R. Reitz, pp. 23–52. New York: Oxford University Press.

Skocpol, Theda, and Margaret Somers. 1980. "The Uses of Comparative History in Macrosocial Inquiry." *Comparative Studies in Society and History* 22 (2): pp. 174–97.

Slate, Risdon N., Jacqueline K. Buffington-Vollum, and W. Wesley Johnson. 2013. *The Criminalization of Mental Illness: Crisis and Opportunity for the Justice System: Second Edition*. Durham, NC: Carolina Academic Press.

Small, Mario Luis. 2009. "'How Many Cases Do I Need?' On Science and the Logic of Case Selection in Field-Based Research." *Ethnography* 10 (1): pp. 5–38.

Soss, Joe, Richard C. Fording, and Sanford F. Schram. 2011. *Disciplining the Poor: Neoliberal Paternalism and the Persistent Power of Race*. Chicago: University of Chicago Press.

Southern California Public Radio. 2010. "LA County Hospital Services Faces $204M Deficit." *Southern California Public Radio*, May 18. https://www.scpr.org/news/2010/05/18/15210/la-county-hospital-services-faces-204m-deficit/.

Spaulding, Anne C., Ryan M. Seals, Victoria A. McCallum, Sebastian D. Perez, Amanda K. Brzozowski, and N. Kyle Steenland. 2011. "Prisoner Survival Inside and Outside of the Institution: Implications for Health-Care Planning." *American Journal of Epidemiology* 173 (5): pp. 479–87.

Stahl, Lesley. 2017. "Half of the Inmates Shouldn't Be Here, Says Cook County Sheriff." CBS News, May 21. https://www.cbsnews.com/news/cook-county-jail-sheriff-tom-dart-on-60-minutes/.

Stiles, Matt. 2019. "'No More Jails,' Just Mental Health Centers. Is That a Realistic Policy for L.A. County?" *Los Angeles Times*, August 26. https://www.latimes.com/california/story/2019-08-24/jail-replacement-mental-health-facility-inmate-supervisors-criminal-justice-reform.

Streeck, Wolfgang, and Kathleen Thelen. 2005. "Introduction: Institutional Change in Advanced Political Economies." In *Beyond Continuity: Institutional Change in Advanced Political Economies*, edited by Wolfgang Streeck and Kathleen Thelen, pp. 1–39. New York: Oxford University Press.

Stuart, Forrest. 2016. *Down, Out, and Under Arrest: Policing and Everyday Life in Skid Row*. Chicago: University of Chicago Press.

Subramanian, Ram, Ruth Delaney, Stephen Roberts, and Nancy Fishman. 2015. *Incarceration's Front Door: The Misuse of Jail in America*. New York: Vera Institute of Justice.

Sundararajan, Radhika L., Andrew L. Miner, William Paolo Jr, and William Chiang. 2012. "Police Detainees in the Emergency Department: Who Do We Admit?" *Webmed Central*. https://www.webmedcentral.com/wmcpdf/Article_WMC002849.pdf.

Sutton, R. John. 1988. *Stubborn Children: Controlling Delinquency in the United States, 1640–1981*. Berkeley: University of California Press.

Tahaouni, Morsal, and Emory Liscord. 2015. "Managing Law Enforcement Presence in the Emergency Department: Highlighting the Need for New Policy Recommendations." *Journal of Emergency Medicine* 49 (4): pp. 523–29.

Tavory, Iddo. 2016. *Summoned: Identification and Religious Life in a Jewish Neighborhood*. Chicago: University of Chicago Press.

Tavory, Iddo, and Stefan Timmermans. 2014. *Abductive Analysis: Theorizing Qualitative Research*. Chicago: University of Chicago Press.

Teplin, Linda A., and Nancy S. Pruett. 1992. "Police as Streetcorner Psychiatrist: Managing the Mentally Ill." *International Journal of Law and Psychiatry* 15 (2): pp. 139–56.

Thelen, Kathleen. 2003. "How Institutions Evolve: Insights from Comparative-Historical Analysis." In *Comparative Historical Analysis in the Social Sciences*, edited by James Mahoney and Dietrich Rueschemeyer, pp. 208–40. Cambridge: Cambridge University Press.

Thelen, Kathleen. 2004. *How Institutions Evolve: The Political Economy of Skills in Germany, Britain, the United States and Japan*. New York: Cambridge University Press.

Thompson, Frank. 2012. *Medicaid Politics: Federalism, Policy Durability, and Health Reform*. Washington, DC: Georgetown University Press.

Thompson, Frank, and Courtney Burke. 2007. "Executive Federalism and Medicaid Demonstration Waivers: Implications for Policy and Democratic Process." *Journal of Health Politics, Policy, and Law* 32 (6): pp. 971–1004.

Timmermans, Stefan, and Pamela Prickett. 2018. "Today is L.A. County's Crucial Annual Memorial for the Living and the Dead." *Los Angeles Times*, December 5. https://www.latimes.com/opinion/op-ed/la-oe-timmermansandprickett-county-burials-20181205-story.html.

Torrey, E. Fuller. 2008. *The Insanity Offense: How America's Failure to Treat the Seriously Mentally Ill Endangers Its Citizens*. New York. W. W. Norton.

Torrey, E. Fuller, K. Entsminger, J. Geller, J. Stanley, and D. J. Jaffe. 2008. "The Shortage of Public Hospital Beds for Mentally Ill Persons." *Montana: The Magazine of Western History* 303 (20): pp. 6–9.

Torrey, E. Fuller, Mary Zdanowicz, Aaron D. Kennard, Richard Lamb, Donald Eslinger, Michael Biasotti, and Doris A. Fuller. 2014. "The Treatment of Persons with Mental Illness in Prisons and Jails: A State Survey." Treatment Advocacy Center.

United States Congress Senate Committee. 2003. *Hospital Emergency Departments: Crowded Conditions Vary among Hospitals and Communities: Report to the Ranking Minority Member, Committee on Finance, US Senate*. Washington, DC: General Accounting Office.

Van Cleve, Nicole Gonzalez. 2016. *Crook County: Racism and Injustice in America's Largest Criminal Court*. Stanford, CA: Stanford University Press.

Van Cleve, Nicole Gonzalez. 2018. *The Waiting Room*. The Marshal Project.

Van Cleve, Nicole Gonzalez, and Lauren Mayes. 2015. "Criminal Justice through "Color-Blind" Lenses: A Call to Examine the Mutual Constitution of Race and Criminal Justice." *Law & Social Inquiry* 40 (2): pp. 406–32.

Vaughan, Diane. 1996, *The Challenger Launch Decision: Risky Technology, Culture, and Deviance at NASA*. Chicago: University of Chicago Press.

Vaughan, Diane. 2004. "Theorizing Disaster: Analogy, Historical Ethnography, and the Challenger Accident." *Ethnography* 5 (3): pp. 315–47.

Vera Institute of Justice. 2019. "Incarceration Trends: Vera Institute of Justice." Accessed March 1, 2019. http://trends.vera.org/incarceration-rates?data=pretrial.

Wacquant, Loïc. 2002. "Four Strategies to Curb Carceral Costs: On Managing Mass Imprisonment in the United States." *Studies in Political Economy* 69: pp. 19–30.

Wacquant, Loïc. 2009. *Punishing the Poor*. Durham, NC: Duke University Press.

Walker, Michael. 2016. "Race Making in a Penal Institution." *American Journal of Sociology* 121 (4): pp. 1051–78.

Washington, John. 2019. "'How Do You Address Disappearance?': A Q&A with Valeria Luiselli." *The Nation*, April 1. https://www.thenation.com/article/archive/valeria-luiselli-interview-lost-children-archive/.

Western, Bruce, and Becky Pettit. 2010. "Incarceration & Social Inequality." *Daedalus* 139 (3): pp. 8–19.

Wildeman, Christopher. 2011. "Invited Commentary: (Mass) Imprisonment and (Inequities In) Health." *American Journal of Epidemiology* 173 (5): pp. 488–91.

Williams, Timothy. 2015. "Troubled Inmates, and a Psychologist as Warden." *New York Times*, July 30, pp. A1–13.

Wilper, Andrew, Steffie Woolhandler, Karen E. Lasser, Danny McCormick, Sarah L. Cutrona, David H. Bor, and David U. Himmelstein. 2008. "Waits to See an Emergency Department Physician: U.S. Trends and Predictors, 1997–2004." *Health Affairs* 27 (2): pp. 84–95.

Wortham, Stanton, Katherine Mortimer, and Elaine Allard. 2009. "Mexicans as Model Minorities in the New Latino Diaspora." *Anthropology & Education Quarterly* 40 (4): pp. 388–404.

Yuan, Jada. 2020. "Burials on Hart Island, Where New York's Unclaimed Lie in Mass Graves, Have Risen Fivefold." *Washington Post*, April 16. https://www.washingtonpost.com/national/hart-island-mass-graves-coronavirus-new-york/2020/04/16/a0c413ee-7f5f-11ea-a3ee-13e1ae0a3571_story.html.

Zuckerman, Stephen, and Amy Westpfahl Lutzky. 2001. "The Medicaid Demonstration Project in Los Angeles County, 1995_2000: Progress, but Room for Improvement." The Urban Institute.

Index

For the benefit of digital users, indexed terms that span two pages (e.g., 52–53) may, on occasion, appear on only one of those pages.

Figures are indicated by *f* following the page number

Printed in the USA/Agawam, MA
March 31, 2021

772369.024